MW01535954

Lejeune

Lejeune

The Napoleonic Wars Through
the Experiences of an Officer
on Berthier's Staff

Volume 2

Louis-François Lejeune

LEONAUR

Lejeune: The Napoleonic Wars Through the Experiences
of an Officer on Berthier's Staff—Volume 2
by Louis-François Lejeune

Originally published under the title
The Memoirs of Baron Lejeune

Published by Leonaur Ltd

Copyright in this form © 2007 Leonaur Ltd

ISBN: 978-1-84677-168-2 (hardcover)
ISBN: 978-1-84677-166-8 (softcover)

http://www.leonaur.com

Publisher's Notes

In the interests of authenticity, the spellings, grammar and place names
used have been retained from the original editions.

The opinions of the authors represent a view of events in which he
was a participant related from his own perspective,
as such the text is relevant as an historical document.

The views expressed in this book are not necessarily
those of the publisher.

Contents

CHAPTER 1

Vienna, Cracow, Paris

I left General Rusca at Klagenfurt, and set out once more for Vienna. The journey back was one long delight to me, for I was now able to examine at comparative leisure the interesting places I had had to hasten past all too rapidly on my way to the Tyrol. I had scarcely passed the quaint little town of Friesach, picturesquely situated at the foot of the lofty chain of mountains separating Carinthia from Styria, when I was overtaken by another of the storms of such frequent occurrence in these lofty districts. On August 15th, the Emperor's birthday, which is generally oppressively hot, I was in such a deluge of rain that I thought I should be washed away. This was succeeded by a heavy fall of snow, which lasted several hours, but I at last reached and passed through the ugly little town of Leoben, where the preliminaries of peace were signed, which saved the town of Vienna from the entry of the troops of General Bonaparte in 1797. Leoben is situated on the Mur, which winds backwards and forwards in a remarkable way, as if loath to leave the lovely valley it waters. At Burg, the Mur, the waters of which are as clear as crystal, widens out at the base of a huge rock, whose foundations it is gradually eating away. This isolated mass of stone, rising up like some defiant giant, is covered with venerable trees, the mighty, sombre-hued, drooping branches of which are reflected in the placid mirror of the waters beneath, as they gently lave the marble they are powerless to overturn.

At the Sommering pass a wall of rocks rising up into the clouds seems so completely to shut in the valley, here extremely narrow, as to leave absolutely no means of passing out of Styria into Austria. But for all that the traveller is able to reach the summit of the pass crowned by an ancient manor house, the walls and towers of which have been partly destroyed by the storms which have swept over them. The view from this point is magnificent, embracing as it does the rich plains of Austria and the banks of the Danube, with the towers and belfries of Vienna rising up against the horizon.

When I got back to the Emperor at Schönbrunn, I found him engaged in distributing rewards to those who had served him in the arduous campaigns just over. He could not without disorganising the whole army give promotion to all who deserved it; and, moreover, many of his bravest soldiers were illiterate men, whom it would not do to make officers. Anxious, however, to confer some real distinction on those brave fellows who had taken part in the actual defence of the flag, the eagle of their regiment, he conceived the idea of giving them a costume and equipment which should mark them out as specially honoured, and at the same time be suitable to the duties they had to perform.

The Emperor, therefore, sent for me, and asked me to make a sketch of a costume such as he wished to give to what he called his Eagle Guard, or those non-commissioned officers whose office it was to surround and defend the actual standard bearer. The chief weapons of each one were to be a pistol, a sword, and a lance, so that in the heat of the battle they would never have to trouble themselves about loading a gun. There was to be gold on their epaulettes, sword belts, and helmets. I made a drawing and took it to the Emperor, and he sent it with his own instructions on the subject.

Napoleon then asked me to draw, under his own eye, a design for the new Order he intended to institute. 'The Order of the Golden Fleece,' he said, 'was typical of victory; my eagles have triumphed over the Golden Fleeces of the Kings of Spain and the Emperors of Germany, so I mean to create for the French Empire an Imperial Order of the Three Golden Fleeces. The sign of this Order shall be my own eagle with outspread wings, holding in each of its talons one of the ancient Golden Fleeces it has carried off, whilst hanging from its beak it will proudly display the Fleece I now institute.' He then took a pen and roughly marked out the size I was to make my drawing. He also said he wished the chain on which the Order would be hung round the neck to be of very rich workmanship, with martial designs. 'The chain of the ancient Orders,' he explained to me, 'consists of bits of flint which emit fire when they rub against each other; the new chain must be made of gleaming splinters of burning grenades.' I made the drawings as desired, and he issued his orders accordingly. The institution of the new Order was duly announced in the *Moniteur*, but the terms of the treaty of peace compelled him to suppress a distinction the chief aim of which had been to humiliate the conquered countries of Spain and Austria.

Peace had already been signed on the 14th, and the Emperor now returned to France.

Major-General Prince Berthier remained in Vienna at the head of the army. The important arrangements for the withdrawal of our troops, and the various precautions taken in case of any infringement of the conditions of the treaty, did not prevent us from devoting a good deal of time to amusement. The wives of several generals came to rejoin their husbands. The Countesses of Daru and Bertrand had also lately arrived in Vienna, charming every one about them with their grace and courtesy. Fêtes and balls succeeded each other rapidly, leaving us little time for repose. The young Viceroy, Prince Eugène, who was just at the age when pleasure is so fascinating, was not the least active in promoting the festivities.

Eight days had passed happily away in amusements when Prince Berthier sent me to Prince Poniatowski, at Cracow, to inform him of the additional clauses of the treaty of peace, to tell him where his future cantonments were to be, and to ascertain from him the condition of his troops, the state of his fortresses, and what his requirements were.

When the first news of the armistice of Znaim reached Prince Poniatowski, his army had already ascended the Vistula beyond Cracow, and he was master of the strongholds of Mod-

9

lin, Sierosk, and Zamoski, which he had placed in a good state of defence. I went to Galicia by way of Brünn and Olmütz, the latter a strong fortress, where the Austrians put considerable difficulties in my way, detaining me for five hours, and passed thence by way of Teschen into Austrian Silesia, finally arriving at Cracow, where I found the Prince.

I had already frequently met him at Warsaw during our campaigns, and he now received me with all courtesy and honour. Prince Poniatowski was much beloved by the Poles, who all hoped the Emperor would place him on the throne of Poland. His handsome person was set off by his easy, graceful manners, the outcome of the truly chivalrous nature which made him the hero he was in war and in gallantry. No soldier was ever braver than he, and though perchance others may have been more faithful, no lover was ever more respectful. Very often was he to be seen sleeping on straw at night, as did the rest of us. He was always most careful for the welfare of his soldiers, and I used to see him sometimes in the midst of his cares toying with a very small gold ring, which he tried to get on to his little finger. No doubt when he took this ring from the willing hand which had bestowed it on him, he had promised never to part with it; and as he could not wear it, he was in constant dread of losing it.

I dismounted at the Prince's quarters at Cracow, and found him surrounded by many of the chief nobles of Poland, who had flocked to his banner. Amongst them were Princes Lubomirski, Radzivil and Czartoriski, Counts Potocki, Kaminski, Sarekowski, &c., who all loaded one with attentions. The Russian General, Prince Suvaroff, son of the General who had fought against us in Italy, was at Cracow with his division, supposed to be there to cooperate with the Polish army in the interests of France; but the probability is that these troops were really waiting to profit by our defeat rather than to aid in our success, and everything Suvaroff did pointed to this conclusion. For all that, the Poles and Russians lived together in Cracow on very good terms, and Prince Suvaroff, to whom I went to pay my respects, received me as a friend. Near him, stretched out upon a big rug of sable fur, was a very beautiful woman, to whom he presented me. Her long black hair, into which were twisted strings of large pearls, hung about her shoulders in studied negligence, and her snow-white neck and arms were also decked with chains of magnificent pearls. The expression of her face was pleasing and gentle. I thought she was the Princess, wife of the General, and I began to address her, when the Prince said: 'She does not understand you; she is a Circassian, whom I bought not long ago.' He then acted as interpreter, and I had quite a long chat with her, feeling as if I were transported for the moment to an Eastern seraglio.

On November 3rd, Prince Joseph Poniatowski held a review of 20,000 of his Poles on a fine plain six leagues from Cracow. We went to see it, escorted by more than a hundred officers. The Prince had sent me a magnificent and richly caparisoned horse, the only white one in the army; and when we arrived opposite the troops I noticed that the donor of my steed drew back a little, so as to give me the place of honour. I manoeuvred in the same way to give place to him, and not succeeding, I begged him to excuse me from going first. Then with perfect grace and dignity he said, as he reined in his horse to allow me to pass, 'You are here as the envoy of the Emperor.' 'Prince,' I replied, ' your orders must of course be obeyed;' and giving the reins to my horse, I let him show off his grace and docility before the eyes of the whole army, as I rode between Prince Poniatowski and Prince Suvaroff, but slightly in advance of them.

Before the march past the Prince had several manoeuvres executed, and I congratulated him on his skill in achieving evolutions so much more rapid than those of our infantry, which always loses an incredible amount of time in deploying. This slowness of movement may add to the precision of a manoeuvre, but it is dangerous under the fire of the enemy. I fought against it whenever I had anything to do with manoeuvring troops, and I rejoiced greatly when, as long afterwards as 1840, the corps known as the Chasseurs d'Orléans was formed, and the so-called *pas gymnastique* with greater rapidity of formation was introduced into the French army.

The 20,000 Poles, whether infantry, artillery, or cavalry, all wore uniforms similar to those of the French, and they seemed

11

delighted at being reviewed by their Prince in sight of a French officer sent to them by the Emperor. I had been charged by him to congratulate them on the courage they had shown in the campaign, and to distribute rewards, such as increase of pay and crosses of the Legion of Honour, all of which were received with loud cheers.

Our return to Cracow after this fine review was like a cavalry charge, for we dashed at full gallop through the deep mud of Poland, which just now was at its worst; and when we arrived we were so completely coated with mire from head to foot, that we could only recognise each other by our voices. We had started all gleaming with gold – we came back reduced, men and horses alike, to one uniformly hideous state of chocolate colour. We all had baths and changed everything, so that when we appeared at dinner no traces were left of our mad ride; and our costumes at the ball after it were by no means the least brilliant there.

On the 4th I took leave of our allies and of their fair companions. A little later I met the Archduke Ferdinand at the Posoritz posting station, and he did me the honour of chatting with me for a few minutes. He asked me how I liked the country and if I knew it well, and I answered, smiling, that I had bivouacked in the garden of this very house on the eve of the battle of Austerlitz. The Prince frowned as he looked round on the memorable scene, but for all that he asked me to explain certain points, and as I did so I vividly recalled the glorious and interesting memories of four years before, over which, however, I could not very well gloat in the Archduke's presence. The damage to his carriage, which had delayed him, having been repaired, he resumed his journey, and I went on to Brünn, where I found Austrian troops. I got back to Vienna on the 7th, having traversed 300 leagues going and returning.

The few days I had at Vienna were spent in fêtes given by Prince Eckmühl, the Countesses Daru and Bertrand, the Princess Czartoriska, and others, and when I left the city I had but just come from a ball. A little incident of my departure will give an idea of the Viennese mode of speeding their parting French guests. A coach-builder had made for me, and duly delivered, a handsome barouche, for which I paid him two hundred florins before I started in it for Cracow. The paper money I had given him had lost a twentieth part of its value during my absence, and on my return, hearing that I meant soon to be off again, the man demanded a hundred francs to make up for his loss. I refused, and the matter seemed at an end; but as the carriage – which was to be drawn by four horses – was to start before daybreak, my postillion went to look at the wheels, to see whether they were well greased, so that we might go at a good pace. Great was his surprise at discovering that the coach-builder had removed the screws of the wheels, evidently intending me to break my neck the first time the horses felt the whip. How these good Germans did love us, to be sure! And we fully returned their feelings. I sent some guards to the coach-builder to take all the screws he had, and having picked out those which fitted my wheels, I started.

I had the pleasure of meeting my brother with his regiment en route, and I reached Munich on November 14th, where I joined Major-General Prince Berthier, now the Prince of Wagram.

The Prince of Wagram presented me to the Queen of Bavaria, and the King assigned me apartments in his palace next door to those of the sister of the Prince of Linange, whom I had met, as related above, in the Tyrol. The King, who was always good to me, showed me his fine pictures, and invited me to dinners and fêtes at Court, where I heard the celebrated Mademoiselle Longiu play the harp, and Mademoiselle Blangini, the well-known amateur, perform on the violin. The King congratulated me on having got back my nose, which he had heard had been shot off at Saragossa, and I took leave in very good spirits of my amiable host, to follow the Major-General, who was returning to France.

I was scarcely back in Paris before I found myself in a perfect whirl of fêtes, balls, and festivities of all kinds.

On the 4th the Municipality of Paris gave a grand ball at the Hotel de Ville in honour of the Emperor. More than 6,000 persons were invited to this fête, and it was kept up until long after daybreak.

13

On the 6th the Prince of Wagram invited to his hunting seat, known as the Château de Gros Bois, all the kings and foreign princes who were in Paris, and during the few hours devoted to the chase the neighbouring forests resounded with the blowing of horns and the firing of guns. A splendid repast, a theatrical entertainment, and a ball concluded the day's festivities.

Many of the attendants of the guests had on this occasion partaken too freely of the good things provided for their masters, and we soon discovered that our drivers were dead drunk. In fact, my men fell off the box of my carriage. It would have been inhuman to leave them lying helpless on the road, so, with the aid of a friend who was with me, I picked them up and put them inside, whilst he and I took their places outside, and drove them back to Paris. Many of the royalties would have been wise to follow our example, but of course they did not dare to do so, and they ran great risk of losing life and throne by being turned over or smashed up through the overpowering of their coachmen by the fumes of champagne.

On the 7th there was a grand theatrical entertainment at the Tuileries, and, as the Emperor expressed it a little later at Erfurt, 'There was a regular *parterre* of kings.' Talma, Crescentini, and Grassini were the chief stars of the evening, and surpassed themselves. I have some cause to remember that night, for I seem to have been so much absorbed in contemplation of a particular box that the Emperor asked the Prince of Wagram, 'Which of your aides-de-camp is it who turns so persistently towards that one box?'

It was not till the entertainment was over that the Prince could see my face, tell the Emperor my name, and make fun of me.

Four days later, on the 15th, the divorce took place. It was a regular day of mourning to all who loved the Emperor and the Empress Josephine, whose very name was synonymous with grace and benevolence. Public opinion agreed in looking upon the union between that Princess and the Emperor as a talisman indispensable to the fulfilment of his lofty destiny. When the Empress, with her gentle grace and her ever ready sympathy for the unfortunate, descended from the throne, the star of the

Emperor lost something of its lustre, and his prosperity perhaps received something like a check. That was, at least, the opinion of all the good-hearted men of the time, who looked upon Prince Eugène, the son of the Empress, and the adopted child of the Emperor, as the possessor of the right qualities for carrying out, after the Emperor's death, all the grand schemes which that great man might leave unfinished. Politicians, on the other hand, considered a grand marriage and a union with some one of royal blood and long descent indispensable to the consolidation of the Empire and future fortunes of France. The Emperor, too ambitious from his very childhood, was greatly flattered at the idea of the Emperor of Russia being willing to give him his sister, and the Emperor of Austria his daughter. The latter was of the same religion as Napoleon, she was descended from the old Hapsburg family, and it was to her that French politicians wished the Emperor to pay court. The winning of such an ally as the Emperor of Austria could but increase his power, and there seemed no longer any doubt as to his choice.

On the 17th the Empress left the Palace of the Tuileries, and retired to the Château Malmaison, whilst the Emperor went to Trianon near Versailles, whither he was accompanied by his three sisters and their ladies-in-waiting. The Prince of Wagram followed him thither with a few officers, including myself. During the ten days Napoleon spent at Trianon he gave up his mornings to visiting the late Empress Josephine at Malmaison, and we witnessed a renewal of the heartrending partings, accompanied by protestations of an eternal affection sacrificed in the interests of the Empire alone. The men were full of admiration for the courage and strength of Napoleon the politician, the women were astonished at the inconstancy of Napoleon the ambitious conqueror, but for all that they did their best to please him.

During my stay with the Court at Trianon, a little episode occurred in which I did not figure exactly as a hero. A lady to whom I took all the greater fancy because she had reason to complain of her husband's inconstancy, but who had hitherto repelled my advances, had at last consented to grant me an interview.

15

I was very much afraid of being prevented from keeping my appointment with her, and did my utmost not to fail her. On the day named I mounted my fleetest steed, got to Paris in capital time, took up my post in a half-open carriage, drew back out of sight, and awaited events. Some twenty paces off, in the same avenue of the Champs-Elysées, a second hired carriage drew up, evidently also waiting for some one. Our two coachmen were on the watch, and the first person to appear was my fair one, who, trembling and so closely veiled that I did not recognise her, sprang furtively into the carriage she thought was mine, and was driven off at a brisk trot. I waited for two hours, but no lady came. I learnt afterwards that she had flung herself into the arms of her husband, who was waiting for another lady, and that each had explained the rencontre by expressing jealousy of the other. The peace thus restored remains still unbroken, so that I had my journey and lost my time for nothing. Anyhow I have the pleasure of knowing that I aided in re-establishing harmony in a somewhat unsettled home. I got back to Trianon before I was missed, but, as may be imagined, I felt somewhat crestfallen. On the 28th the Emperor returned to Paris, and until December 31st our time was spent in Court festivities, parades, brilliant reviews of the corps returning from the army, or in balls given by the Queens, sisters of the Emperor, and others, at which the display of costly materials, embroideries, jewels, &c., gave an immense impulse to the trade of Paris.

Amongst these balls a very remarkable one was given by Marescalchi, the Italian Minister, at which a grand quadrille was danced, representing a game of chess, the thirty-two dancers being dressed in exceedingly rich costumes, as the kings and princes of Egypt and Persia with certain of their subjects. On account of my height I was told off to be Sesostris or the great Ptolemy, the lovely Madame de Barral was my queen, and our purple and gold garments sparkled with the rubies with which they were lavishly sprinkled. The beautiful Duchess of Bassano, her costume one blaze of lapis lazuli and sapphires, and M. de Legrange, who was called Apollo, sat side by side opposite to us on the throne of Persia, which was assaulted, taken, and checkmated by the soldiers of Pharaoh. These soldiers were the most beautiful of the princesses and duchesses of the day. My pawn was the Princess of Aremberg. These charming battalions, who had no offensive weapons but the bewitching glances from their eyes, were attacked, supported, and defended by men dressed up as fools, bells and all, who gambolled about in true fool's style; and by horsemen amounted on docile yet fiery steeds, caparisoned in silk and gold, whose cardboard feet were not likely to trample any one down, whilst behind them rose frowning but gilded towers with battlements unmanned by archers, representing the ramparts of the Empire. The brilliant actors of the scene manoeuvred on a floor marked out to represent an ivory and ebony chess-board. The Queen advanced in a cold, imperious, and threatening manner; and the good King, compelled to submit to the laws of the game, greatly regretted not to be able to advance more than one step at a time in the direction of her pretty soldiers.

The news of the divorce and of the approaching marriage of the Emperor was received with considerable grief by the army, and great was the dismay when it was found that his choice had fallen on a foreign princess. But no notice was taken of this feeling of regret; diplomatic notes were exchanged between the French and Austrian Courts, and the marriage of the Emperor with an Archduchess was definitely arranged.

The Emperor now named the ladies who were to form the household of the new Empress; and the Duchess of Montebello, widow of Marshal Lannes, who had been created Duke of Montebello before his death, was made one of her maids of honour. On the same day the Emperor addressed a message to the Senate to announce that he was sending the Prince of Neuchatel (Marshal Berthier) to Vienna as ambassador extraordinary to represent him at the ceremonies of betrothal and marriage. The Prince did me the honour of taking me with him, and I started for Vienna once more on February 24th. This time I arrived in a carriage drawn by six horses, and not, as before, on horseback with drawn sword. The cannon greeted us yet again, but only to do us honour. I took my friend M. le Paillot with me, for I wanted him to share in the festivities; and as it was carnival time, we had a good deal of amusement of one kind and another.

I alighted at the Imperial Palace, where apartments had been prepared for the ambassador; and when I took possession of my quarters in the evening of the same day, a little accident occurred to me which gave me a strange insight into the real nature of the apparently rich appointments of the Emperor's grand residence.

My rooms were adorned with a profusion of gilded bronzes, and the chandelier of the salon was of specially elegant design. I noticed the rich gleam from it and its delicacy of finish, and an unlucky impulse made me think I should like to try and lift it to see how much the twenty-four branches of which it consisted weighed, for the golden chain from which it hung looked very thin. I climbed a chair, and what was my surprise at finding, when I lifted the chandelier, that it weighed no more than pasteboard or the lightest wood! I was so taken aback that I was perhaps not quite careful enough in removing my hands, and the four chains all gave way at once; the magnificent chandelier, falling with a crash, broke into a thousand pieces on the floor, revealing that the material of the whole thing – ornaments and all – was nothing more than larchwood. There was a fire burning in a magnificent grate, so I hastened to fling all the rubbish which had thus fallen a victim to my curiosity into the flames, and I never heard another word about the matter. But my thoughts involuntarily turned to the illusions of one kind and another which had led our Emperor to fix his choice on a foreign princess, and I feared that some day worse deceptions would be practised on him by the Court of Austria than that which on this occasion at Vienna made me realise so sadly the truth of the old proverb, 'All is not gold that glitters.'

I afterwards learnt that the Tyrolese have made quite an industry of copying French bronzes in wood, which the Germans buy at a small cost as decorations for their residences, the brilliant imitations passing muster except when tampered with by clumsy visitors.

Soon after I got to Vienna I had to go and officially inform M. Otto, the French Ambassador, and all the principal personages at the Court, of the arrival of the Ambassador Extraordinary. A few hours later the Prince of Neuchatel, who had to make a public and ceremonious entry, went with his suite to the palace of the Prince von Schwarzenberg in the suburb of Carinthia, whence he was escorted with a pomp worthy of the heirs of Charlemagne – his party, all in gala costumes, driving in some twenty or thirty gilded chariots, each drawn by six horses and surrounded by valets and footmen running before and beside them. Hungarian squadrons formed the escort, and the procession traversed the most densely populated quarters of the town, between two lines of regiments, who presented arms.

Arrived at the castle, where the staircases were lined by the halberdiers, the Imperial Guard, the lifeguardsmen, the arquebusiers, and the Hungarian 'Noble Guard' in their antique costumes, the Ambassador was ushered into the anteroom; the wide folding doors between it and the Great Hall, which had been prepared for the audience, were flung open; and with equal ceremony he was announced to the Emperor, awaiting him surrounded by his entire Court.

After the three salutes prescribed by etiquette, the Ambassador made a short speech to the Emperor, to which that monarch replied; Prince Berthier then presented each of us in turn as the gentlemen of his suite. From this audience the Ambassador went to the apartments of the Empress, where the same ceremonial was observed. That Princess, one of the most remarkable women of the day, distinguished for the highest qualities alike of head and heart, though suffering greatly just then, did not refuse to receive us. Her Majesty replied to Prince Berthier's speech with such purity of language and in terms so flattering and touching that we were deeply moved. We were all presented to her, and she addressed a few most gracious words to each one of us.

The Ambassador Extraordinary then passed to the apartments of the five young Archdukes, four of whom had commanded the armies with which we had been at war. These four wore the white field marshal's uniform, but the fifth and youngest was dressed as a cardinal. Their Imperial Highnesses were ranged in a row according to their age and rank on a dais covered with green cloth and raised some two feet above the body of the hall. They looked not unlike motionless wax figures. The Prince of Neuchatel addressed a few complimentary remarks to them, and the eldest replied but could find little to say to us. They had provoked the war in the hope of conquering France, and had not yet forgiven us for their defeat.

After all these solemn interviews the Ambassador went to the palace of Prince Charles, where I had the good fortune to see that illustrious warrior, who during the last fifteen years had caused us to pass so many anxious nights by the Rhine and the Danube. There was nothing in his quiet face with its grave and gentle expression, or in his simple, modest, unassuming manner, to denote the mighty man of war; but no one who met his eyes could doubt him to be a genius.

The Ambassador asked his Imperial Highness if he would represent the Emperor Napoleon at the marriage ceremony, and in a voice the genuine tone of which went straight to our hearts, he replied, 'I accept with pleasure the proposal made to me by the Emperor of the French. I am flattered by his choice of me, and feel convinced that the projected alliance will result in a happy future for the two nations so worthy of each other's esteem. I shall count amongst the happiest moments of my life that in which in token of a frank and loyal union I shall offer my hand to the Archduchess Maria Louisa in the name of the great monarch whose delegate you are. I beg of you to convey to the whole French nation my desire that this union may cement for ever the friendship of our sovereigns and assure the happiness of their people.'

In the evening there was a public ball in the Apollo Hall, to which 6,000 persons were admitted. This Apollo Hall is a good-sized building used for public gatherings, and the Emperor is often there with his family, mixing as a friend or rather as a good father amongst his Subjects. Every one dresses just as he likes on these occasions, some going masked or otherwise disguised, others with faces uncovered, but the members of the higher nobility keep their hats on and wear a false nose; they also sport a little black cloak on their shoulders – these three peculiarities signifying that they are incognito. The conversation is as free as if they were completely masked. The people are all so full of respect and affection for the upper classes, that the Emperor, his ministers, and indeed his whole Court, mix familiarly with the lower orders without ever meeting with anything to annoy them. A band played the minuets, waltzes, and quadrilles, and nothing amused us more than the exceeding gravity with which the good Germans danced the melancholy minuet they are so fond of. Several rooms were decked out to represent groves full of flowers and shrubs, caves with fountains playing, or Chinese summer houses. Rivers of beer were poured out on every side, and the roast chicken and ham, without which no fête can be held in Vienna, were washed down with tokay.

There were plenty of seats everywhere, but nevertheless many young ladies sat on the knees of gentlemen (probably of very low degree), and no one seemed to think it at all bad manners to behave in this way in public. It all appeared to amuse the Emperor very much, and like any good citizen he received the congratulations of his subjects on his daughter's approaching marriage without showing the least annoyance at the indiscreet zeal displayed by some few.

On March 6th, after having paid a great many visits and admiring the extraordinary collections of curios belonging to the Count of Fries, which included ancient and modern violins, valuable on account of the great performers who had played on them, fine statues by Canova, &c., we returned to the Palace, where the Emperor received us at a grand gala banquet.

Hitherto only those who could prove thirty-two quarterings of nobility, which involved a genealogy to be traced back for seven or eight centuries, had been admitted to the Imperial table, but victory had broken through this superannuated etiquette, and here were we, twenty children of the people, raised up by the fortunes of war, courted and petted by the descendants of Charlemagne and Charles V. After the meal the salons were thrown open, in which were assembled many no-

21

ble dames in disguise, whilst the beauty and grace of others who remained unmasked made us feel how much we lost in not being allowed to look upon the charms of those who had disguised themselves.

The salons presented a most dazzling appearance. Several rows of gleaming white stucco columns upheld the ceiling, from which hung a great number of chandeliers formed of oblong-shaped pendants of Bohemian crystal, in which the light of countless candles was reflected in rainbow hues. I had never seen any illumination in France to compare in brilliancy with this. Equally unrivalled were the variety and richness of the costumes worn by the ladies, whose necks, waists, and arms were encircled with strings of the finest pearls I ever set eyes on, and who together made up most bewitching groups. The Hungarian ladies especially excelled all others, and amongst them I may name the beautiful young Countess Zicky, the Princess Kraschalkovitz, and Princess Esterhazy, whose hair was golden and whose shoulders were as white as alabaster. Her husband wore the rich Hungarian costume which is handed down in his family from father to son. Prince Ludwig von Liechtenstein, who was good enough to tell me the names of the chief people at the ball, called his friend Esterhazy to his side and said to him, 'Turn round so that the Colonel can see your clothes.' We had met before in Paris, and the Hungarian Prince was very polite to me, allowing me to examine in detail the huge pearls and diamonds forming the buttons of his pelisse, dolman, and even of his boots, and he assured me that the harness and trappings of his horse were even more valuable. The complete get-up was said to be worth more than six million francs, for which sum it had been several times pledged. I asked him to meet me at the next battle, and he promised laughing to do so in that very costume.

The Emperor, Empress, and the Archduchess Maria Louisa spent several hours at this fête, the young Princess attracting all eyes.

On the morning of the 7th the French Ambassador held a grand reception, and at two o'clock he went to dine with Prince Charles. At this dinner I saw many of the illustrious men whom

I had learnt to know and honour in our wars. All these princes and veteran field marshals, whom I might well have dreaded meeting in the camp, now received us as friends. I sat near the old Marshal, the Prince von Ligne, who was in his eighty-seventh year. He was still very handsome; his white hair was brushed up and curled as if he were still but thirty years old; he was full of life and spirits, and his memory was excellent. The conversation turned on his extraordinary journey in the Crimea with Potemkin in the suite of Catherine, Empress of Russia; and on the bombardment of Lille, when his only son was killed beside him. I reminded him of that son, as I was about the same age as he had been at his death, and the old man's eyes filled with tears. He also spoke a good deal of his friend the Duchesse de Coigny, a very witty woman, whom I also had the honour of knowing.

On March 8 there was a great gathering at the Palace for the ceremony of asking the hand of the Archduchess in marriage. The Emperor, surrounded by all the chief dignitaries of the Court, received the Ambassador Extraordinary, who made the formal proposal of marriage, which concluded in the following words: 'The Princess called to a great throne will make the happiness of a great people and of a great man.' The Emperor made a gracious reply, ending with the words, 'I grant the hand of my daughter to the Emperor of the French.'

The Empress then appeared leading the young Archduchess, to whom the Ambassador addressed a few courteous words, concluding by saying, 'Political considerations may have influenced the decision of the two monarchs, but the Emperor Napoleon cares more to win your heart, Madame, than anything else.' To which the Archduchess replied, 'I have always made my father's will my own. I consent with my father's permission to my union with the Emperor Napoleon.'

The Prince of Neuchatel then took the portrait of Napoleon, set in big diamonds, from the hands of the Comte de Laborde, and handing it to the Emperor begged him to give it to our future Empress, who seemed pleased to receive it. After this interview there was a grand matinee in the fine hall known as that of the Columns.

The next day the Court went in state to the Grand Theatre, the Emperor having the Empress on his left and the Archduchess on his right. The Ambassador and his suite were admitted to the Imperial box, where the light was as strong as sunshine. I was very near the Archduchess, and without being seen by her, for I was hidden by the feathers of the ladies, I made a drawing of her profile. My neighbours made signs to me that they thought it a capital likeness, whilst we listened to the music of Gluck in the opera of *Iphigenia in Aulis*, and admired the easy grace of the Viennese dancers.

On the 10th, part of the day was occupied in witnessing a far more interesting scene, recalling the days of chivalry, for there was a solemn distribution of the orders of chivalry of the Empire. The Emperor, wearing the robes, mantle, and big antique cap of the Grand Masters of the Teutonic Order, went attended by a huge retinue to the palace of the Grand Master, there to hold a chapter of the orders. When I entered the great hall enriched with the beautiful armour, banners, portraits, and emblazoned escutcheons of the great barons of the Empire, with the quaint antique arm-chairs, now occupied by some fifty knights, each wearing a robe and mantle of purple velvet similar to those of the Emperor, I felt for a moment as if I were transported back ten centuries to a feudal gathering of the Middle Ages. The speeches were made in Latin. The diplomas, written on parchment, to each of which were appended the huge sigillum of the Order and the seals of the Empire, were given to the recipients as they knelt before the Emperor, who then placed the chain of the Order round their necks.

Then came the knights who were to receive the Order of the Golden Fleece, succeeded by the Grand Cross Knights or cordons bleus of the Order of St. Stephen, originally instituted as the National Order of Hungary, now adopted by the Imperial Family and the grand dignitaries of the Royal Order of Leopold of Hungary for personal merit, of which I was made a Knight.

More interesting than anything else in this grand spectacle was, however, the distribution of the decorations of the Maria Theresa Order, founded by the Empress of that name for officers distinguished in war only, which could be given to none but those who had performed some brilliant feat of courage in the service of their country, duly recorded in the official army reports and attested by incontrovertible witnesses. The account of the historic deed which has merited the decoration is read aloud in German in the presence of the whole chapter of the Order, and no one ever becomes a Maria Theresa knight without the whole nation being informed of what has won him that great honour.

On the 11th we all went in a grand procession to the Imperial Palace, and thence to the Cathedral of St. Stephen, where the marriage ceremony was performed with the greatest solemnity beneath a canopy in the presence of the Imperial Family, the Prince Archbishop, his numerous clergy, and the whole Court. A drawing room was then held in a vast gallery, at which from eight to ten thousand persons were present, the greatest silence and decorum being preserved. The Imperial Family sat on a raised platform, the newly made Empress of the French occupying the seat of honour in the centre of the group, and wearing the brilliantly set portrait of Napoleon. We were presented, and the ceremony of kissing hands began, the young Princess taking off her glove. The Ambassador was the first, and I was the fourth or fifth, to have the honour of doing reverence to our Empress.

In the evening a drawing room was held at Court in the big Throne Room, after which there was a grand supper at the Imperial table, the good burghers circulating about the room meanwhile in the most respectful silence.

Thus ended the marriage ceremonies at Vienna, and the departure for Paris of those of us who were to precede the Empress was fixed for the next day.

Just as I was getting into my carriage, a dealer in precious stones came up to me, and asked me to take to a fellow merchant in Paris a little green round box about the size of an apricot. I consented with great readiness, but thought I would just ask him what was in it. 'There are two diamonds,' he replied as he opened the box; 'this one is worth 30,000 francs, and that one, though not so large, is worth 100,000 francs.' 'Oh, indeed!'

I exclaimed. 'Well, take your box back; I should not like you to risk losing all that, and I might be robbed on the way.' He insisted, however, on my doing as he asked, adding that I should be rendering him a very great service. Much against my will, I consented at last, and fortunately the only inconvenience I experienced was that of being afraid of thieves for the first time in my life. I arrived at Stuttgart before the Empress on the 20th. I find that my notes made when in that town express my astonishment at the luxury and magnificence displayed at the Court of Würtemberg, which resembled that of Louis XIV. at Versailles, though on a very much smaller scale. The richness of the uniforms and accoutrements of the bodyguards, the splendour of the furniture, table services, illuminations, &c., the extraordinary *éclat* with which the grand opera of *Solomon* with Winter's music was put upon the boards, all alike appeared most remarkable at a German Court of secondary rank. We were all received, lodged, and feasted at the palace as if we had ourselves been grand princes.

In the midst of the pleasures of the Court, when I was thinking of anything but my duties, I was suddenly summoned to the presence of Caroline Murat, then Queen of Naples, and the Prince of Neuchatel, who had arrived at Stuttgart with the Empress. They entrusted me with a message for the Emperor, and before daybreak the next morning I was rolling along in the midst of clouds of dust in a carriage drawn by six post horses, taking with me a note from the Queen and many regrets of my own. It was March 20th, a day I never forgot.

The Prince of Bauveau, one of the old noblesse of the former Court of France who had rallied round the Emperor, and was now his Grand Chamberlain, was also on his way to Paris with a letter from the Empress. I joined him at Strasburg, and we travelled together, finding the Emperor at Compiègne, where he was awaiting his new bride. The Emperor received the Prince with great honour in the salon, and then took me into his private apartments, where, altogether laying aside his regal manner, he began chatting away with the most delightful abandon, making me tell him all about the festivities at Vienna, Munich, and Stuttgart. He had the portrait of the Empress brought to him, and asked me if was really like her. I showed him also the profile sketch I had made, and he exclaimed at once, 'Yes, she has the regular Austrian lip of the Hapsburgs!' Then he pointed out the same peculiarity in some medals, and making me stand close to him, he leant over the table so as to get the light of the lamp on the portrait, with which he seemed quite in love. He asked me yet again if I thought it like her – if it were flattered. 'And are her eyes really like that? as blue as that? Is not her nose smaller? . . . It really is the Austrian lip, isn't it?' he went on, as he pouted his own lips a little. 'Is she taking at first sight? Has she a bright smile? Is she as tall as that? (indicating his own height). Is she this, that, and the other? Tell me! tell me! tell me everything about her!'

'Yes, sire! Yes, sire!' I kept on repeating; and then, rubbing his hands together like a thoroughly happy man, he began again. 'Well, how did the Vienna fêtes go off? I hope those we are going to give will please every one still more. We mean to astonish them. France is the only place for real good taste. So the King of Würtemberg had a fine display too? Yes, he has the grand manner, he is a regular Louis XIV. in miniature; he'll ruin himself. The people of Germany seem very pleased about the marriage, then?' In a word, his Majesty was in a most charming mood, and would have liked to ask me a great many more questions, showing how eager he was to see the Empress, only some one interrupted us to tell him that a wing of the Palace had caught fire, and he dismissed me.

A few days later the Emperor's longing was fulfilled by the arrival of the Empress. He rode out unattended for several miles to meet her, and as soon as he caught sight of the procession he galloped up to her carriage, sprang off his horse, made the attendants open the door, and flinging his arms round his bride embraced her tenderly, much to the surprise of the Princess, who was in the singular position of finding herself being kissed by a stranger who had given no one time to introduce him.

When I got to Paris, I really had had enough of festivities, and I enjoyed being able to take up my brushes again. In the ceremonies which now rapidly succeeded each other, I only took the share forced on me by my position. The civil marriage of the Imperial couple took place with great pomp at Saint-Cloud on April 1, and I remember that some of those who had opposed it from the first whispered to me that they looked upon the perjury of that day as a very ominous augury for the future.

The Emperor wore his imperial robes, and the Empress had on her head the crown set with diamonds.

After the ceremony of the civil marriage there was a grand banquet, and in the evening Paris was brilliantly illuminated.

On April 2nd, a day of bright sunshine succeeding a night of storm, the religious marriage was celebrated in the grand salon of the Louvre, which had been converted into a chapel consecrated and decorated for the occasion. On their way to it the august pair walked through the great gallery of the Louvre, lined on either side from end to end by platforms on which were seated several rows of ladies in full dress. It would be impossible to imagine a more brilliant scene, and I for one never saw anything equal to it. Temporary staircases were erected along the quays and on the Place du Carrousel to facilitate the exit of the crowds invited to the fête.

A calm and very dark night added to the lustre of the millions of cressets, variegated lamps, Bengal fires, and other illuminations, which outlined alike the form and the ornamentation of every building, the arches of the bridges, &c. At a great height above the towers of Notre-Dame rose a brilliant Temple of Hymen, and the whole of Paris resembled a sea of fire which was reflected in the waters of the Seine. The Place de la Concorde, especially surrounded as it was by richly decorated and illuminated buildings, presented a most extraordinary appearance. The Champs-Elysées were crowded with bands of music, dancers, and various shows. But when daylight came every one had dispersed, and nothing was left of the magnificent display but the memory of it.

This great 2nd of April was marked by a happy innovation. It had been the custom in Paris for centuries on all occasions of public rejoicing to have the fountains run with wine, and for all manner of good things to eat to be flung from platforms and balconies to the crowd below. Horrible scenes used to take place amongst the people jostling each other round the fountains and beneath the platforms, the strongest of course getting the best of everything, whilst the weak were often trodden under foot and rolled over in the dust amongst the men who had fallen down dead drunk. For many a long day the ignoble spectacle of broken glasses and tipsy men stained with wine had been an inseparable adjunct to every outdoor fête; but the Emperor, who was most anxious to raise the tone of public manners and morality, determined that there should be no coarse vulgarity about the largesse he bestowed, although it was in fact on a more liberal scale than had ever before been known. He ordered good food to be taken to the homes of the indigent, and organised a distribution of lottery tickets, the thousands of prizes including such things as pies, hams, loaves of bread, &c. The distribution took place in perfect order, very little liquid was spilled, and I only saw a few men staggering about tipsy who had brought nothing to receive their wine in, and had drunk their share off at a single draught.

The panorama of the battle of Wagram from my sketches was making rapid progress, and I received orders to put in the movements of the troops. I was already looked upon in Paris as the chief historical painter of our campaigns, and I received the kindest advice from the celebrities of our day, especially from David. Not depending as so many did on my art work for my daily bread, I was never afraid of giving too much time to details. One day, when I was making an excuse to David for having been so long over a painting, he reassured me by saying, 'What is quickly done is quickly seen, and would not bear the test of careful examination.'

The Imperial Guard was anxious in its turn to give a fête in honour of the Empress. The vast plain of the Champ de Mars, the buildings of the Military College, and the great courts connected with it, were crowded with those invited to witness the display. The grand balcony and all the apartments of the College, which was a regular palace, were richly decorated for the recep-

29

tion of the Imperial pair and their Court, who were to witness during the day numerous chariot and horse races, great numbers competing at a time, the winners amongst the drivers and riders, got up in gala array, coming up to receive their prizes from the hands of the Empress. All manner of equestrian games and tournaments were organised to amuse the crowds, and one excitement succeeded another for several hours. At last as the sun began to set a number of balloons, launched at a considerable height, were seen to traverse space, catching and reflecting the dying beams as the twilight gathered about us. The atmosphere was perfectly clear and calm, and we could distinctly follow the course of the balloons through the air. Then, as a climax to the whole fête, Mademoiselle Blanchard, the celebrated aeronaut, having received the signal to start, had the cords cut which held down her huge balloon, richly decorated with mottoes and various devices, and as it rose majestically into the air she flung down amongst the spectators baskets of flowers and thousands of light silk scarves, handkerchiefs, fichus, &c., which as they fell assumed the appearance of many-coloured flames. The delight of the people below at receiving these dainty ornaments of the toilette knew no bounds. Night soon fell, and from the balloons, which still slowly floated above us, were flung fireworks representing luminous meteors, which lit up the whole sky for a great distance and fell in golden showers. The beautiful face and figure with the courage of the fair young aeronaut excited the greatest interest among us, and we trembled for her when we realised the danger she ran of setting herself on fire as she lit the many fireworks launched by her. Fortunately, however, she escaped this time, though she met a terrible fate later, for having ascended above the clouds she was flung upon a roof in Paris and killed on the spot.

After the grand display of fireworks, Marshal Bessières, as president of the fête, went to beg the Empress, as he presented to her the golden wand of Medea, to act as the enchantress and by a touch from it set free the dragon who was to light up all the palaces of fairyland.

At this every one around the bride began to laugh, and the

Emperor with the warriors of his suite shouted with merriment as they saw the terrified hesitation with which the young Princess received the alarming request that she would set fire to a dragon, for she evidently thought that was what was meant, and that the animal would go off with a roar like that of a cannon. The Emperor, however, insisted on her complying, and guided her trembling little hand. She shut her eyes, and when she opened them again there was a magnificent dragon just flinging itself like a thunderbolt from the balcony, to go to the Champ de Mars and with the flames issuing from it light up one after another the grandest illuminations ever seen, including representations of palaces and temples, allegorical scenes, inscriptions, all manner of devices in coloured fire, sheafs of flames, showers of stars and sparks, and one huge volcano, by the light of which we could see as in broad day the crowds, numbering some 600,000 persons, drawn to the slopes of the Champ de Mars by the magnificent spectacle. It was eleven o'clock before we could tear ourselves away, and retire to the rooms prepared for dancing.

The courts of the College were transformed for the nonce into grand halls, in one of which supper was served, whilst a ball was held in the others. The decorations, all of a martial character, were very effective and tasty. Every one of note in Paris was present, and the most perfect order was maintained.

My evenings were now all happily spent at balls, now at the house of Count Daru, now at that of one or another of the Ministers, and I spent the days working at my pictures, which many distinguished visitors came to look at, encouraging me very much. Amongst those I should like to name with gratitude on account of the interest they took in me were Prince Eugène, the Prince and Princess of Wagram (Marshal Berthier and his wife), the Princesses Jablonowska and Sapieha, &c.

At last came the fête given by the Prince von Schwarzenberg, then Austrian Ambassador at the Imperial Court, in honour of the august marriage he had done so much to bring about. The Prince's mansion, situated in the Rue de Montblanc (now the Rue de la Chaussée d'Antin), was surrounded by a beautiful garden, in which were represented many of the

31

places where the young Empress had passed her childhood, in each of which some of the dancers connected with the Opera, wearing Austrian costumes, acted scenes from the early life of her Imperial Highness. This delicate attention made the first part of the fête very charming to the Empress, who was evidently greatly touched.

For the reception of the twelve or fifteen hundred invited guests the Prince had had a big room run up of boards, which was richly decorated with mirrors, flowers, pictures, and draperies, and lit up by an immense number of candles. The ball had been going on for about an hour, and in spite of the stifling heat a Scotch reel was being vigorously danced. The Empress, the Princess Borghese, the Princess von Schwarzenberg, sister-in-law of the Ambassador, and a hundred other ladies, were eagerly engaged in treading the energetic measure of that dance, when a candle in one of the lustres near the door fell and set fire to some drapery. Colonel de Tropbriant rushed with one bound to the curtain to try and drag it down, but his sudden clutch at the drapery only spread the flames, and in less than three seconds they had reached the ceiling, which had been smeared with spirit to make it dry quickly, and was moreover baked with the heat of the July sun, and further heated by the immense number of lighted candles. The flames rushed from end to end of the ceiling with the rapidity of lightning, and with a roar like that of thunder. In a moment all present found themselves beneath a vault of fire.

When the Emperor saw that there was no hope of extinguishing the conflagration, he calmly took the Empress by the hand and led her into the garden. The rest of the guests imitated the example of his coolness – there was not a single cry of alarm, and many of the dancers were still ignorant of the cause of the great increase in the light and heat. There seemed at first to be plenty of time to escape, and the company went towards the entrance to the garden without any hurry or crowding. Presently, however, the heat became insupportable, and those behind began to press on those in front, which led to several persons being thrown down on the steps leading to the garden. Fragments of the ceiling now began to fall, burning the hair and shoulders of the ladies, and setting fire to their clothes. In the terrible struggle which ensued the thicker garments of the men also caught fire, and many even of the strongest were flung down and trampled on. The sight of all these people in flames was truly awful. I had been able to get out easily amongst the first, escorting the Countess Sandizelle and Madame de Mathis, who were not hurt in the least, and having placed them in safety I made my way back to the entrance to the dancing room to try to help others. One of the first I was able to drag out of the fiery furnace was Prince Kourakin, the Russian Ambassador, who was in a horrible condition. One of his hands, all burnt away and bleeding, rested on my breast, and left its impress on my uniform. Beneath his body lay several half-burnt ladies, whom it was very difficult to extricate from the flames, as the swords of the men had got entangled in their clothes, and greatly hampered our efforts. On every side rose cries of agony and terror – mothers calling to their daughters, husbands to their wives. The garden, which was as light as at midday, was now full of distracted men and women seeking those they loved with heart-rending shrieks of despair, or flying with burning garments from the fiery furnace, struggling to extinguish the flames consuming them. Two mothers, the Princess von Schwarzenberg and the Princess de Layen, who had escaped to the garden and could not find their daughters there, impelled by their maternal love, heroically flung themselves back into the burning room to seek their children. The roof fell upon them, and only one, the Princess de Layen, got out alive. She died an hour afterwards, and the Princess von Schwarzenberg was never seen again until at the close of the awful scene her body, so terribly disfigured that it was only recognised by her diamonds and other jewels, was found amongst the debris left by the conflagration. Her diadem had been melted by the heat, and the silver setting had left its mark in a deep groove on her skull. Several ladies died the same night from their injuries, and others a long time afterwards, all in dreadful suffering. The men, whose clothes had protected them more, escaped better. Prince Kourakin, one of those who were the most hurt, did not fully recover for six months, and it was not till a year after the fire that the Countess Durosnel was able to leave her bed.

As soon as the Emperor had seen the Empress into her carriage he hastened back to the scene of the disaster to aid the sufferers, and remained until the morning, eagerly superintending all that was done on their behalf.

Amongst the victims was a lady, whom my friend Colonel Bontemps and I succeeded in dragging out of the flames on to the steps going down to the garden. She was so terribly burnt that her body was one wound, presenting a shocking spectacle. She bore the pain with marvellous courage, but we could not carry her or place her in a carriage, so we supported her one on each side by placing our arms under her armpits, the only part of her whole frame which was not burnt, and succeeded in getting her to her house in the Rue Royale after a most arduous and painful walk. One of her people ran off to fetch a doctor, and waiting for his arrival, which might be long delayed at this time of night, the happy idea occurred to my friend of sending for some olive oil, some fresh water, and the white of an egg. These he had all beaten up together, and then, soaking some rags in the liniment, he ordered them to be laid over the wounds. When the doctor came, long after we had left, he said we could not have done better. Our treatment was continued, and at the end of six weeks our patient had completely recovered. She turned out to be the wife of one of our best friends, M. Prévost, then holding a post in the War Department.

Ten people died from their injuries in the fire, and some hundred others were very badly hurt. The dismay in Paris was extreme when the news of the catastrophe was received; and all the veteran officers of the army, who had so regretted the union of the Emperor with the daughter of the hereditary enemy of France, did not fail to look upon the tragedy as an evil augury for the future, and to compare it with the catastrophe on the evening of the marriage of Louis XVI. with Marie Antoinette, when 3,000 persons were crushed to death or wounded in the Place Louis XV.

CHAPTER 2

Mission to Spain

On the evening of February 14th, I was at a grand masked ball at the house of Prince Cambacérès, Lord High Chancellor of the Empire, when a black domino of medium height and in a very simple toilette, who was standing near me, fixed his eyes on mine in a meaning manner, put one hand on my shoulder, and with the other made me a sign to keep silence. He then said, in a low voice, 'Hush! you are to go to the Tuileries at ten o'clock to-morrow – the Emperor wishes to speak to you.' I bowed respectfully, but gave no answer beyond an affirmative sign. The black domino, who was Prince Berthier, returned to the crowd of pleasure-seekers, and I purposely avoided watching him. I was extremely anxious to know what the Emperor could want with me, but I passed the rest of the night in amusing myself at the ball, and the next morning, February 15th, I went to the Tuileries to keep my appointment.

The aide-de-camp on duty at once ushered me into the Emperor's room, where Napoleon, in uniform and evidently just going out, said to me without preamble, 'It is a long time since I left Spain, and news comes slowly and with difficulty; go and see my brother. Remind him that with the forces I have placed at his disposal he ought to second me energetically. I insist on that point. Inform yourself as to the feeling in the country and the needs of the army. Examine the state of the troops, see Marshal Soult, with the other marshals and generals. Tell Dorsenne at Burgos to beware of N. N——. He is to give an account to the Duke of Istria of what he hears about him. You will go to Granada and see Sebastiani's army. You will tell that General to take as much quicksilver as he can get from the mines of Almaden to the magazines at Malaga. I'll send a man-of-war at once to Malaga to fetch the quicksilver, of which we are beginning to run short in France. The business must be conducted with all secrecy, lest the English cruisers should get wind of it and intercept the return of the vessel. Visit the arsenal at Seville, press on the siege of Cadiz. Examine everything in detail, men and stores; take note of everything, come back without loss of time, and give me such an account that I shall feel as if I had seen everything myself. Go to the Luxembourg and ask my sister-in-law if she has any messages for her husband, and then start at once. Berthier will give you his despatches.' Then, as he dismissed me, the Emperor added graciously, 'Go and win your promotion!'

As requested by the Emperor, I went to take leave of the Queen of Spain, who was a perfect angel of beauty and kindliness. She sent for her pretty children, so that I might tell the King about them. I then went to receive my instructions from Major-General Prince Berthier. I filled the belt of my valet de chambre Williams with gold pieces, and took with me the son of a friend of mine, for whom I promised to find a good appointment at Burgos. I felt well, for I had had a good rest since the war and was really almost tired of peace and festivities. My preparations were quickly made, and I started the same evening.

At Bayonne I left my carriage, to continue my journey on the good posting nags which can be had everywhere in Spain. The Baron de Soulages and M. Clouet, two engineer officers, friends of mine, who were going to join Marshal Ney, went with me, and our little cavalcade took the road to Madrid. As far as Tolosa the country was quiet and the road pretty safe, but beyond that we were warned by the postillions, wherever we changed horses, of the dangers by which we were threatened. We soon discovered that they were right, for the band under Mina fired at us, and when we reached Pancorbo, where the road winds between huge perpendicular rocks, at the foot of which a stream has hewn out a narrow channel so wild and forbidding that it resembles the entrance to a dungeon or to hell, some twenty brigands belonging to the guerrilla band under the chiefs nicknamed the Bourbon Brothers, who lay in ambush amongst the rocks, fired upon us, but, taken by surprise through the rapidity of our march, not one of them succeeded in hitting us. Several other bands made the approach to Vittoria very dangerous, and no one attempted to reach it without a strong escort. The road was no longer the beautiful camino real which but two years before had been strewn with flowers and shaded by thousands of triumphal arches made of laurel branches and set up in honour of the Liberator by the people of the country, who lined the route in eager enthusiastic crowds to see the Emperor go by. Now the road looked melancholy and deserted, and was encumbered with fragments of broken carriages, shreds of clothing, the bleaching bones of the unburied dead, the bodies of horses which the vultures were tearing to pieces, the effluvia from which poisoned the air, whilst here and there the corpses of brigands or peasants who had been taken with arms in their hands hung from the trees, and swayed to and fro in the wind.

We got to Vittoria in very low spirits, for the state of things made us anxious and depressed. General Joseph Caffarelli, one of the Emperor's aides-de-camp, gave us a hearty welcome in that town, where he was much loved and respected. I left my travelling companions here, and the General gave me a strong escort for the next stage of my journey.

It was always very annoying to me to have to wait for these escorts, or to give the men I had secured time to rest at every posting station. I was impatient to arrive at Madrid, and when I did at last get them to start they would creep along at a foot pace. When I heard a favourable account of the state of the country, I always galloped on without waiting for my escort, so that the enemy's spies should not have time to give notice of my coming, and this boldness was nearly always successful. I got to Burgos without accident, and dismounted at the residence of General Count Dorsenne, commanding a brigade of the Imperial Guard. When I arrived, the Count, who was preparing to give a fête to the people of the town, which was to include a ball, a lottery, &c., was in the hands of his hairdresser, who had so far only curled half of his beautiful long black hair, but he received me with open arms and begged me to allow him to finish his toilette. He asked me a great many questions about friends in Paris, and then inquired if the Emperor had sent him any special message. 'Yes.' I replied, 'I will tell you about it later.' 'Oh, tell me – tell me now!' 'No,' I said, pointing to the valet, who was watching and listening with eager eyes and ears to our conversation, evidently determined not to lose a word; 'no, no. I'll wait till you have finished.' 'Well,' replied the General, 'you might just as well speak before him; he is a trusty fellow.' I knew, however, that it was thanks to just such trusty fellows, who abused the blind confidence of the French, that the enemy was informed so promptly of all our movements, so I repeated, 'No, it is a serious matter.' 'Oh, never mind; speak out.' 'I have no right to let any one but you hear the message, but you can tell your valet what it is afterwards if you think fit to do so.' This remark, made with great gravity, seemed to surprise him, and he regretfully dismissed his man. I then informed the General of the Emperor's intentions, and dwelt upon the way in which the army had suffered from the indiscretion of those by whom the generals in Spain were surrounded, and of whom they apparently had themselves no suspicion.

I spent the night at the ball given by General Dorsenne, but I met none of the people I had known at Burgos two years before, for they had all emigrated. I was pressed to remain, but instead of doing so, I started early the next morning, when every one thought I was asleep.

The further I went in this unhappy country, the more cause I had for anxiety, and I was everywhere told, 'Yesterday or the other day such and such a courier or escort was assassinated . . . let us get on as quickly as we can.' The men would say, 'Beware of that wood, look out on that plain,' and so on. I got to Valladolid after many such alarms, where General Kellermann was then in command. It was even more dangerous to leave this town than it had been to enter it, so well organised was the system of espionage of the numerous guerrilla bands in the surrounding districts. I had great difficulty in finding a postilion who would brave the chance of meeting the brigands, and it was not until I had secured an escort of 200 Swiss soldiers that I managed to persuade a boy to go with me to bring back the post horses.

When we got to Valsequillas we found the whole place in an uproar after a struggle which had just taken place between a French battalion, escorting a number of prisoners, and a guerrilla band which had endeavoured to rescue them. The French, who had been terribly harassed on their march, had had to fall back on Olmedo, or they would certainly have lost their prisoners; and though my Swiss were very tired, I found they were willing to join in the fray, so I gave them plenty of bread and wine, which I was able quickly to secure on the spot, and led them in pursuit. The guerrillas, who were still fighting as we advanced, were thus between two fires, but as they had been strong enough to repulse a whole battalion they might easily have turned back and annihilated our little party. God did not, however, give them the courage to attempt it, and at sight of our 200 bayonets gleaning in the sunshine as our men advanced at the double, they separated like a flock of frightened birds, and ran away in every direction, leaving many wounded on the ground. When we entered Olmedo, every one rushed out to embrace us as so many liberators, and we were congratulated on having escaped the imminent danger we had braved. The next day the Swiss went back to rejoin the rest of the garrison of Valladolid, reinforcing on the way the battalion escorting the prisoners; and as I thought that the brigands of the day before were not likely to venture out of their retreat again directly, I started with one postilion and my faithful Williams, who was in a great fright for his own safety and for that of the contents of his belt. We sped like the wind across the wide plains leading to Coca, near to which I noticed the grand ruins of a great Moorish palace, which had belonged to some wealthy sultan. I wanted to go and examine the ruins more closely, but my guide stopped me with the Spanish proverb so applicable to the ways of his country just then, 'The spider hides in ruins to dart out on flies.' He urged me rather to pass them as quickly as possible, and he was evidently more than ever on the alert as long as we were near them. I, too, felt uneasy, but my real reason for crossing the plains in broad daylight was that I had been told the brigands themselves generally retired to a distance for their siesta, lest they should themselves be in their turn surprised. I reached Segovia without mishap before night.

There I found the old Count de T——. acting as French commander of the province of the same name, who was powdered and frizzled in the style of the generals of the army of Louis XVI. He had served in the American war. His great delight now was to give fêtes in honour of the French who happened to visit Segovia. He overwhelmed me with courtesies and offers of service. I knew that the old gentleman was unfortunately like a child in the hands of a lovely woman of Piedmont, who had him so completely in her power that she was able to betray him with the greatest ease to her handsome young lover, Don P., chief of the bands surrounding the town. Thanks to the information she gave him, this Don P. carried off nearly every courier or convoy which left Segovia, in spite of their escorts. I therefore pretended that I should like to remain some days in such pleasant company and to examine the various objects of interest in the town, such as the well-preserved Roman aqueduct, which is still in use. I passed the evening with the happy couple and some officers, and started, without a word to any one, before daybreak, with no escort, to cross the dangerous Fonda San Raphael passes and the Guadarrama mountains, which are almost always infested by brigands. I was again fortunate enough to escape all dangers, and arrived at Madrid on March 5th, having met no living thing except the numerous vultures quietly waiting by the roadside for the booty which the war—waged apparently in their interests – was sure to bring them every day. In spite of all the haste I could make, it had taken me eleven days to get from Bayonne to Madrid, whereas three years before I had done the same distance in forty hours.

I alighted at the residence of General Belliard, chief of the Staff to King Joseph, and went thence to the Royal Palace, where I was at once taken to his Majesty. That monarch, whose fine face reflected all his amiable qualities, had always loaded me with benefits, and he now did me the honour of receiving me as a friend. I little thought then that I should become his nephew a few months later!

After his Majesty had heard the news I brought him from Paris, he took me aside, and walking up and down alone with me in a spacious gallery, he gave me a most piteous account of his position. 'It is simply untenable,' he said; 'gladly would I consult the happiness of the people of Spain, over whom my brother chooses me to reign; I try to induce them to do as the Emperor wishes, but everything is against me. The exchequer is exhausted; the national debt is immense. The distress here is extreme, and discontent is on the increase. To try and win friends I have granted largesses, and the ungrateful recipients have simply gone over to the enemy with their hands full. My protection is absolutely powerless to save the Spanish from extortion, and as a result no one is in the least disposed to back me up. These disorders are the cause of the dilatoriness of which the Emperor complains.' The King then, with very great reluctance, gave me the names of those he complained of, with an account of the acts of insubordination which troubled him the most. 'My good Spanish subjects are irritated,' he added, 'and the number of guerrilla bands desolating the country to the very gates of Madrid is daily increasing. The beautiful provinces of Andalusia submitted voluntarily, and now they are oppressed. I suffer from this state of things more than I can express. Misery and famine will reduce my good Spanish subjects to despair. Unable to govern them as I wish, I am compelled to let them suffer. Still, I do not mean to abdicate. No; I will never abdicate. I will do all I can to ameliorate the lot of the Spanish, and I will remain faithful and devoted to the Emperor, to whom I owe everything. But make haste, I entreat you, to report to him all the sad details I have told you, and to describe to him the melancholy position in which you found me. Assure my brother that his presence here would put everything right, and that I beg him to return.' I explained to the King that all France was at that moment awaiting the accouchement of the Empress, and that the Emperor was not likely to be able to leave her immediately, so that he must not hope to see him yet awhile; that I too must also continue my journey, and complete the mission entrusted to me, so that I could not take his Majesty's messages to France till I had had the honour of seeing him again at Madrid on my way back. The King expressed his very great regret that he could not write all the details he had given me to his brother, explaining that if he did so and his letter were intercepted, it would only make his position worse than ever. He therefore made me promise to get back as soon as possible.

A good many of those I had to visit, amongst them some even of the *Josephinos*, as the friends of King Joseph were called, added to what he had told me other details which left me in no doubt whatever as to the cause of the misfortunes of the country.

'Your generals,' they said to me, 'are young, handsome, and already covered with glory; they win the hearts of our women, and under their rule all the laxity of morals is reproduced which led to the revolt against Don Godoy and Charles IV. No one fails to recognise the amiable qualities and good intentions of the King; every one appreciates the benefits which ought to accrue to the country from the introduction by him of the French Constitution. In speaking of the King the people say in their naïve way, "This foreign prince is a good fellow and governs us as if he meant to stop here all his life; we like his pleasant manners, he is good-looking and well set up; we are already fond of him, but we dare not attach ourselves to him too much, for he has a certain look about him which makes us think that he really wants to be off and will soon abandon us." The dread of the terrible reprisals we are threatened with by the Junta of Cadiz damps the ardour of those Spaniards who would otherwise loyally adhere to the cause of Don Joseph: some fight with the courage of despair, others fling down their arms at the first encounter with their opponents. The brave fellows would serve the Emperor better anywhere else than in their own country, torn asunder as it is by the various parties.'

From yet further confidences I learnt all about the opinion in Madrid of the army serving in Spain. The courage of the French troops, I was told, is incontestable, and they are now well inured to guerrilla warfare. The foreign soldiers, too, serving with them are as brave and skilled in war as the French. Amongst others, the Nassau infantry regiment has specially distinguished itself. The Poles are simply terrible in their gallant intrepidity. The men from Baden are also very brave, and they are humane and well disciplined; but unfortunately they all hate being sent away from their own land to fight in the service of France in a cause about which they care nothing, and the authorities, instead of sending regular conscripts, make up the numbers of the regiments by buying men from the very dregs of the people. These substitutes bring their vices and their habits of insubordination with them, and many desert to the enemy. Those that are left are indignant at the way they are treated if they fall into the hands of the guerrilla bands devastating the country, and when their turn comes they are guilty of the cruellest reprisals on the banditti. 'The war,' my informants added, 'has in fact assumed an atrocious character, which can, however, easily be removed if, instead of punishing with death insurgents taken with arms in their hands, the Government were to send them all to France, or, still better, if there were an exchange of prisoners after each battle. Many of our soldiers die of misery in the hulks of Cadiz. Exchanges of prisoners would save their lives, and they would return to our ranks more eager than ever to defend themselves bravely.' I also learnt that the guerrilla bands are chiefly made up of escaped convicts, who, assuming the name of insurgents, join the smugglers and choose the boldest amongst them as their chief. Deserters from both armies flock to these lawless bands, preferring their wandering, bloodstained life, with the many opportunities for pillage it offers, to the regular discipline of the camp.

After collecting all this very far from satisfactory information, I left Madrid on March 7th to make my way into Andalusia. I went without escort again, and was fired at in several passes. Twice my guide pointed out to me the clouds of dust behind me raised by a party of some dozen horsemen riding in my pursuit, and each time I only escaped them by making a detour round the next posting station, so as to double on them and let them pass me. Harassed in this way, I was only able to get a passing glimpse of the battle field of Almonacilde, between Ocaña and Mora, which was still covered with debris. At Mançanares, where I paid a flying visit to General Lorge, and Santa Cruz, where I also halted for a moment, I had scarcely time to taste a glass of the celebrated wine of the beautiful Peñas Valley, the rocky picturesque districts of which I was traversing.

I had a strong escort assigned to me for crossing the narrow richly wooded passes of the Sierra Morena. Whilst my troops were examining the ground and cautiously advancing, so as to guard against surprise in the narrow defiles, where the road was dotted with the dead bodies of brigands hanging from trees, I was free to enjoy the wild beauty of nature in these mountain solitudes, which resemble the Pyrenees in their geological structure, but are even snore beautiful, as they have not yet been deprived of their primeval forests. I was told that I was very lucky to reach the top of the pass without being attacked.

At Andujar I took the Granada road, which passes through Jaën, where I found Colonel Tinseau, who had just beaten General Black's corps. I pressed on now across deserted districts, where we rode sometimes for ten leagues at a time without passing a single cottage, though the soil evidently only needed culture to be very fertile. I should have made much of the annoyance caused me by the tremendous downpour of rain which drenched me to the skin on the 12th, if it had not been for a still greater trouble which befell me on the same day. The Guadalbolo torrent was so swollen that we had to choose between going back some eight leagues to avoid it, and trying to cross it as it was. We were already wet through, and I did not therefore hesitate to plunge into the muddy waters; but my guide's horse and mine both stumbled over a rock and fell. The torrent swept us down with it, and my clothes, being heavy with the rain they had absorbed, weighed me down and greatly embarrassed me. I was already half choked with water, and should certainly have been drowned had not Williams, who had kept his feet, managed to save both me and himself. I am, however, so passionately fond of nature that, though I was as saturated with water as a sponge, I could not think of anything but the marvellous beauty of the cloud effects and of the colours of the rainbow spanning the mountains, amongst which the storm was still raging. The wind soon dried us, and in the evening we arrived at an isolated stronghold on the road commanded by a young Alsatian officer named Kat, who spent all his time shut up in it with his garrison, except when he had to lead his men out to the pursuit of brigands – a perilous task enough. He assured me that but for the rain, which had dispersed the robbers, I should have fallen into the midst of a band who would have killed me, or at least have stripped me of everything. Kat also told me that hardly a day passed without his having to give chase to brigands, and practice had made him quite an adept at this kind of warfare.

The next morning at daybreak I arrived at the point from which I ought to have a grand view of the beautiful amphitheatre of Granada, at the base of the Alpuxarras range, the summits of which are crowned with snow and ice, whilst its strata are rich in veins of silver and of mercury. How ardently I longed for the wind to tear aside the veil of mist which hid everything from me! and presently Heaven did deal kindly with me, for a scene of absolutely divine loveliness was spread out beneath me. The atmosphere became warmed by the sunbeams, and the mist rose like steam from a boiling lake, breaking into a thousand light and airy columns, which in their turn changed into floating wreaths and garlands of fleecy clouds, soon dispersed by the wind, till there was nothing left between me and Granada but a luminous atmosphere, through which I could make out the ancient ramparts once owned by the Abencerrages, and the minarets of the Alhambra, where they met their fate. As soon as ever I got to Granada I went over the Alhambra with several officers, and I really do not know which I admired more, the beauty of the site or the wealth of delicate ornament in this ancient monument, which has been preserved for six hundred years, and much of which still looks as if it had been built but yesterday. My companions gave me some plans and views of the finest aspects of the Alhambra, and deplored with me the barbarism of the Spanish, who, to destroy the verses from the Koran, which they could not understand, engraved in Arabic on the walls, smeared whitewash over all the mural decorations.

It was not without deep emotion that I strolled through the rooms where my friend General Franceschi had been shut up after being taken prisoner by the Spanish. That young sculptor, who had joined the Compagnie des Arts at the same time as I did, and later risen to the rank of General of Division, married the daughter of General Matthieu Dumas. A short time afterwards, in a cavalry charge, he fell into the hands of the Spanish, who imprisoned him in the Alhambra. Franceschi, separated from his country and his bride, wrote some touching verses on the walls of his prison, and the air of the now deserted room seemed to be vibrating still with the heartrending lament he had addressed to the wife he was never to see again. He had made no fewer than twenty sketches representing the different phases of his captivity. The officers with me were as interested as I was in these drawings and verses, and were eager to help me make copies of them. The elegies in which he bade farewell to her and to his friends were seen some time later by Madame Franceschi herself, who directly she heard of the death of her young husband shut herself up in her own room, which she had draped with black cloth like a mortuary chapel, and lit only by a funereal lamp. There, refusing all nourishment, she spent her time in prayer awaiting the death which should reunite her to her beloved. She was inexorable to the pleadings of her father and sister, repelling their caressing attempts to console her; and until she needed its aid to look at my drawings, she never admitted the daylight to her sanctuary. She had no tears left to shed, or she would doubtless have wept afresh over these touching words of love from the grave, and she died almost immediately after she had read them.

I also visited the arsenal, the army stores, and many fine Moorish buildings in Granada, some of them still retaining in their gardens groves of laurels said to have been planted by the Abencerrages. I greatly admired these well-preserved and graceful Oriental residences, which seemed to me to need but a few curtains and carpets to make them most comfortable; and I was struck by the beauty of the white marble fountains, from which silvery mercury had once gushed forth, now replaced by water pure as crystal. My obliging guides then took me to the points of the town commanding the best views, and I made a few hasty sketches before returning with them to head-quarters, where, as I had expected, I received a very hearty welcome.

Before I left Granada, I climbed on to the ramparts to take a farewell look at the beautiful view, which quite fascinated me, and which I still recall with delight. There, picturesquely perched on the slope of an isolated mountain rising from the plain, was the little village of Atarfé; there was the river Jenil, fed by some twenty little streams flowing amidst an almost African vegetation, including regular forests of oleander trees laden with masses of bloom, pomegranates and fig trees weighed down with fruit, all alike draped with tropical creepers and vines bearing the famous Corinthian and Malaga currants, &c. &c. All this charmed me so much that it was with difficulty I tore myself away from a scene so fraught with pleasure of the purest kind, when I was told that my horses were ready. The direct road for Cordova via Alcala was so infested with brigands that I was advised to avoid it, and I went back to Benalva by way of Jaen and Andujar. Being over-taken by the darkness, I took refuge at the castle already mentioned, occupied by Commander Kat, who was waited on by three old women in the ruins of what had once been the home of their ancestors, with a gateway emblazoned with thirty-two quarterings. As the three old creatures, who reminded me of the Parcæ, moved about preparing our supper of *podrida* flavoured with pimento by the light of a lamp hung from the wall and of a small fire, I imagined myself to be transported back for several centuries, and the illusion was heightened by the accounts given me by my host of his various pursuits of the brigands and of the danger he ran of being surprised and strangled by them some night. The precautions taken to make all secure before I was allowed to retire to the rush mat which was the only bed Kat could give me, lent quite a touch of romance to the situation.

'After you left me the other day,' said my host, 'I went and placed myself in ambush with thirty of my men in a deserted *ventena de cabillas*, where I knew the brigands often go to rest. After waiting some thirty hours, I saw about fifty of them arrive. I let them unharness their horses before I stirred, and then opened fire on then before they had discovered our presence. Seven fell dead, and the others, all more or less wounded, got off, but I took thirteen horses, and you shall have one of them when you leave.'

I left Kat the next morning, and the only living things I saw in the mountains I had to cross were numerous vultures quietly resting on the trees near the road. At Jaen, Colonel Tinseau, of the 55th Regiment, received me as kindly as before, passed his troops in review for my benefit, and gave me a plan of the town, with some views taken from it. At Andujar, the Marquis de Contadero had his horses saddled and accompanied me for some distance along the road to Cordova, where I arrived on March 19th, to find the inhabitants celebrating the birthday of King Joseph.

General Godinho was anxious that I should have my share in the festivities going on, and took me to the fine mosque which is now the Cathedral of Cordova, a perfect specimen of Moorish architecture. The first building in which the characteristic horseshoe arch was largely employed, the Cathedral owes much of its beauty to the massive pillars, which originally numbered twelve hundred, and are now reduced to about a thousand. Most of these pillars came from Rome, from Greece, and Carthage, and were the spoils of old heathen temples; others were sent from Constantinople by the Emperor Leo, and yet others from France, whilst a smaller number are of Spanish origin. These pillars form more than fifty naves, and their arcades uphold a number of cupolas and domes which may perhaps be described as resembling an onion in form with the point upwards. The onion has long been largely cultivated as an article of food in the East, and it is not unlikely that it may have suggested the form of the Moorish cupola, which harmonises well with the other details of the same architectural type.

I also went to have a look at the antique marble bas-reliefs on the old Roman bridge still spanning the Guadalquivir, which represent the tragic death of the two sons of Pompey, and are appropriately placed at the entrance to the town as a warning to conquerors.

I brought good news from the Emperor and the King, and a place of honour was assigned to me at the banquet and the ball succeeding it. The General proposed the toast of the King of Spain and the Indies; the Prefect that of the Emperor of the French, King of Italy; and as for myself, I drank to the happy deliverance of the Empress Maria Louisa and the birth of a prince. I little thought that only fifteen hours after I expressed this wish the most ardent desires of the Emperor and of all France would be realised, and that volleys from hundreds of cannon would be announcing and celebrating the happy event throughout the length and breadth of the Empire.

As a special favour I was introduced at the ball to Doña Luisa Plateres, the most beautiful young woman in all Andalusia, that district in which the beauty of the women is proverbial. My partner, whose height suited mine admirably, had, however, never waltzed before, and she seemed greatly distressed when she found herself being carried along by a stranger to the music of the orchestra. One of her little hands trembled in mine, and she scarcely dared to rest the other on the shoulder of the man who seemed to be saying, 'Have no fear! I will support you.' After we had taken a few turns in view of a large concourse of spectators, I saw a kind of mist gather over her eyes; her cheeks, which had before been flushed with pleasure, grew pale; her steps faltered, her beautiful head fell upon my breast, and I felt that she had fainted. I supported her to the door leading to the garden, so that she might breathe the fresh air. Several ladies hurried after us, and as there was no seat near I knelt on one knee and supported my fair burden on the other. Salts were brought and placed to her nostrils, and after a few moments of the greatest anxiety she began to show signs of returning animation. Her father, who had brought her to the ball, ran off to fetch a chair, and I was obliged to place her on it. We waited thus till her carriage could be fetched. Then, escorted by lakeys bearing torches, the flickering light of which made her sweet and languid features look more beautiful than ever, her father and I supported her trembling steps till the door was reached. It was opened, and I had to leave her. Her father shook hands with me, and the carriage drove off. I was too much agitated to return to the ball, which seemed dull enough after the thrilling emotions I had experienced; I was too much preoccupied to hope for sleep, so I went and asked for an escort and horses, and long before daybreak I was on the way to Ecija.

The beautiful Andalusian sky, as blue and clear as that of Naples, was spread out above a smiling landscape looking so peaceful that I felt secure from attack. Whether from eagerness to get back to Cordova as soon as I could, or from any desire to reach Seville quickly, I found my escort went far too slowly to please me, so I soon dismissed it, and thinking of something very different from any danger to myself, I set off at a gallop, arriving at Seville before daybreak, having seen nothing of brigands except between Ecija and Carlotta, where I was pursued by a few rogues. I met Colonel Château at the gates of Seville, just starting for Paris, so I told him to take news of me there, pointed out to him the dangerous spots on the road where he would have to be careful, and went to fulfil my own mission.

Marshal Soult received me with all honour. After talking to me for a long time about the position in which he found himself and offering me the most lavish hospitality, he told some of his aides to go with me on the round of visits I had to pay to the various French army departments. I stopped three days at Seville, reviewing the troops, and examining the arsenals, foundries, hospitals, and in fact all the establishments, whether civil or military, connected with our service. Everywhere I found the greatest activity and the most complete order prevailing. I then went to see the old Alcazar and the celebrated royal tobacco factory, which is really a model of a big public manufactory. I never sneezed so much in my life, and I shall not forget in a hurry the huge piles of tobacco powder, which rather resembled red pepper, or the hundreds of workmen engaged in the making of cigars.

I also visited the fine mosque, now the Cathedral of Seville, which is surrounded by a garden still retaining the white marble fountains at which the Arabs performed their ablutions before entering the sacred building, the waters now moistening the roots of the venerable orange trees always laden with flowers and fruit, and of the stately palms which now give shade to Christian worshippers in the court of what was once a Moorish temple.

The principal entrance of the cathedral is surmounted by one of the finest Moorish rose windows in existence. The interior, like that of the Mosque of Cordova, is a perfect forest of columns of various antique orders, symmetrically arranged beneath the Oriental arcades. The precincts are enclosed within an enceinte flanked by crenelated towers, one huge square minaret rising to a great height with a terraced platform at the top commanding a grand view of the beautiful country round Seville. Within this tower is a gently sloping passage, up which the sultans used to ride on horseback to enjoy the view, and it can still be used for the same purpose.

Generals Senarmont and Ruty, of the artillery, General Lhéry, of the engineers, with some twenty of my fellow officers, made a great fuss over my visit, and complained greatly of being left in this remote isolated spot away from all chance of reward or promotion. They all begged me to get back to Paris as quickly as possible, so as to give the Emperor a true account of the state of things, which they believed had been misrepresented to him.

Marshal Soult was especially bitter at having to command men of equal rank with himself, and said he was often very much worried by being obliged to show so much consideration for them. 'Of course,' he said, 'I feel greatly flattered at having Marshals de Treviso and de Belluno under my orders, but I should much prefer generals on whose passive obedience I could rely.'

This remark led me to suggest to Marshal Soult that he should grant to the Duke of Treviso the leave I knew he had been trying to get for some time, and he consented. I now left

Seville to go to Cadiz, then besieged by our troops. The road from Seville to San Lucar not being very safe, I had to embark on the Guadalquivir, and I went down that river without any disagreeable encounters.

At San Lucar, I was warned against the great danger of crossing the wide plains between it and Santa Maria, for I was told three men belonging to an escort were killed yesterday. This, however, led me to suppose that as the brigands had had a tussle so recently as the day before, there was less chance of meeting them on the road to-day, so as I was able to secure some good horses I again started without escort. About halfway across Williams suddenly shouted, 'Oh, sir! sir, do stop! I entreat you to stop!' but I pushed on. He galloped after me, crying, 'Oh, sir! my belt has come undone, and all the money has run out.' 'Come on, come on,' was my only reply. 'But, sir, we shall lose everything.' 'Never mind, never mind, let's save our lives; we can get some more money later.' 'Oh, sir! everything is gone now; do stop!' 'So much the worse, but come on.' At last, two leagues further on, when I had got to the other side of a brook and felt pretty safe, I stopped. Williams, now in a regular temper with me, said, 'And high time you did, for I have lost simply everything.' We dismounted, and I said, 'Look in your boots, man; perhaps a few pieces have slipped into them. I helped him to pull them off, and sure enough there was all the money except two napoleons. We congratulated ourselves on having lost so little, and on escaping what might have been an awkward fix.

Marshal Victor gave me a very hearty welcome at Santa Maria, told me all about the operations at the siege of Cadiz, and gave me a detailed account of the battle which had first taken place opposite Chiclana and Barossa. General Garbé, of the engineers, General Nourri, of the artillery, and Generals Leval, Barrois, and Beaumont, of the infantry and cavalry, showed me all their troops and the important works they had constructed, of which they also gave me plans. I visited at their request the whole line of forts, including those of St. Catherine, Porto Real, Santi Petri, &c., opposite Cadiz, occupied by our forces. The enemy cannonaded us hotly from the island of Leon whilst we were visiting the Matagorda and Trocadero forts, where the French had placed the cannon and Villantroi mortars, with which they were bombarding Cadiz, and which were capable of sending hollow projectiles to the very end of the port, that is to say for some 6,500 to 7,500 yards.

As we went along the beach, my guides pointed out to me the shells, more than half burned, of three decked vessels stranded at about two hundred paces from the shore.

Many of our soldiers were still engaged in diving into the submerged remains of these vessels, and often brought up objects of considerable value. M. d'Hérize, one of the officers who were with me, said to me, 'I owe my deliverance from captivity to those vessels having been wrecked.' This roused my curiosity, and I begged him to tell me what he had to do with English ships. As we walked on he showed me the wrecks of two other vessels stranded at a short distance from each other, some few hundred paces from the shore, and gave me the following account of what had happened.

'Those old hulks, are all that is left of the Argonaut and the Castile, from which two thousand French prisoners managed to escape some five weeks ago, after braving the most terrible dangers.

'For two years we had languished in those floating prisons, deprived of money, of clothes, and almost of provisions. Nothing could have been more miserable than our condition. Officers and men were mixed up together, and we had not even the melancholy consolation, which has so often cheered those in captivity, of intercourse with others as well educated as ourselves. A number of women and children, who had been arrested during the Revolution, were shut up with us, and their weakness made them less able to endure their sufferings, whilst the sight of those sufferings added to ours. Every day death carried off several victims; mothers lost their children, children their parents, friends were torn from each other. The chance of any amelioration of our lot was so remote that it could do nothing to sustain our courage.

'We were, in fact, in a position so terrible as to baffle description, when one day one of the three vessels over there was torn from its anchorage by the force of the wind and carried by the current to the beach, where it was stranded, as you see, in spite of every effort on the part of the crew to turn it in another direction. This incident was as a flash of light to us, and what was dreaded as certain destruction by others became the most earnest desire of our hearts. As we watched the rising of the tide we began to feel a hope of our own salvation; we flung bits of straw or anything which would float into the sea, and eagerly watched them drift away to the shore, on which they would be flung. When, however, we examined the cables and chains with which our vessels were fastened to their moorings, our hearts sank again, for it seemed simply impossible to detach them. Moreover, a Spanish guard kept watch as border police, and we had no weapons.

'On board the Castile, however, where I was, the desire for liberty was so strong, that some new idea occurred to us every day, and we managed by hook or by crook to collect a lot of hatchets, which we stole from the carpenters who came to patch up our old hulks.

'The possession of these hatchets did not seem much towards silencing the two hundred cannon which might open fire on us at once, but it was enough to set our brains to work and encourage us to further efforts. Six officers and I therefore concocted a plan of escape together. We took Captain Derolles, of the navy, a man of high courage, into our confidence, and he fell in with our views, suggesting a yet more audacious plan than our own, which we carried out.

'We kept our secret religiously, for we knew that it was not given to many to await calmly a moment fraught with such consequences, and the fears of the more timid of the prisoners might have undone us. We decided that the time to get off would be at four o'clock in the morning six days later, when the highest tide of the month just beginning would occur. We sent news of our intention to the bravest officer on the Argonaut, wrapping our message up in a ball of bread, which we flung on to the deck of his vessel. He accepted our proposal eagerly on behalf of himself and those with him, and we spent the intervening days in trying to make every one desire and believe in the success of our venture, even threatening with death any of those to whom we communicated our intentions at the last moment if they either opposed or betrayed us.

'He was the first to climb on deck, and the sentinel on guard tried to push him back, but he felled him with a blow from the hatchet, and flung him upon the great cable, which he cut with two strokes of his weapon. The guards shouted, 'To arms!' but they were strangled or flung into the sea, and whilst several shots gave the alarm to the town and its batteries, all the moorings were cut, and our two vessels, without masts or rigging, slowly drifted with the tide. Several cannon shots were at once fired from the ramparts, and one of our women was struck down by a ball. Two or three others, terrified at this sight, screamed to us to take them into port, and we should all have been glad to do so, but it was quite impossible. All our men shouted at the tops of their voices, in the hope of attracting the attention of the French on shore, and our courage and resolution seemed to increase with our danger.

'The two hulks were a little distance from each other, and the strong current had already taken us for about half the distance we wished to traverse. The absence of wind was a help to us, as it retarded the progress of the gunboats, which were firing at us, though a good many were killed by the shots from them. At last day began to break, and we could see our fellow countrymen hurrying down to the beach to help us.

'As soon as they had heard our cries, and recognised that we were French, they had flown to our aid, some bringing planks and ropes, and running far into the water, so as to make out our signals better, they waved their hats to us, as we did to them. Others dragged cannon into the water to bridge over the space between us and safety, and we soon found ourselves slowly advancing between two fires, one aiming at our defence, the other at our destruction. When we got near the shore, all who could swim, and many who could not, flung themselves into the water. At last, after an hour and a half of terrible suspense, we saw the Argonaut stop near enough to the land for every one on her to jump out and land in safety.

'We, on the Castile, were a little behind, and from this moment the enemy concentrated all their fire upon us. Still we felt our vessel touch ground a few minutes later, and the shock made us all shout for joy, though we were still in eight feet of water, and more than two hundred paces from land. In spite of that, every one who was not wounded jumped into the sea, not hesitating a moment between the risk of being drowned and the certainty of being taken or killed. Many tied their children on their shoulders, others dragged their wives along by the hands, determined to save them or to perish with them, while many intrepid swimmers quietly gained the shore in spite of the hail of grapeshot poured into us by the enemy. Some brave fellows saved as many as twenty others besides themselves.

'The shells now set fire to our hulk, and Derolles with a few others, hatchets in hand, rushed to extinguish the flames wherever they broke out, and their noble courage saved the lives of many of the wounded, whom they dragged out of danger. When we at last got to shore we had the grief of finding that but half of our numbers had escaped, but the delight of finding ourselves safe and the generous warmth of our reception by the French forces soon made us forget our regrets. We were literally overwhelmed with the clothes, the money, and the eager attentions lavished upon us by our fellow countrymen.'

As M. d'Hérize concluded his narrative his eyes were wet with tears, and he pressed the hand of an officer near whose share in this noble treatment he was about to relate; but his friend, who was as modest as he was generous, would not allow him to go on.

As we strolled along the lines of our army whilst M. d'Hérize was talking, all the Spanish batteries continued to fire at us, hoping to destroy our little group, and the warlike sound fell pleasantly on my ears, for it was now more than a year since I had heard it. It was with considerable anxiety that I recognised the difficulty our forces would have in traversing the deep mud of the beach on our side of the canal of Santi Petri; but for this obstacle the canal could have been crossed as easily as a river, for we had boats and everything necessary for the transit. Thousands of wading birds, such as cranes, spoonbills, and flamingos with scarlet plumage, circulated in security on these swampy tracts, a sure proof that they were inaccessible to man. In addition to all the usual contrivances for crossing a difficult river, a number of rafts were prepared made of square pieces of leather joined together and inflated with air, which were connected by light woodwork and were broad enough, though drawing little water, to carry troops across the mud. Cork belts were also made to help the swimmers, who were to form an advanced guard. The copper pontoons of the artillery were to serve as bridges over the Santi Petri canal itself, and a French fleet was to come from Toulon or Brest so as to engage the English cruisers during our passage and attack, which there would be no hope of achieving without some such diversion. Our batteries had been ready for action for some time. The arrival of the French fleet had long been anxiously expected, when, on March 5th, an unexpected attack called the attention of Marshal Victor to the rear of his army.

The English, to the number of some five or six thousand, commanded by General Graham, came from the camp of Saint Roch near Gibraltar with 15,000 Spanish under General Lapina from Algesiras, who, leaving Cape Trafalgar on their left, attacked the French army, which was scattered on the heights of Santi Petri, Chiclana, and Porto Real, hoping by falling upon our centre to force us to abandon our redoubts, and by destroying our batteries, which were bombarding Cadiz, to make us raise the siege of that town.

In the first moment of surprise our rearguard was compelled to fall back upon the main body composed of the Rufin and Leval divisions, which were able to keep the enemy in check. Marshal Victor, promptly informed of this attack, hurried to the scene of the struggle with all his available forces, and the battle which had begun so suddenly at once became a very serious affair. The head of the Spanish force, thrust back at the outset, as our rearguard had been, and the rest of the column giving way also, the English general immediately pressed into the front line.

The Rufin division met the shock of the English attack, and both sides fought with extraordinary valour amongst the trees of the wood above Chiclana. Twice in succession the Rufin and English regiments met face to face and charged each other with the bayonet, a mêlée ensuing such as is very rare in modern warfare, for as a rule one of the corps engaged is demoralised, to begin with, by the firing, and draws back before the enemy is near enough to cross muzzles.

The lines occupied in this glorious struggle remained marked out by the corpses of numerous heroes, which looked as if, having dispensed with burial, they were awaiting the erection of monuments to their honour to transmit their names to posterity. There was one peculiarity about this sanguinary struggle, and that was, that when the English had broken their weapons by striking with butt or with bayonet, they never seemed to think of using the swords they wore at their sides, but went on fighting with their fists. Their officers, too, kept up the old custom of angrily striking with their canes any of their men who fell out of the ranks, whilst our non-commissioned officers, placed as a supernumerary rank, crossed their muskets behind their squads, thus forming buttresses which kept the ranks from giving way. On this occasion the French officers picked up the muskets of the wounded and flung themselves into the gaps made in the ranks of the common soldiers.

It was in one of these terrible *mêlées*, in which the 95th Regiment was engaged, that Colonel Mengarnaud was killed, and General Rufin, one of the handsomest men in France, was mortally wounded. His horse had received several wounds, and the furious animal carried his master into the English ranks, where he was thrown on to the points of the bayonets. He fainted away and was taken prisoner. The General's handsome features, set off by his long curling hair, and his fine figure aroused the admiration of the English, who did all they could to restore him and took the greatest care of him on the way to England, but he died just as he was about to disembark.

The English cavalry furiously charged ours, and were received with equal valour. At last their squadrons were driven back, and they were obliged to withdraw to the beach by the same narrow gully which the Spanish had taken in their retreat on Cadiz. During the struggle the Spanish threw a bridge of boats from the island of Leon across the narrowest portion of the Santi Petri Canal in spite of the cannonade from that fort. The Spanish column under General Lapina flung itself upon this bridge in its retreat, and some of our detachments pursued it to the other side and beyond. Meanwhile General Graham, who was very badly supported by the Spanish, having recognised the impossibility of penetrating further into our lines and making us raise the siege, took up his position on the height crowned by the Barossa tower, and there successfully repulsed several attacks from the Leval division, thus covering until nightfall the retreat of the English army. Our advanced guard, therefore, having the English in their rear, retired from the further side of the bridge and contented itself with cannonading the passage. The English finally retired to the island of Leon and boasted as of a victory, which they call the battle of Barossa, of the advantage they had gained in sending to the relief of Cadiz the ten or twelve thousand men who were all that were left of the combined forces.

On their side the French, weakened by the vast extent of the coastline they had to defend, taken by surprise by this attack on the scattered outposts of their rear, and arriving as they did in small detachments on the battle field, might with equal justice look upon the issue of the struggle as a brilliant victory, in which, their courage making up for the absence of any settled plan, they baffled the schemes of their enemies, and compelled them to retreat. They gave the name of the battle of Chiclana to the affair.

Amongst the many remarkable incidents of this day, the following were related to me. During the preceding days some five or six hundred Spanish had been taken prisoners by the French, and were crossing the battle field when the English attack was made. The prisoners thought this gave them a good opportunity for escape, and they all refused to go on, but the officer in command made them lie flat on their faces, left a few of his men to guard them with orders to shoot the first who raised his head, and marched against the enemy with the rest of his troops. At the end of the battle he had not lost a single prisoner.

Some other officers told me how a vivandière of the 95th Regiment, Catherine Baland by name, ran about through the French ranks during the battle giving the soldiers brandy to raise their spirits, as she gaily said to them in a bright encouraging tone, 'Drink, drink, my brave fellow; you can pay me to-morrow.' She must have known full well, however, when she saw so many men falling around her, that most of her debtors would not answer the roll-call the next day. The fair Catherine, who became quite a celebrated character in the army, and whose praises were sang by Béranger, was never wounded. She received the Cross in 1813 for many such acts of disinterestedness and courage as that above described.

From the heights of Barossa and Chiclana I could see the towers of Tangier rising up from the coast of Africa, beyond the Straits of Gibraltar, the whole of the island of Leon, the monuments, forts, and roadstead of Cadiz, with the far-stretching salt marshes, where thousands of heaps of salt at regular intervals looked like long lines of troops. The picturesque beauty of the site, and the extraordinary character of the struggle in which I had lost my dear friend the brave and handsome General Rufin, with whom I had made my first campaigns in Germany, decided me to try and paint a picture of the battle at some future day, and I made a number of sketches on the spot so as to give to my work the stamp of truth.

The claims of all the different corps were entrusted to me, to be put before the Emperor, and I took care to make myself thoroughly informed in every case so as to secure the rewards deserved. Before leaving, I urged on the operations of the siege, which ought not to have been delayed by the brilliant affair related above, although of course the troops had been a good deal fatigued. I got back on March 27th to Santa Maria, where Marshal Victor gave me a long account of the necessities of his army, and told me how important it was that the Emperor should come in person to settle the affairs of Spain. I left with regret the delightful residence assigned to me by the Duke of Belluno at Santa Maria, the windows of which, always open in the wild climate, looked down upon the roadstead and Cadiz, which I could see in the distance through the orange trees laden with flowers and fruit. The branches of these trees came into my very room, so that I could enjoy the fragrance and eat the fruit on the spot. This fascinating residence appealed alike to every sense, and I shall never forget that, in addition to the beauties of natural scenery, the fortunate inhabitants of Santa Maria enjoy the presence of some of the loveliest women in the world. Of course my visit was too brief for me to make their acquaintance, but what I did see of them fully confirmed all that I had heard of the charms of the ladies of Andalusia.

After our interview Marshal Victor gave me his despatches for France, and I started for Seville with an escort, arriving the same evening at San Lucar. There I hired a decked boat in which to ascend the Guadalquivir, and whilst waiting for the escort assigned to me, and for the tide to float our boat, which was still high and dry, I strolled about on the sandy banks of the beautiful river. It was a dark night, and I was much interested in noting two phosphorescent phenomena of which I had previously been told. As I was hesitating which road to choose amongst the many on the beach, the sand disturbed by our footsteps emitted a brilliant light of the colour of flames, and for a moment I fancied I was walking over still glowing cinders. At the same moment I saw some hundreds of tiny gleaming lights circulating round the boats, and I thought they too were on fire. But my boatmen caught several of the lights to let me look at them closely, and I then saw that they were fireflies, which, when they move their wings, give out a much stronger light than do the glow-worms of France. Fireflies also abound in Italy, where they are called *lucciole*. All these details of natural history were of great interest to me, and I made a collection of insects and plants, and of specimens of minerals, sulphur, &c., from various districts, which I kept with my sketches of the places where they had been found, as aids to my memory, intending to study them closely when I reached home.

Our progress up the river, easy enough at first, became difficult as the tide rose, for the wind, being against the current, lashed the water into great waves, which seemed bent on driving us back. With all sails set, however, our bark ploughed its way on, but we were all too sea-sick to care to look at the sun rising over the beautiful landscapes on either side. We had already got about a third of the way, and had not once raised our heads from our pillows to look about us, when our crew warned us of approaching danger. They had caught sight of a sentinel, who at our approach had hidden himself in a little grove of orange trees on the left bank. We were already close upon him, and it was necessary to guard against a surprise, a fact which roused us all to action. When we were about half musket range from the grove, two armed men came out, and seeing no one but a boatman at the helm, shouted to him to come ashore. He took no notice, but calmly pursued his course. Then the two men were joined by several others, also armed, who threatened to fire if our boat did not stop. I then called up my little guard of fifteen men, and as soon as they showed themselves on deck, the brigands, whose numbers had still further increased, fired a volley at them. They did not, however, wait for their reply, but, turning tail, took refuge amongst the trees. We were threatened with several similar attacks, but none of them really came off, and our worst danger was from the wind, which now amounted to a regular gale, the waves dashing over the deck and threatening to swamp our little boat. We were so much knocked about that we made our boat-men land us at a village some two leagues from Seville, where M. Blagnac, an officer in the service of King Joseph, supplied me with horses. I got to Seville that same evening, but the boat did not arrive until the next day.

I wound up this stormy and fatiguing day by supping with Marshal Soult, and going to the theatre with him. We had a good deal of talk together, and he grumbled at being ham-pered in everything he undertook. He was, he said, perfectly hemmed in by enemies, having to contend not only with the English, the Portuguese, and the Spanish, who were in front, on the right and on the left, but by the guerrilla bands, which harassed him in the rear, and circumvented him at every turn. He added that the sinews of war were wanting, that the coun-try was drained of its supplies, provisions being very scarce and very dear. 'The reinforcements promised me never arrive,' said the Marshal, 'for Belliard keeps them at Madrid. The siege operations at Cadiz drain my feeble resources. There are no medicines at the hospitals. The army of the Junta has appropri-ated all the horses suitable for cavalry, and I can get none for my men.' Then, his excitement increasing, Soult added in a voice full of emotion, 'Would you believe it? I am surrounded by jealous men, eager for my recall, I am badly seconded by officers of too high rank to obey me without criticism, and I have not a single friend in whom I can confide, for I have long been separated from my family, who are all in Paris.'

The Marshal did not, as so many others had done, express a wish to see the Emperor come in person to take the command of his army, but from all I saw and heard I felt sure that it was absolutely necessary that some very decided step should be tak-en to reconcile all these jarring elements. Until something was done there could be no hope of the campaign being brought to a successful issue. I determined, therefore, to hasten back to France to tell the Emperor how things stood, and I obtained a strong escort. Five or six couriers with despatches, and several travellers, availed themselves of this opportunity of travelling safely, and started with me.

I got to Ecija the same evening, and put up at General Dijon's quarters. The next day my friend Colonel Lallemande, of the 27th Dragoons, escorted me with his regiment as far as Cordova. There General Godinho entrusted some jewels to me to be taken to his wife, and I packed them with many other tokens of affection which were confided to my care. Many were the hearts I was to rejoice with good tidings of those they loved when I got to Paris, and everything combined to make me eager to reach the end of my journey. General Godinho told me that a few days before my fair partner Doña Luisa had left Cordova with her father, who had been appointed to a position of great trust in another province. The terrible news of the massacre of the whole family by brigands, which I heard on my way to Madrid, had not yet reached Cordova. They had fallen into an ambush by the way, the father was shot as a Josephine, and the poor daughter perished after the most infamous treatment. It was at Consuegra that I learnt with horror all the revolting details of this hideous crime.

When he took leave of me and sent his loving greetings to his wife, General Godinho probably knew that he would never see either her or me again. Soon after I left Cordova I heard that, having received a severe and very unjust reprimand from Marshal Soult, the General, unable either to avenge or to endure the insult put upon him, went straight down to the sentinel at the door, and said to him, 'Is your gun loaded?' Then, on the man replying in the affirmative, he added, 'Give it to me.' And resting the butt-end on the ground, he put his foot on the trigger and blew out his own brains before any one had time to stop him.

The melancholy accounts I everywhere received as to the state of the unhappy country of Spain were not calculated to reassure me as to what I might expect on my return journey. I left Cordova on April 1, at a time when the fine weather and the warmer nights encouraged the brigands to leave their mountain haunts and lie in wait on the roads for parties of travellers with escorts smaller than their own bands, when they would spring out upon them with the cruelty and treachery of wild beasts. At Andujar, at Baylen, and at Caroline, where I changed my escort,

I was warned of the presence of these guerrilla bands and of the necessity of constant vigilance on the march. At Santa Cruz the officers of the 13th Dragoon Regiment told me about a battle they had had that very day with a pretty large party of brigands, whom they had beaten; and agreeing with me that the enemy would be likely to keep quiet for a bit after this defeat, they approved of my wish to push on during the night. This we did, arriving safely at three o'clock in the morning at Val de Peñas, at six o'clock at Mançanares, where we called on General Lorges, and at noon at Villa Rubia. There we learnt that the escorts were all out, and as the state of the country was too threatening for us to risk travelling by day without a strong body of troops, we were obliged, much to our regret, to wait till they had come back and had a rest. I availed myself of this delay to send a message to General Neuenstein, of Baden, then at Consuegra, by a Spaniard in his service, telling him to have an escort ready for me when I should arrive. The day seemed very long to me, for there was absolutely nothing of interest in the town but a number of donkeys of a peculiar breed, which were, without exception, the biggest, the ugliest, and the worst-tempered brutes I ever saw. I could not have believed that a donkey could attain a stature of more than four feet! Looking at these animals was not a very cheerful recreation for us, preoccupied as we were in thinking of how best to get out of a very awkward position.

All the talk of the couriers and merchants who had joined my party was about the dangers they had run owing to the atrocious guerrilla warfare which had been going on for the last two years, and though they were all brave enough and ready to defend themselves, they could not help grumbling at the injustice of being subjected to all this worry and suffering in a bad cause. Williams sadly counted the louis d'or still in his belt, and found he had now only 150 left. The men and horses I was waiting for did not come back till sunset, but I did all I could to hurry them over their supper, begging them to be quite ready to start as soon as my messenger came back; and then, very much worried at the delay and worn out with fatigue, I stretched myself on a bench with my cloak for a pillow, to try and get a little sleep.

My repose was not long, for I had scarcely sunk into oblivion of my woes before a horrible nightmare came on, making me start up, tumble off my bench, and run in the dark into the next room, where Williams was sleeping. I called him several times before he answered, for he was in a profound sleep, but at last he replied, 'Here I am!' That was all I wanted, and, reassured as to his being still alive, I felt sorry I had disturbed him; but in my horrid nightmare I had fancied I heard him crying out to me for help, and had seen him fall dead at my feet in the midst of a terrible struggle. I was still feeling melancholy after this horrid dream, when my express messenger returned from Consuegra to tell me that the road seemed clear, and that troops were awaiting me there. My escort of dragoons was ready soon afterwards, and we started again at two o'clock in the morning.

CHAPTER 3
I am Taken Prisoner

When I got to Consuegra, General Count Neuenstein, of Baden, dissuaded me from taking the Aranjuez route, infested by guerrillas, with whom he had to fight every day, and the escort of cavalry he gave me took me to Mora, where I arrived the same evening. Here I was again delayed, and was not able to start until one o'clock in the morning; and though the road was anything but safe, forty dragoons were all the escort I could secure. I arrived at Toledo with them a little before daybreak. The old general in command there could only spare me twenty-five dragoons, who had returned during the night after marching all day, and I was obliged to let them rest for a few hours before resuming my route.

Whilst waiting for my little escort to be ready to start I had a look round Toledo, most picturesquely situated at the summit of a number of lofty rocks, with the Tagus, by which the site is surrounded on three sides, flowing at their base. The number of fine old buildings gives the city a dignified appearance, and I was specially struck by the cathedral, which I entered at six o'clock, just as day was beginning to break. It was the 5th of April, and Easter time. A grand service was going on, in which a regular orchestra with a number of singers in galleries were taking part, and the angelic voices of the children in the choir seemed to those in the nave to be coming straight from heaven.

The body of the church, but for a few flickering torches, was still wrapped in the twilight of the dawn, and the solemn service, with its exquisite music and clouds of incense, through which the figures of the numerous clergy loomed dimly, combined with the utter stillness of the nave, where but a few scattered women, completely hidden in black woollen mantles, giving them the appearance of spectres, knelt on the stones, made a deep impression on me. But one solitary man in military uniform appeared suddenly amongst the prostrate worshippers waiting at the foot of the altar for the benediction, for I also felt impelled to say a prayer and bless God for having brought me safe and sound so far.

In those few moments of meditation, when I thus performed a religious duty, the petitions I put up seemed to calm my spirit, still vibrating with the agitation resulting from the many struggles in which I had been engaged. I thought to myself then that it is at moments such as these, snatched in the midst of war, that the heart of a soldier is more sensitive to the influences of religion than at any other time. I, too, in the very depth of my soul tasted that indefinable and soothing sense of peace and serenity which comes from prayer. Nor was there a man in our army who would not have felt as I did, for in all our wars I never saw one of our brave fellows, whether amongst the common soldiers or the elite of the army, behave like an atheist or an infidel or commit sacrilege, for they were all ever ready to do homage to God, who alone gives courage, victory, and honour. I put up a prayer for a happy issue of my journey, and then I went to join my feeble escort, leaving Toledo at eight o'clock. The officer in command of my twenty-five dragoons, Duhamel de Bellenglise by name, warned me that the district we were about to cross had for the last eight or ten days been infested with an immense number of brigands, all the different bands having joined forces, and said that it was therefore very imprudent to travel with so few troops. I quite agreed with him, but I knew how important it was that I should get to Paris quickly, and how dangerous it would be to lose time by any further delay at Toledo. So we started, keeping, however, well on the alert, and neglecting no precaution as we went along. It was a splendid day, and we got to Cavañas before noon without any adventures or hearing anything of the brigands, except in the stories about their daily fights with them with which M. Duhamel and his dragoons enlivened our march.

Cavañas is a big village surrounded by a weak wall, and standing quite alone in the centre of a plain. The commandant had had this wall loopholed to aid in the defence of the place against the guerrilla bands occupying the surrounding districts, who had made several attempts to take the village. The commandant blamed me very much for my imprudence in attempting to reach him with such a small escort, and as he could not spare me any mounted men just then, he tried to persuade me to remain with him.

I was, however, so near Madrid, where I hoped to arrive that evening, and so anxious to push on, that I could not bring myself to lose any time. Moreover, the commandant told me that six or eight hundred men of the band under one Dr. Padalea, surnamed El Médico, feeling sure that I must return soon, had been scouring about on the plain looking for me for the last eight days and nights, and had only moved off the evening before, weary of the long waiting. The commandant insisted on sending an express messenger to ascertain the whereabouts of this band, and make inquiries about the state of the district to be traversed, before I left, and I employed the time whilst waiting for the man's return in resting and feeding the horses of my twenty-five dragoons, so that they might be able to go as far as the next halting-place with me. The peasant sent out returned to say that he had gone a considerable distance across the plain, and seen no sign of any one, and I set out with my same party of dragoons, who were all well-seasoned troopers, and who were supplemented by sixty good infantry soldiers with their officers, belonging to a Baden regiment. I arranged my little party in the order of an army corps, sending nine dragoons out in front to reconnoitre as an advanced guard, placing the couriers and travellers, all of whom were armed, in the centre of the rest of the dragoons, and making the infantry bring up the rear as a reserve.

It was a beautiful day, and we were marching peaceably on in this order, without our advanced guard having noticed anything alarming of which to warn us, when I noticed the dead bodies of several men and horses on the road. The Baden officer with me then told me that a very short time ago eighty French grenadiers, who were escorting a courier, were attacked by the band under El Médico, and, compelled to yield to superior numbers, they took refuge in a square chapel some three-quarters of a mile from Illiescas, where they were besieged for two days, refusing to surrender. Every effort they made to get out was frustrated, and all who ventured to leave the chapel were at once struck down dead. The brigands then fetched ladders, and great quantities of straw and faggots, from the village. With the aid of the ladders, they put the straw and wood on the top of the chapel, and set fire to them. The burning roof fell on the grenadiers, who flung themselves in a body on the enemy, but, like the cowards that they were, the brigands opened their ranks to them, and then shot them all down, not a single one escaping. During this melancholy recital we had reached a little wood consisting of about a hundred olive trees, some eight or nine paces from the chapel. The quiet bearing of our advanced guard, and the utter stillness of the plain before us, added to our sense of security as we passed the scene of this tragedy, and I was turning over in my mind what would have been the best thing for the luckless grenadiers to do under the circumstances, when I suddenly saw two priests in cassocks and broad-brimmed hats spring out from behind the walls of the chapel and wave their handkerchiefs wildly. There was nothing to be seen on the plain, and it seemed as if these signals must be meant for us. We were too far from the priests to hear what they said, so I told one of my dragoons to gallop up to them, and ask them what they meant. He obeyed, but his horse was very tired, and he did not go half quickly enough for our impatience to find out what it all meant.

As the man approached them the priests gesticulated all the more wildly, and, eager to understand what they were aiming at, I sent a second better mounted dragoon after the first. But he was as slow as his comrade, and, unable any longer to control my eagerness, I set spurs to the fresh horse which I had secured at the fort, and in a very few seconds I had traversed the space dividing me from the priests. Their gestures now expressed the greatest horror, and I began to suspect mischief, especially when I came up with a young peasant who was cutting the harness of his oxen in his terror, so as to get them out of the plough more quickly. I asked him why he was unharnessing in the middle of a furrow, but he did not answer, and the wild, fierce expression of his eyes as he looked at me made me think it would be wiser to return to my people, so I wheeled round after another good look at the priests and the peasant. As I rode back to my escort, I remembered the dream which had made such a vivid impression on me a few hours before. I may have been wrong, I said to myself, in ignoring the presentiment of coming evil I had had then, because silly cowards are disposed to attach too much importance to dreams. I had, however, no time to make up my mind on the point, for I had scarcely ridden a few paces before I heard again the cry of distress which had roused me from my sleep. It was no nightmare delusion this time, but the most terrible reality.

'Master, master, we are lost!' screamed Williams as he rushed up to me. I looked at him, and as I did so I saw advancing upon us in a circle from every quarter of the plain some six or eight hundred horsemen, who, though still at a distance, completely surrounded my escort. Williams went on screaming, 'Oh, master, master, what shall I do?' 'Go behind me,' I replied, 'draw your sword, and do as I do.' But, alas! neither getting behind me nor drawing his sword saved him, for he was struck by a bullet the next minute and fell dead without uttering another word. The fatal omen of the dream was fulfilled! The brigands had let our advanced guard pass without showing themselves, and then closed in upon us, firing as they came.

Our infantry were able to reach the olive grove, and placed themselves in battle order amongst the trees which afforded them some little shelter; they fired in their own defence, but they could do nothing to protect us, for if they had aimed in our direction they might have killed some of us. The enemy saw this, and getting between our foot soldiers and us they rained bullets upon us, not venturing to approach nearer than the length of the weapons with which they were armed. I turned aside the

71

spears with my sword, but I could not get at any of the assailants. Only three or four dragoons remained near me, and those few fought like lions. We managed at last to pierce the ranks of the enemy, and we should have got off and joined our infantry if the brigands had not prevented it by concentrating their fire on our horses, shouting, '*Entrega, entrega Usted!*' (Surrender, surrender!) My horse, which was very strong, was the last to fall. He had already been hit some thirty times, and at last, covered with wounds, and no longer able to feel the spur, he rolled over dead amongst his comrades. I managed to struggle out of the crowd of fallen horses and men, and had defended myself for a short time with my sword, when I received a blow from a spear which was quite enough to kill me, but it only cut open my right hand, causing me such terrible pain as to paralyse my sword arm. My weapon fell, I was disarmed, and my assailants, athirst for blood and plunder, flung themselves upon me and began to tear off my clothes. In four seconds I was stripped naked from head to foot, but I was fortunately unwounded except for a few cuts from spears. Those of the brigands who were not too much encumbered with the spoil they had taken from me, now raised their muskets above the shoulders of their comrades and pointed them at my breast. I made no effort to shield it, but rather exposed myself as much as possible, my only hope being that I might die at the first discharge, and not have to endure a lingering anguish. But, strange to say, though seven or eight primings flashed, the charges did not go off! In their rage at having missed me, four of the brigands, threatening to have done with me in a moment, took fresh cartridges from their belts, and having loaded again they pointed their weapons at my breast, which I once more presented to them without flinching. But the primings hung fire again! Recognising the divine protection in this extraordinary incident, I seized with both hands one of the muskets which were being banged about my head, and with it parried the blows which would otherwise have killed me, for they bent out of shape the weapon which protected me. The terrible struggle sent a rush of blood to my heart, my strength failed me, and I was on the point of succumbing, when a man on horseback, wearing some of the insignia of an officer, dashed into the fray, shouting down to me from above the heads of my assailants, '*Quien es Usted? Quien es Usted?*' (Who are you, who are you?) I was too much occupied in parrying the blows from the butt-ends of muskets which were raining on me from every side, and from which I was all but stunned, to answer him, and it was not until he had compelled his rearing horse to come close up to me, and repeated again and again, '*Quien es Usted?*' that I answered, 'A colonel.' '*Ah! es un coronel,*' he cried; '*no matad le!*' (Ah, it is a colonel; do not kill him). The men were, however, so furious at my long resistance, that it was all he could do to make them listen to him, and spare my life. The officer was Don Juan Padalea or El Médico, the chief of the band, who got his name from the fact that he practised medicine before he became a leader of brigands. Seeing how done up I was and that I was about to faint, he shouted out to me, '*No tenga Usted miedo!*' (Don't be afraid). At the word 'afraid,' which wounded my self-respect, I raised my head proudly, and whilst he kept on saying, '*No ten miedo,*' I kept on replying, '*No tengo miedo*' (I am not afraid). Again and again he set spurs to his horse, making it rear against the men, who still wished to kill me, and finally told two mounted men to carry me off the field of battle. My little band of infantry saw the whole struggle without being able to interfere, and continued to fire in their own defence. The two brigands told to take me away each seized one of my hands, and as they galloped off I had to run between them. They cared nothing for the suffering this inflicted on me, compelled to rush along with bare feet and legs over the rough ground and through hedges and ditches. What pained me still more, however, was passing the dead bodies of my dragoons stripped as I was of all clothing, whom the miscreants had literally hacked to pieces. They had evidently not dared to face them even when they were dying, but had stabbed them from behind with the long swords they had robbed them of. The poor fellows had died in my defence, and I was filled with despair at their fate.

After dashing along for a league or two we approached the mountains, and my two brigands halted for a moment to allow the rest of the band to come up. The Médico, who seemed in very good spirits, told his men as he joined them, with a view to enhancing the value of their capture, that I was the *sobrino del Rey Pepe* (nephew of King Joseph). He ordered them to show me every attention, and assured me that he was too generous to ill-treat his prisoners when they no longer had arms in their hands. My two horsemen now vied with each other in their generosity to me, and offered to give me back some of the booty they had just taken from my party. As the band, now reassembled, galloped off again, one of my guards gave me a big pair of boots, and the second threw me a shirt, soaked and dripping with blood, shouting, 'You can wash it in the next stream.' Never did I receive a more horrible gift, and I shuddered with disgust. Still, I kept it in my hand, and as I was hurried along again I felt the blood from it mingling with that from my own wounds. I did not, however, have to carry the revolting burden long, for the guard, whose name was Dorringo, soon snatched it away again, not liking, after all, to part with it, and the only advantage I derived from the gift was a fresh access of horror. I had to run on like this between the two horses till we got to the village of Casarrabis, where the band passed the night. There I saw four others who had been taken prisoners, namely, Lieutenant Duhamel de Bellenglise, of Lille, who had commanded the dragoons, M. Massart, a merchant, a French dragoon, and a soldier from Baden. The rest of the mounted men had apparently all perished. I learnt afterwards, however, that the Sieur de Laval, a courier in Government employ, who had been left for dead on the scene of the combat, had survived his many wounds and managed to drag himself to the road, where he was succoured by some passers-by. He recovered and returned to Paris a year later.

The terrible emotions we had all gone through, and the long run under such horrible circumstances, had made us dreadfully thirsty, and a charitable peasant woman, who was rather like and quite as beautiful as her celebrated fellow countrywoman Madame Tallien, was generous enough to bring me a big earthenware pitcher containing a couple of quarts of water, with a dash of vinegar. I should quickly have drunk it all if my companions' sufferings had not been as great as my own. I tore the pitcher from my lips and offered a share of the refreshing beverage, which reminded me of that offered to Christ on the cross, to my fellow captives. The kind woman filled the pitcher for us again, and showed no embarrassment at waiting on perfectly naked men.

Don Juan Padalea and his band passed the night in the village, and we were shut up in a stable with a sentinel to guard us. Massart, Duhamel, and the soldier from Baden yielded to their despair, and it grieved me to see them give way before such contemptible enemies as ours, so I urged them to follow my example and that of the dragoon, who still held his head up proudly, though he was much weakened by his wounds. The sentinels were relieved every hour, and some of the men told me that but for the fact that the humidity of the last eight or nine nights had damped the powder of their cartridges, not a single one of us would have escaped the massacre of the preceding day. They spoke of this as a contretemps, but we thanked God for it.

Just before daybreak Don Juan sent us a little bread to eat, and a mule for me to ride, with the order to start at once, for he wished to get to a village some distance off, where he would be more secure from being surprised by the flying column, under the commandant Soubiran, which had been in pursuit of his band for several months.

As we went along I had the mortification of seeing various brigands sporting my uniform, my decorations, my cap and my epaulettes, and they added insult to injury by riding up to tell me how much they regretted not having been able to kill me. Presently their anger against us became greater than ever at hearing that the French general in command at Avila had just had two *guerrilleros*, as they called their comrades, whom he had taken prisoners, hanged a couple of leagues off. Don Juan had the greatest difficulty in preventing them from killing us on the spot, and the march was resumed. A little further, however, fresh accounts reached them of the tragedy, and Don Juan was compelled to yield to their eager desire for our blood. They made us enter an orchard, where the low trees afforded plenty of branches on which they could easily hang us, and, abusing us all the time for the cruelty of the French to their comrades, they took off the thongs for tethering their horses ready to hang us with them. Approaching death and the touch of the running noose already flung round my neck gave me an eloquence in speaking the Spanish language which I had never had before. I told them what a shame and a dishonour I thought it was to add to the inevitable horrors of war those of needless cruelty, that I agreed with them in thinking the French general very wrong to set them such a horrible example and provoke them to such terrible reprisals, and I tried to induce them to think it their duty to put an end to such deeds on both sides. 'You know,' I went on, 'from my insignia with which I see you decked out now, that I hold high rank in the army; make haste to exchange me for some Spanish prisoner, and I give you my word of honour that I will use all my influence with the King and with the Emperor himself to stop such extreme measures on our side, so that there may be no further justification for the reprisals which those measures lead you to make. Then if the war must continue, it will at least lose the ferocious character which is a disgrace to men who ought only to bear arms in defence of their country and of liberty. None but public executioners should ever hang their fellow men.'

This harangue, which strangulation nearly cut short, did but make the human tigers hesitate a little, and our horrible position only provoked a ferocious laugh from them. Several of them had already climbed into the plum trees to begin operations, and though Don Juan seemed to think there was something in what I urged, the fatal moment was evidently close at hand, and there seemed no hope of escape from a violent death. The rest of the men formed a circle round us, all eager to see us die. I held the running noose round my neck tightly with both hands to prevent it from strangling me, and went on talking. The other end of the thong was actually in the hands of one of the men in the tree above me, and I could get no hearing. In fact, a good many of the spectators were shouting angrily, '*Horcad los! Horcad los! al corniolo, al corniolo!*' (Hang them! Hang them! To the plum

76

tree! to the plum tree!) Then in my rage I in turn shouted with a mocking laugh, '*Que malos ciruelos haran ustedes!*' (What bad plums you are going to make!) This cry of mine in extremis made them all laugh in a ridiculous way, and stopped the terrible preparations for a moment, but whether they would have resumed them or not I cannot say, for just then five or six shots were heard in the distance.

All the men shouted together, 'Soubiran! Soubiran!' Those in the trees jumped down, the band remounted, and Don Juan told off twelve men to guard us, saying in our hearing, 'You will kill them if we have to run away; they would only hinder our escape.' He then rode off at the head of his band in the direction of the firing, the sound of which alternately approached and receded for more than an hour of horrible suspense for us, during which our hearts were torn by cruel anxiety, and I mentally bade farewell to my old father, to all who were dear to me, and to France, which my safe return to Paris would have done, so much to serve. It was indeed hard to be cut off from friends and country in the very springtide of my life. No night immortalised by Young in his celebrated 'Night Thoughts' was as long as that one hour of alternations of hope and fear during the night of April 6th, 1811, to us poor prisoners condemned to death, and with nothing to serve as our shrouds but the splashes of dried blood on our naked bodies.

We now learnt that a courier and his escort on the way from Escalona to Madrid had been surprised by the scouts of El Médico, whom they had imagined to be far away from the district at the time, as they were quietly winding along by the Alberge, intending to turn off for the capital at Valmojedo. El Médico's men seeing that the escort was but a small one threw themselves upon it, and we now found ourselves in the cruel position of not knowing what to wish. If the escort were beaten it would mean death to Frenchmen, and we dared not hope for that; if, on the other hand, the French were victorious, our guards would have to take flight and our doom would be sealed. At the end of an hour, which seemed two to us in our terrible suspense, we had to look upon a scene more horrible if possible than anything which had yet met our eyes, for the escort was beaten and driven back to Escalona, leaving many dead and five or six wounded on the ground. Three of the poor wretches, who were stripped naked, were dragged to where we were waiting, but the dread with which Soubiran had inspired the brigands was such that they dared not linger, and therefore decided to kill those too much hurt to go with them. The next moment in spite of my entreaties the poor fellows were massacred, and as they fell I caught them in my arms. The points of the swords which were driven through their shoulders actually pricked my breast, and the unfortunate creatures were literally hacked to pieces in my hands, all powerless to help them.

It is thirty-five years ago now, but the sound of the blows rained upon the unhappy victims, with the cracking of their bones, still rings in my ears, and the remembrance of the scene makes me shudder with horror.

The blood they had just shed seemed to have satiated the brigands' lust for slaughter, as they said no more about hanging us. The mule I had ridden before was led up, and Don Juan, whose features wore an angry frown, gave the order to start riding on again in silence.

During the further journey three or four of the brigands kept close to me to protect me from their comrades, who with many insulting gestures kept expressing their regret at not being allowed to kill me. On the other hand, our guards began to talk to us in quite a friendly way, and we began to indulge in hope once more. I was now able to observe the men about me a little more closely. They were all dressed in a fantastic manner, in a most heterogeneous collection of garments, and presented a very wild and ferocious appearance. Their complexions were swarthy and sunburnt; their black eyes, of the Arab type, were shaded by heavy eyelids; their hair, shaved away on the forehead, was allowed to grow long elsewhere, and was gathered at the back into a mass called a *catogan*, which hung down on the nape of the neck. All of them, chiefs and men alike, wore a coloured handkerchief knotted about the head, and hanging down the back in a *négligé* manner. Above the handkerchief was worn a round felt hat, with a high pointed crown, varying in colour from black and russet-brown to grey, according to its state of decay, and decorated with a few cock feathers and a twist of red cord. The chest and one shoulder, black or red from constant exposure to the weather, were left bare. Some of the men wore jackets like those of our hussars of different colours, and others brown, black, or blue vests; but all had broad red silk or woollen sashes, whilst many had belts over the sashes which could hold several dozen cartridges, as I had good cause to remember. The short black velvet or leather breeches were open at the knee, and the calves of the legs were protected by leather gaiters coming down over Spanish sandals or big shoes with spurs on the heels. The men all shouted at the top of their voices, showing their pointed white teeth, which looked like those of angry wolves.

The clumsy saddles had wooden stirrups, the bit was fastened on to the reins with bits of twine, and the steeds with these primitive trappings resembled the quaint and shaggy nag of Don Quixote. The men who had rather better horses were very proud of them, and kept saying to me: '*Mira que buen caballo por una retirada!*' (Look what a fine horse to run away on!) These words were a very good revelation of the character of the speakers, and whilst I had the honour of being dragged along amongst them, I always heard them say when they approached an enemy, '*Son muchos, salvemos*' (There are a lot of them, let's escape), or, '*Son poca gente, acometamos*' (There are only a few, let's attack them!) On the present occasion they trotted along in good spirits, rejoicing at their success. After crossing a forest and climbing up a steep rocky ascent, we came down to the banks of the Alberge. The ferry boat was broken, and the river was deep and difficult to ford; but the fear with which Soubiran inspired him made Don Juan wish to put the water between him and the French. He noticed a herd of oxen grazing in a meadow some distance off, and sent some men on horseback to fetch them. He then had the oxen driven to the edge of the water, and his men forced them to enter it by pricking them with their lances. The poor beasts tried to escape by swimming, and when they were all about twenty paces from the bank and had broken the force of the current, the guerrilla band forded the stream, their horses, having to swim part of the way, whilst the prisoners were dragged along by the hands to save them from being drowned. The torrential mountain streams are very cold at the beginning of April, but that was the very least of our woes. The bath was really a good thing for us, and we came out looking a little less hideous than when we went in. We pushed on through forests and amongst rocks, and arrived, as darkness was beginning to gather, at the village of Prado, where the robbers thought they would be safe. We were again put into a stable, and the division of the booty took place almost under our eyes. I recognised with grief the clothes of my poor Williams, the faithful servant from Auvergne, whose real name was Guillaume Bariol, but whom I had christened Williams so as to be in the fashion. The savage fellows who had killed him were puzzled by the collections of small stones, minerals, bits of sulphur, and other geological specimens which I had made Williams pack in his valise, and asked me what in the world they were for. Nothing which would not bring in money seemed of any value to them. Don Juan understood a little French, but he pretended not to know a word, as it would have roused suspicion if he had talked to his prisoners in a language unknown to his men. In looking over the despatches seized with my other effects he recognised their importance, and sent them in all haste to the head-quarters of the Spanish army. He then ordered me to be brought before him, and still retaining his severity of manner, he gave me leave to write to France to arrange for my exchange. I wrote immediately on the subject to General Belliard, who had already received and passed on the false report of my death. I was also extremely anxious to inform the Emperor of the melancholy condition of his armies in Spain; but I did not dare to say anything which would be understood by our enemies, and lead to my letter being intercepted, so I merely wrote these few lines to my friend Baron Leduc, secretary to Prince Berthier: 'Tell the owner of the "Pavillon de Flore" that I have seen the person of whom he asked me to obtain news, and that I found his numerous children in a condition demanding the presence of their father at once.' Don Juan sent these letters open to Madrid, and that to Baron Leduc reached Paris safely and was understood at the Tuileries. Don Juan now gave me the remains of an old cloak, such as shepherds wear, to cover my nudity, and was actually good enough to say to me, 'I have no doubt they will consent to your exchange at Madrid, so I shall send you to the head-quarters of Don Julian, where you will await the reply to your letters.' The next day, in fact, he ordered a dozen men to take me to Don Julian, chief of the largest band then infesting Old Castille, and he instructed my escort to treat me with respect. The savage fellows henceforth softened their tone a little, and always addressed me as Excellency or Signor, and so on. One of them, who was wearing my handsome cap with black plumes, even gave me an old pointed sombrero made of some grey linen stuff, which had been dangling by a torn fragment from his saddle bow. It was clothed in these mean rags that I had to make my entry into the towns on our route, and now began a series of vicissitudes, the recital of which I will spare my readers, for after having described the experiences of a fortunate officer on many a glorious battle field, I think it is only natural that I should wish to draw a veil over my humiliating sufferings as a prisoner.

At one o'clock in the morning of April 7th, we started on our way to the head-quarters of Don Julian under the escort of Sobrechero, who was chosen from the band to lead our party. For three days we climbed laboriously along the steep banks of the Alberge till we came to its source. The ascent was very difficult but most picturesque, and at the sight of the wild beauties of nature around me I awoke to fresh enjoyment of the life which had been so nearly ended. The exertion of climbing up and down the rocks, hunting about for the paths through the woods, or scrambling and sometimes tumbling over into the numerous torrents which flow into the Alberge, was really good for us, and our bodily fatigue relieved the tension of our minds. Our escort, too, cheered us by showing their anxiety to bring about our exchange as soon as possible, so as to put an end to the terrible reprisals on either side. The hope of being once more of some use to humanity revived our courage and aided us to bear

81

up, all but naked though we were, against the bitter cold of the mountains, and to rally from the many accidents which befell us in spite of the fact that we never got enough to eat.

We passed the first night at the house of a Spaniard, who heaped reproaches on our escort for not having killed us and so saved themselves the trouble of bringing us so far, and him that of having to receive us. The next night we spent with a more hospitable host, a priest named Don Pablo, who killed for us, he said, the last fowl left to him by the French, but, as you see, he bore us no malice. The third night we were received by another priest, one Don Mauricio, who, poor fellow, was very well educated, and enjoyed a chat for once with civilised people. He insisted on my accepting two or three of his shirts before I left. I appreciated this gift greatly, for to a naked man on the crest of a mountain covered with snow a shirt is worth more than a lot of gold on a plain!

At last, in a heavy downfall of snow, we reached the all but inaccessible village of Piedra Lavez, the head-quarters, I had almost said the den, of our brigands, perched at the top of lofty rocks. At the sight of this spot, which resembled the eyrie of an eagle or the stronghold of some feudal noble of the middle ages, in the keep of which he hoarded his treasures or the booty he had seized in his raids, we expected to be received in a manner as coarse and rude as the appearance of the place, and as cold as the flakes which were falling on our shoulders. Imagine, then, the effect produced on us when the leader in command at this wretched robber haunt came forward, and, addressing us in a friendly way in French, said, 'Welcome, gentlemen. I was a prisoner of war for three years in France, and during that time I was so kindly and generously treated that I consider myself fortunate in getting a chance to do something in my turn to help Frenchmen whose evil fate has brought them to me. I am sorry that my position in these poverty-stricken mountains prevents my giving you the reception I should have liked, but I will do my best to alleviate your sufferings.'

The robber chief, whose name was Joseph Ribero, was captain of a band he had levied in the hope of replacing Ferdinand

VII, on the throne of Spain, and though he was of course our political enemy he treated us as if we were his brothers. He gave us a hat, some neckties, pocket handkerchiefs, and even a few *piastres*, but he had such a very poor opinion of his own men that he advised us not to let them see the money, as they would be quite sure to take it away from us.

Ribero treated me especially with very great respect, for I had been brought to him as the nephew of King Joseph. He said I was sure to be exchanged soon, and added, 'The chances of war may turn in your favour, and I may be your prisoner some day; be good enough to remember, if that day ever comes, that we are enemies only on the battle field.' At the frugal repast which was all he was able to put before us, the monk Ursulo, who was one of the chief instigators of the insurrection, did full justice to the wine provided, of which a large quantity had been brought with us on a mule in goatskin bottles. The manners of this monk justified the contempt which the brigands with us seemed to have for all the Mendicant Friars.

Before we left, Ribero again expressed his great regret at not being able to supply us with clothes or to entertain us better, and he also earnestly recommended our escort to treat us well.

On the 8th we reached Naval=Donda, near the source of the Tormes, where we put up at the house of an old woman who was more bitter against us than any one else had yet been. Furious with rage at having to provide for Frenchmen and for our escort of brigands, she would have murdered us if we had not been protected by our guards. We dared not touch the food she offered us for fear of being poisoned; and not content with urging our escort to complete the work of destruction which divine intervention had arrested on the field of battle, the old fury hurled curses after us as we rode away. Needless to add that there was nothing in our calm and resigned demeanour to pro-voke such treatment.

After a long weary journey, with many a detour to avoid the French outposts, and many an adventure, the recital of which would only weary the reader, we reached Placenzia on the 17th. Our arrival in that beautiful city was expected, and all the inhabitants were at the windows or in the streets to witness the entry of the sobrino del Rey (the King's nephew). The women were far more incensed against us than the men, but fortunately our guards had orders to protect us from the fury of the populace. Well-dressed women filled the balconies, and angrily brandishing their fans they shouted to our brigands, '*Ahorcadle, degollad le*' (Hang him! Cut his throat!). The women of the lower classes yelled at us in an even more furious manner. When the execrations were at their worst I looked up at the ladies in the balconies, and said with a smile, '*Muchas gracias, señoritas, sois deliciosas, hechizas*' (Many thanks, fair demoiselles, you are charming, fascinating). This unexpected reply, which I gave with an imitation of Castillian grace and animation, this gay demeanour instead of the shrinking tremor they had expected, astonished them all so much that the balconies now literally shook with the thunders of amused applause, and every one cried, '*No, no, no ahorcad; tratad le muy bien*' (Don't hang him, don't hang him. Treat him very well!). Fans and handkerchiefs, held in pretty little Spanish hands, were now waved so vigorously in token of the favour of their owners, that they would have created quite a breeze if the soft April wind had not already been blowing pretty strongly, making the simple linen shirt, which I owed to the good priest Mauricio, and which was the only thing that saved me from appearing before all these ladies in the garb of Paradise, cling closely to my limbs. This very light apparel scarcely reached to my knees, and floated behind me on the back of my steed, who, proud of figuring in such a triumphal procession, halted to bray with joy at every street corner.

Don Julian had already received an answer from General Belliard, who proposed sending to him in exchange for the French Colonel Baron Lejeune, Colonel MacMahon and General Obledo, both prisoners at Madrid. This proposal, which was as honourable as it was generous, made Don Julian think the French attached great importance to getting me back, and to gain time he ordered my escort to take me across the Tagus to the headquarters of the Marquis de Castaños, Commander-in-Chief of the Spanish army, where a fresh series of woes awaited us.

Our guards told us every day that if one of us should escape, the other three would be put to death. We knew only too well that it was no good hoping for any mercy from the brigands, and this cruel announcement took away the last consolation of our miserable condition, for as long as we could occupy ourselves in making plans for each other's escape, our situation did not seem altogether desperate. Twice certain generous, kind-hearted ecclesiastics had seemed willing to co-operate with us in evading our keepers. The priests at Coria and at Minofol on the Tagus very nearly compromised themselves on our behalf, but the vigilance of our guards had frustrated their efforts. Then again at Caceres our hostess, whose name was Mariquita, was much distressed at seeing four young men, in the flower of their life, going about with scarcely more clothing than they had had at the hour of their birth; and when our guards boasted of having charge of the nephew of the King, she secretly determined to restore me to my uncle, the good *Rey Pepe*, whose generosity and kindness she extolled to me. 'This very night,' she said to me, 'my husband will take you to Truxillo, and you will be with your fellow countrymen the French before daybreak. I've planned the whole thing. I mean to hide you in my daughter's mattress; she will lie down on it with you beneath her, and even if any one went into her room no one would guess you were there. I will come and fetch you at the right moment. My daughter will then get into the bed I shall pretend I have given to you she will be taken for you, the guerrilleros will not have the slightest suspicion of your escape, and you will be in safety before they are ready to start again. There are no troops in the town, and you will find it quite easy to get away.' 'But can I take my three companions?' I asked. 'That would never do,' was the reply; 'the brigands watch you all very closely, and it would be impossible for four to disappear at once.' 'But, dear lady,' I answered, 'if I go alone my flight will be their death-warrant; I could not make such an odious sacrifice as that, my remorse for it would haunt me all the rest of my life.' 'Come, come,' she said, 'no more of that; I can save you, but it is quite impossible to save four.' This short talk was several times interrupted by our very vigilant guards. I passed a night of cruel agitation, and when we left the next morning I could only express my gratitude to Mariquita by pressing her hands, for our brigands watched us, jealously. She understood this mute language, however, for her eyes filled with tears.

A few leagues further on we passed through a burnt village, the inhabitants of which wished to strangle us, our guards having the greatest difficulty in preventing it. Beyond this village the country was deserted, and we often suffered from hunger, having nothing to eat but a few lettuces and a little chicory, which we found in the fields. One day our guards, worn out with fatigue and also suffering a little from hunger, though, thanks to the habitual abstinence of the Spanish, not quite so much as we did, halted in a little hovel beneath the shade of one of the very biggest chestnut trees I ever saw. The fruit had all disappeared, but the ground was completely covered with little snakes, which tried to escape at our approach. Though the idea of eating them made us shudder, famine drove us to attempt it, and we caught a number, which we proceeded to grill. They were, however, so emaciated that when they were skinned there was nothing left but their backbones and a few eggs, so we threw them away. We heard that the Spanish and Portuguese armies in the border districts were suffering as much as we were from dearth of provisions.

Although very much weakened for want of proper nourishment, our spirits rose as we approached the end of our journey, and I enjoyed the beauties of the country we were traversing perhaps more than I should have done in a state of repletion.

We arrived the same evening at Albuquerque, where we were lodged in a palace occupied by the descendants of Pizarro, who rivalled Hernando Cortés in cruelty to the peaceable inhabitants of the New World. The stern character of the chief of the race had been transmitted to his descendants. When we got to a palace we hoped we should be better received than we had been by peasants ruined by the passage of our armies. But it was not so. The great-great-granddaughters of the conqueror of Mexico were laughing with some Spaniards, who, as they looked at us in a menacing way, said to our escort, 'You had better have killed then instead of bringing them to us.' And these young ladies, in spite of the rich coat of arms carved above the entrance to their home, approved of the bloodthirsty suggestions of their companions, and behaved in such a manner that our very guards were indignant. But so great was our misery that we rejoiced indeed when a few hours after our arrival some food was brought to us in a big tureen. It was only a little coarse army bread, over which a few drops of oil with a lot of red pepper were sprinkled in our presence, whilst a quantity of boiling water was poured over the whole, but to us it seemed a delicious meal after our eight days of abstinence.

The only notes I made on the three days it took us to get from Albuquerque to Merida were: 'Scarcely anything to eat,' 'Nothing to eat,' for the district was an entirely uncultivated desert, in which we met only a band of ragged peasants who wanted to kill us. We followed for several leagues the ruins of three Roman aqueducts covered with the nests of storks which lived on the numerous snakes frequenting these wastes. The largest of these aqueducts still retains three rows of arches one above the other, so that it rises to a great height. They served to conduct the water from the mountains to the circuses and *naumachiæ*, of which many ruins still remain, about three-quarters of a mile from the town of Merida, built by Titus, and given by him as a reward to the legions he left behind him in Spain. It was long the capital of the Roman Lusitania.

Near the ruins of the Temple of Mars, opposite the triumphal arch begun by the soldiers of Titus in his honour, but not completed, some twenty English officers were awaiting the arrival of the French Colonel and his companions, of whose capture they had heard. They came forward and received us in quite an affectionate manner, and offered to do me any service in their power. It would be impossible to describe the delight I felt in finding myself once more amongst civilised men, but it may be imagined when it is remembered that I had for the last twenty days been with some of the roughest characters in the world, about whose very care for and protection of us there was something wild and ferocious. To give but one example of their ways, I will quote a solitary but very significant custom of theirs. Their abstinence makes them often a prey to low spirits, and to relieve their depression they would plunge one of their hands in very hot water; it, of course, at once became swollen, and then with a sharp razor they would open the most prominent vein. When enough blood had been lost, they cauterised the wound with a bit of burning tinder, and feeling better, they remounted and rode on. This reminded me of the wild horses of Hungary, which I had often seen bite a vein in their own necks near the shoulder. The copious bleeding which ensued seemed to do them good.

The English officers, with the considerate courtesy of true gentlemen, brought me underlinen and clothes enough to cover me from head to foot. They were also generous to my companions in misfortune, and took me to their officer in command, who received me most cordially. Major-General Sir William Lumley, who still limped in consequence of a severe wound, made much of me, kept me to dinner, asked me to stop at his house, and, in fact, loaded me with kindness. Having learnt from the papers and despatches which had been taken from me that I was an engineer, and interested in the fine arts, he instructed his officers to take me to see the numerous antiquities, such as the Roman bridge over the Guadiana, the porticos, monuments, Roman fortifications, &c., which render the town of Merida so interesting.

In the evening the young officers asked me to go and have some punch with them. They had nearly all been to Paris, and asked me a great many questions about it.

The evening was spent in telling each other amusing stories, and I contributed my share, forgetting all about the misery of the preceding days. Far more abstemious than I expected to find them, not one of the officers took too much wine. The witty chief of the staff and the worthy commissary officer, Hook and Wilkinson by name, with the rest of the officers escorted me back to my quarters. We parted very good friends, and they all promised to come and see me in Paris after the

war. Several kept their word, including Hook, whom I introduced to a friend of mine, whose daughter he married. She
was perhaps the prettiest girl in France at the time.

Good heavens! what a contrast there was between the manners of these Englishmen and those of my keeper Sobrechero,
to whom I had now to return to resume my journey with the
barbarous brigands under him! The English officers lent us their
horses, and we soon reached Almendralejo, where we were received by Lieutenant-General Lord Beresford, commanding the
Anglo-Portuguese army, who treated me with the same kindness and courtesy as his fellow countrymen had done at Merida.
His staff of officers were equally eager to make up to me for
my misfortunes. The Marquises of Mello, Lima, and Alva, all scions of noble Portuguese families, with Colonels Walker, Wilson, and other Englishmen, seconded their General in his efforts
on my behalf; but noticing that all these delicate attentions to
me aroused the jealous suspicion of Sobrechero, who visited his
spleen on my three companions in captivity, they appeased him
by giving large bribes to his brigands.

At last, on the 27th, we reached the head-quarters of the
Marquis de Castaños at Santa Maria, where our guards left us. I
gave them some of the things I had received when I was at Sir
William Lumley's, and thanked them for having preserved our
lives. Their departure took an immense weight off my heart,
and when they were gone I felt able once more to breathe like
a free man.

The Marquis de Castaños, who was a very intelligent man,
with prepossessing and dignified manners, had three generals
with him, namely, General Curera, Don Martino, chief of the
staff, and Don Carlos, now a marquis of Spain, who was, however, really a French émigré, descended, as he told me himself, from the Conites de Comminges, and connected with the
Montesquieus. Don Carlos made me stop with him for several
days, treating me like a brother; and he provided clothes for my
fellow prisoners at his own expense. During this quiet resting
time, the Marquis de Castaños sent for me again and again,
less to talk about my exchange – for which he was arranging

– than to impress on me how anxious the inhabitants of the Peninsula were to put an end to the war, which was ruining Spain for the benefit of England. At the same time Lord Wellington was writing, 'What folly it would be to risk anything further for the deliverance of Spain whilst the inhabitants, for whom we have done ten times as much as they ever deserved, hold themselves aloof in the midst of the storm!' Don Carlos also sounded me to find out whether I would be discreet enough to take a message to the Emperor from the Junta of Cadiz unknown to the English. 'It will be possible for us,' he said, 'to let you embark for France under the pretext of an exchange, and you shall propose to the Emperor the restoration of Ferdinand VII., to whom he should give in marriage one of the princesses of his family. Spain would then become his most devoted ally, and will aid him against all his enemies, even against England, whose behaviour wounds the self-respect, and is really against the true interests, of the Spanish.' I was certain that the Emperor would never consent to withdraw his brother from the throne of Spain and replace Ferdinand. I was bound by the commission I held to work against any such arrangement between the contending parties, but I disguised my real sentiments in the presence of the enemies of France, and gladly hailed the chance of being the bearer of messages tending to conciliation and peace. Whether in bona fide belief in my consent, or as a stratagem to catch me, I never knew, but Don Carlos told me with an air of great frankness on the third day of these conferences that the Marquis de Castaños had despatched a courier to the Junta of Madrid to assure them of my willingness to undertake this pacific mission.

'The Marquis de Castaños,' said Don Carlos, 'in so doing has met the desire several times expressed by the Junta of making advances to the Emperor in an indirect manner, but by means of a trusty messenger, before treating with England.' Whilst waiting for the reply of the Junta, I must be kept away from the operations of the army, and should be sent to Elvas. So I had to resign myself to fresh delays. We all went together to take leave of the Marquis de Castaños, who had copies given to me of the letters he had written to Marshal Berthier and General Belliard, urging my exchange. In this interview the Marquis spoke of Generals Dupont, Marescot, and Vedel, expressing his regret and making excuses for the melancholy results which had ensued, as he said, quite against his will. He also alluded to Marshal Soult, and expressed his great veneration for Marshal Mortier. In taking leave of me he said cordially, 'We shall meet again soon.' Don Carlos begged me to take with me an impression of his seal, on which was his coat of arms, and to recall him to the memory of his family in France. As an escort to Elvas he gave us his aide-de-camp, Captain Don José Cabrera, with four non-commissioned officers of dragoons of the Sagantum Regiment, who treated us with the greatest courtesy, and we started all mounted on horses lent by Don Carlos.

The English Governor of Olivença, commanding the Portuguese forces there, received us and gave us rooms in his own residence. It was now May 1, and the sun was very hot. It amused me to see the English officers riding about in uniform holding parasols above their heads. The fact that they use parasols and umbrellas, though it is not the fashion to do so in the French army, does not prevent them from being very brave soldiers in battle; but for all that, I must say that I was surprised and amused when I looked out of my window to see several groups of officers, on their way back to their quarters, followed by a very picturesque though unusual suite. First came the captain in his scarlet uniform, mounted on a very fine horse, and carrying a big open parasol; then came his wife, in a pretty costume, with a very small straw hat, seated on a mule, holding up an umbrella and caressing a little black and tan King Charles spaniel on her knee, whilst she led by a blue ribbon a tame goat, which was to supply her night and morning with cream for her cup of tea. Beside Madame walked an Irish nurse, carrying slung across her shoulders a bassinet made of green silk, in which reposed an infant, the hope of the family. Behind Madame's mule stalked a huge grenadier, the faithful servant of the captain, with his musket over his shoulder, urging on with a stick the long-eared steed of his mistress. Behind him again came a donkey laden with the voluminous baggage of the family, surmounted by a tea-kettle and a cage full of canaries, whilst a jockey or groom in livery brought up the rear, mounted on a sturdy English horse, with its hide gleaning like polished steel. This groom held a huge posting whip in one hand, the cracking of the lash of which made the donkey mend its pace, and at the same time kept order amongst the four or five spaniels and greyhounds which served as scouts to the captain during the march of his small cavalcade.

The sketch from nature I made of this party was later the subject of one of the best of the little compositions which I inscribed with the two words, *Utile dulei.*'

The fiction which made me the nephew of the King and of the Emperor had preceded us at Elvas, and when we arrived on May 1 many curious spectators lined our route. General Leyté, governor of the town, gave me the best room in the Dominican Convent, and the mayor and the municipal officers spread a repast for us, to which the chief members of the garrison were invited.

The next morning the officers of the Portuguese army came one after the other to greet the captive French Colonel. A grand meal was again served us on this occasion, and I noticed several persons in black who circulated to and fro behind the guests. I took them at first for the stewards, but their aristocratic bearing puzzled me, and presently I inquired who they were. 'The mayor and municipality, who are doing the honours of their sumptuous hospitality,' was the reply; and I at once got up to beg them to excuse my mistake, nor would I sit down again until they took places at the table with us.

In spite of the courtesy of all these people and of the interesting books which were lent to me to read, the time passed sadly, for from my window I could see in the distance the smoke rising up from the besieged town of Badajoz, and I could hear the roar of the cannon which was probably killing some of the French defending that fortress.

Lord Beresford had probably been informed of the scheme the execution of which the Junta of Cadiz had wished to entrust to me, and he hastened to foil the conspirators by ordering me to be taken to Setubal, beyond reach of the Spanish. This unfortunate contretemps sent me off once more on my travels, and destroyed my last hope of liberty.

General Leyté now ordered Captain Sassarmento, of the Portuguese dragoons, and four non-commissioned officers to take me to Setubal.

At Estremos we received a grand welcome in a fine convent, where there were only three monks left, who had, however, kept four first-rate cooks, and we were served with an abundance and variety of well-dressed dishes.

A little further on, as we were passing Arrayolos, we noticed a telegraph station of three square compartments, having four divisions giving twelve combinations and their multiples ad infinitum. Beyond Montemoro we came to Vendas Novas, where we passed a great underground room, or rather cellar, crowded with French prisoners, who were absolutely naked and who cried out to us to help them. I was of course powerless to protect them – all I could do was to put into the hands stretched out to me through the bars the few things which had been given to me by the English. The thought of their terrible fate, which might soon be our own, saddened our march across the far-stretching desert plains between Vendas Novas and Añas de Mora, a miserable hamlet, but the only place where we could halt after a pretty long tramp.

In the three or four huts which composed the hamlet of Añas de Mora, we found no one but a young and slightly deformed girl, with rather a pretty face, who was preparing food against the return of her absent brothers, and it was with a very bad grace that she set to work to add enough for nine extra people. Whilst waiting for our meal we went and sat down at the edge of the lake which gives its name to the hamlet, and as we were admiring the beauties of the sunset reflected in the quiet waters, the brothers of our hostess and some workmen passed us on their way home, carrying with them their guns, hatchets, and agricultural implements. When they caught sight of us, they glared at us with the fury of tigers. They did not speak a word, but the silent scowl of hatred on their faces, blackened with exposure to the sun, was more eloquent than any speech could have been. Our reception when we got back to the hut showed us that the young girl had aroused against us the bloodthirsty passions of her brothers. Our very frugal repast passed over, however, without a quarrel, though the eyes watching our every movement were full of bitter if taciturn rage. When the meal was over Sassarmento, foreseeing an outbreak, told me it would be prudent to withdraw, and we all went to the next room with the non-commissioned officers, who had been looking after the horses. They now flung themselves on the ground as we did, and were soon asleep; but Sassarmento and I, who were equally anxious, dared not close our eyes. We listened to the whispered conversation of the eight or nine peasants with the young deformed girl, and we both heard her say to her brothers, 'Stanitza is reckoned as good as a man since she helped her husband to cut the throats of three Frenchmen. Well, I'll do even more than she did, for I will dig my *uñadas* (nails) into the eyes of the big one' (that meant me!) 'whilst you cut his throat with your *cuchillo*' (knife). Then, just like the general of an army, she assigned to each of those present the part he was to take in our murder when we should be asleep, and it would be easy to overpower us, whilst her hearers encouraged each other by saying, 'The dragoons won't interfere,' &c.

Sassarmento was very indignant at what he overheard, and made a sign to me that one of the non-commissioned officers had left his rifle in the room with the peasants. Without hesitating a moment, I got up and boldly fetched the weapon, cocking it as I withdrew in sight of the peasants, who were simply trembling with rage. We then loaded the pistols belonging to the captain and the dragoons, and shut the door. Sassarmento lay down across it, and we awaited events. Sleep, however, soon overpowered our enemies as it did ourselves, and they forgot their lust for bloodshed, so that we were able to rest in peace. We left before sunrise the next day, giving the deformed girl a few *piastres* to make up to her for having deprived her of the glory of excelling Stanitza.

94

Beyond Añas de Mora the wide plain was deserted and un-cultivated, but covered with regular forests of marshmallows in flower, beneath which were millions of green lizards and little yellowish snakes, the sand being quite ploughed up by their numerous trails. They retreated slowly and with difficulty at our approach.

At noon on May 8th we reached Setubal, a pretty little town on the river Sadao, which flows into the wide and deep Bay of Setubal, an admirable harbour, then full of vessels which had come to take in cargoes of wine and oil for Russia and America. The contrast between the dreary tracts we had just crossed and the bright picturesque scene now before us was very great. The town with its many belfries and ancient fortifications stood out against the sea horizon, which is bounded on the right and left by lofty heights covered with gardens, vineyards, and woods, dotted here and there with pretty summer houses and mills each with eight triangular sails. The port is crowded with a forest of masts, whilst in the roadstead hundreds of sailing vessels of vari-ous tonnage are constantly arriving from their ocean voyage.

Captain Sassarmento took us to an inn called the *Etalaga Nova*, belonging to a Frenchman, now detained a prisoner in Lisbon, as he was suspected of being in communication with our army. His daughters, however, glad to see fellow country-men once more, were eager to wait upon us, and the English Commissary, Robert Boyer by name, who had been at once informed of our arrival, hastened to offer us his services and to bring us all we needed. We were then taken to the Governor, and Captain Sassarmento took leave of us. The Governor, with a politeness which we took as an earnest of the liberal hospitality we might expect, ordered a boat to be prepared, and we were rowed out to the lighthouse, about an hour's distance from the shore. The Governor showed us the tower of this lighthouse, and with a friendly smile assured us that the air was so pure there that his prisoners had lived in it for fifteen years without ever having so much as a headache. 'Fifteen years!' I cried in horror. 'Yes, fifteen years at least,' was the reply. The boat now touched at the fortress known as the Torre d'Othon, which was to be our abode, and the Governor always with the most exquisite courtesy installed us in two little casemates of hewn stone, which he honoured with the name of rooms, containing one table, one bench, and three old mattresses, the last-named peopled with crowds of the most disgusting and voracious vermin Spain or Portugal could produce. When he took leave the friendly Governor promised often to give himself the pleasure of paying us a visit, and expressed a hope that we should enjoy the beautiful air. He also gave us leave to walk about on the topmost terrace of the fortress.

We were immediately assailed by swarms of jumping and crawling brown insects, who were famished for want of food; but without losing courage in spite of the vigour of the bloodthirsty assault, we at once began in our turn to make war on them, and treating them much as we should a conflagration, we poured quantities of cold water on to them, hoping to sweep our enemies into the sea, their battalions being too numerous for us to be able to crush them all on land. Then having to some extent remained masters on the battle field, we went out on the terrace to rest a little after the struggle. For the last thirty-five days we had been the playthings of hopes continually disappointed, and of circumstances generally, to say the least of it, rather depressing than reassuring. We had no longer any hope of regaining our liberty, and there was nothing left for us to do but to make the best of the position in which we found ourselves. One thing, however, which made us almost happy was that we no longer had the prying and menacing eyes of our gaolers constantly upon us, and were free at least to gaze unmolested on the beautiful view spread out before us, which, leading us as it did to raise our eyes to heaven, did something to console us. We could still think of our lost country, and dream of some day finding means of returning to her.

The next day Robert Boyer came to see us, bringing with him an American merchant, named David Meyer. They were both laden with baskets full of oranges, wine, and dainty loaves of bread. Meyer wanted to bring us a lot of under-clothing, but we would not accept it. When we refused he spoke with gratitude of the kind and generous reception he had several times met with at Bordeaux, and repeated that he was glad of the chance of serving Frenchmen wherever he met them. Boyer also renewed his offers of service, and promised to get me the paper with the brushes and colours for which I asked him.

At the same time the following day he brought me a complete set of colours carefully labelled, and all I wanted for writing or painting. This present was indeed a valuable one, and I hastened to show my gratitude by making him then and there a sketch of the scene when I was taken prisoner, with likenesses of the brigands who had attacked me, for their faces were indelibly graven on my memory. In working at my painting once more I regained something of resignation, for, attractive at all times, it is impossible to describe what an immense resource wielding the brushes became in my dreary captivity.

Talking with my fellow prisoner Duhamel also made a break in the days, which no longer seemed so endless. We drew a chessboard on our table, and made white and yellow pieces with the outer and inner rind of our oranges, and Duhamel often had the pleasure of beating me at the game. Massart, who, though an excellent fellow, cared more for the pleasures of the table than for intellectual pursuits, looked after the kitchen department; we lived on dainty cooked dishes made of the so-called giltheads, which are very delicate eating, and other fishes from the bay, quantities of which were daily brought to us by the fishermen.

Our days passed quietly away in work, and in the contemplation of the grand view of the mountains which protected us from the cold north winds, and of the far-stretching bay, with its many vessels going to and fro under the guns of our fort. The height of our terrace and its peculiar construction enabled me to make a plan of the fortress and its surroundings. I had not the proper instruments for the work, but I made a quadrant and a compass in wood, and by means of the intersections of my principal lines I succeeded in drawing a very exact plan, which surprised the Governor and made him rather uneasy.

The Governor, who was an original character if ever there was one, just the eccentric fellow to figure to perfection on the boards of a theatre, came to see us nearly every day, to ask how we were getting on. He would chat with us quite confidentially, but stop suddenly every now and again with an access of reticence. However, he let out that the Marquis de Villeneuve, a Frenchman, and his wife were shut up in one of the rooms of our fort. The Marquis was an émigré, who was serving in the Portuguese army when Junot entered Lisbon with the French forces, and the Marquise de Villeneuve, who had not been able to get away in time, remained in that city. Her husband, becoming uneasy on hearing that she was in a house full of young aides-de-camp, ran the risk of leaving the Portuguese army and got into Lisbon, where he concealed himself. He was discovered, and Junot, taking him for a spy, ordered his arrest. The Marquis could not have evaded capture by the police had not a young officer whom he specially suspected, and had accused of being his rival, come to the rescue and aided him to escape. The French soon afterwards abandoned Lisbon, and the Marquis de Villeneuve decided to remain, thinking he could now rejoin the Portuguese army, but he was arrested by the Anglo-Portuguese and shut up in the fort of Setubal with the young wife who had been the innocent cause of his misfortunes.

On Sundays we used to go down to hear mass, and we could see the other prisoners in the chapel, though we were not allowed to speak to them. We thought the young lady very beautiful, and we in our turn took to sighing for her notice. We used to go every evening to the very end of our terrace, from which we could see the windows of her apartment, and we all three sang together nocturnes, barcarolles, and love ditties, such as Richards' 'Burning Fever,' &c., and everything else we could remember. Our only recompense was to see the tips of a white-gloved hand waving through the bars, as if in applause of our clumsy and discordant efforts.

David Meyer, the American, not only brought us provisions, but seconded our efforts to obtain our exchange. He even tried to help us to escape, and one day brought a long rope wound round his body under his clothes, for us to let ourselves down with from the fort. He had arranged a plan for our escape. A boat was waiting for us at a point he described to us, where it would be easy for us to embark, and we were to be taken in this boat to his vessel, of which the cargo was now complete. He would hide us on board till he started, and the American flag would protect us. At last everything was arranged for that very evening, and our escape seemed sure, when by order of Lord Beresford an officer and eight men came to escort us to Lisbon. There was no help for it – we had to follow our new guides. We were allowed to go, *en passant*, to bid farewell to Robert Boyer and David Meyer. The latter, much put out by the presence of the witnesses to our interview, could only say in an expressive manner, 'I shall be there with my boat this evening. We shall start before daybreak – do you see, do you see?' and an expressive pantomime made us understand that he advised us to evade our guards and keep our appointment with him, for he would wait for us.

We answered him with our eyes to the effect that we should do our very utmost to get away, and after shaking hands with him we started with our officer on good mules and surrounded by the eight soldiers. After we had been marching some time, we pretended to admire the country greatly, and begged our guides to let us stop to look round. Duhamel, Massart, and I then turned the pause to account to make out our bearings. We noted the rock at the foot of which the boat was waiting for us, and the stretch of ground between us and it, and we could see David Meyer's ship, on which he had purposely hoisted the American flag. We decided how to act, and continued our route, awaiting the moment to carry out our plan.

We had scarcely marched an hour, before, as we were going down from Palmela in the direction of Lisbon, we met a Portuguese escort taking some twenty men to Setubal, all fastened by the neck to one long chain. It was no surprise to us to see amongst them two of the men who had wanted to cut our throats in the house of the deformed girl at Añas de Mora; but what did astonish us was to hear that these twenty young fellows chained together were merely recruits being taken to join their regiment. Their escort, which was on foot, stopped to chat for a few minutes with ours. Our officer, however, continued to press on, and we were presently some eight paces in advance of our soldiers. The officer noticed this, and begged us to wait. We dismounted at once without hesitation, and thinking that the favourable moment had come for us to get off into the wood, we had already stooped to fill our hands with dust to throw in the officer's eyes so as to escape whilst he was blinded by it, when, alas! a courier from Lisbon dashed up at a gallop, and drew rein to exchange greetings with our leader. This gave our escort time to come up. Our chance was gone, and with infinite regret we dropped the sand which might have purchased our liberty.

Arrived at Moita, we embarked on the Tagus, and a few hours after we landed at the royal town of Lisbon, and our officer took us to a fine building which I thought was a palace. After crossing two beautiful rooms I was pushed towards a low narrow opening, rather like a chimney, and told to stoop down and go through it. This curious-looking aperture aroused my suspicions, and I inquired where it led to. 'Oh, to the convict prison, the galleys, where the prisoners are kept.' I knew well enough the shameful way in which prisoners sent to the galleys were treated, and at the words 'convict prison' and 'galleys' I turned upon my guides and swore that they would never get me to enter the infamous place alive. 'You are all,' I added, 'soldiers like myself, and it concerns the honour of every one of you not to allow soldiers to be confounded with criminals.' *'Es verdad! Es verdad!'* (It is true! It is true!) cried all the men together, but the officer continued to insist. 'Very well, then,' I said, 'kill me if you like, for I don't go in alive!' 'I have no orders to kill you – only to leave you here.' 'You can have received no such orders, sir,' I replied. 'for your superiors have promised that I should be treated with every honour.' Then, seeing that he hesitated, I went on, 'Go and find the Governor, and tell him of my resistance.' The officer, seeing that he would not be supported by his soldiers, whom my appeal had aroused to indignation, went to see the Governor, leaving us where we were to await his return. He had scarcely left us when we heard the noise of chains, and in came some hundred convicts with horribly ruffian-like faces, who were being brought back from work, yoked, so to speak, two and two to

100

a long heavy chain dragging behind them on the ground. When they reached the narrow opening the convicts went down on all fours, and creeping through the infernal aperture they disappeared. The soldiers, whom I continued to ply with arguments in my favour, were altogether indisposed to take part against me. When the officer returned he made many apologies to me, telling me that Lord Beresford ordered us to be taken on board the English frigate stationed in the port. We were escorted thither in a boat, and the officer took his leave.

The English captain and his officers left me in the state cabin whilst a meal was prepared for us. The evening was spent in very pleasant company, and the next day we were taken on to a three-masted vessel called the *Thetis*, which was about to start with a convoy for England. Here again a state cabin was given to me, and we shared a first-rate table throughout the voyage. Captain Robert Stolf, who had all the reserve of manner characteristic of the English, always addressed me with a politeness which would have been remarkable even in a Paris salon, and not a day passed without his assuring me that I should be far better treated in England than it was possible for me to be in his ship. I believed all he said to me, and my only regret was that my companions in captivity could not share in the good things I received, but orders had been given that they were only to have the rations of ordinary prisoners.

The voyage took nine days, and the wind being high the sea was so rough that I constantly fancied there was a storm going on. This was the first time I had ever made a voyage, and the creaking of the timbers of the ship alarmed me greatly, for I thought again and again that she was breaking to pieces and would be swallowed up by the waves. Once I said to the captain in my anxiety, 'Is this a storm?' and he replied coldly with a smile, 'I do not think so.' We passed the coast of Normandy in the distance, and I thought of my father mourning for my death, which had been falsely reported to him. Perhaps, I said to myself, he is at this moment walking up and down on the beach indulging in the grief he disguises at home so as not to distress my mother, and I was thinking what a joy it would be to go and comfort him, when we entered the Solent, dividing the Isle of Wight from the mainland. That very day the last honours were being paid by the English, in the form of volleys of artillery, to my friend General Rufin, who had been wounded at Chiclana, was taken prisoner by the English, and died just as the vessel he was on reached Portsmouth. The *Thetis* entered Portsmouth harbour, and I witnessed a singular scene. A few minutes after the vessels of the convoy had cast anchor, and the bells of the various ships had announced their arrival, some hundreds of row-boats full of women appeared, making in our direction, the various crews all shouting and whistling together. I was told that these ladies were the wives and sisters of the sailors, with whom were also some members of the *demi-monde* of Portsmouth, who were allowed to come on board to welcome their relations or their friends.

Captain Stolf, who was so sure that I should be honourably received in England, hastened to go ashore and ascertain what was to be done with me, and it was indeed with a sinking heart that I looked into his face when he returned, for he appeared very sad and was evidently much upset. 'Let us go down into the boat,' was all he said, and I dared not question him, dreading to hear too soon the bad news he had to tell. We were all as silent as he was in the boat, and our uneasiness increased when we passed some twenty old vessels full of French prisoners, most of them wearing only yellow vests, whilst others were perfectly naked. At this distressing sight I asked our captain if he was taking us to the hulks. To which he replied with a frown, 'Yes, just as a matter of form.' At the same moment our boat drew up alongside of the San Antonio, an old eighty-gun man-of-war. We climbed on to it, and there, to our horror, we saw some five or six hundred French prisoners, who were but the third of those on board, climbing on to each other's shoulders in the narrow space in which they were penned, to have a look at the newcomers, of whose arrival they seem to have been told. Their silence, their attitude, and the looks of compassion they bestowed on me as I greeted them *en passant*, seemed to me omens of a terrible future for me.

The captain of the old hulk entered our names on his register, and then apologised for having no better quarters to offer us than those assigned to the other prisoners, for, as he said, he had such an immense number on board. I could scarcely believe my ears, and made him repeat what he said. Then, my rage getting the better of me, I seized Captain Stolf by the arm, exclaiming, 'You have betrayed me! You promised I should be well treated. I would rather have been killed than have allowed myself to be brought hither, and now you shall die with me.' My violence alarmed the captain and the two or three soldiers with him. I then drew back a step, so as to have my back against the cabin and face all my enemies. I snatched a sword from an Irishman standing near, and threatened to kill Captain Stolf or any one else who tried to detain me on the vessel. Stolf assured me he had nothing to do with it, and the other captain endeavoured to calm me, but in the twinkling of an eye all the prisoners on board catching my excitement began shouting, 'Bravo, bravo!' They climbed on each other's shoulders till they towered above the little group of disputants, crying out, 'If every one behaved as you do, the English would not dare to ill treat us so.' The noise emboldened me still further, and the captain of the vessel, who being close to me was in more danger than any one else, became alarmed at the rage of the twelve or fifteen hundred prisoners, who seemed likely to break down the barriers dividing them from us, and to overpower the very small guard. So he hastened to say to Captain Stolf, 'Rid me of this furious fellow; take the French devil to Forton!' Captain Stolf, whom I still held by the arm, needed no second bidding, and quickly making for his boat insisted on my getting in first. The soldier whose sword I had seized called out to me to give it back to him, and I flung it on deck as I went down to the boat. I was thus separated from the two companions who had shared my captivity so long, and I did not see them again till after peace was concluded.

CHAPTER 4
Escape

Forton, which is close to Gosport, was then a depot for prisoners in connection with that at Portsmouth. Before taking me thither Captain Stolf, thinking we both needed something to soothe us after the painful emotions we had just gone through, took me into a public-house and ordered a glass of what he called grog for each of us. This very simple beverage, consisting of rum mixed with warm water with a lump of sugar in it, certainly had a beneficial effect upon us, and as soon as we had drunk it we started for the depot for prisoners at Forton. Arrived there, Captain Stolf told the Commandant that he had orders for me to be treated with every respect during my stay, and at his recommendation a decent lodging was assigned to me for the few days I should be at Forton. Here Robert Stolf left me. A few minutes after my arrival a French captain named Garat, who had been taken prisoner in India, and was confined to his bed in a hospital at Forton, sent by the hand of one of the attendants a bag containing 1,200 francs, which he begged me to accept, though he did not yet know me. I sent it back to him at once, and hastened to go and thank him for this very kind thought for me. He assured me that he would really be grateful if I would take the money, and even larger sums which he pressed on me, for he was himself in danger of losing them. I remained three days at Forton, during which I drew up an account of my journey for Major-General Prince Berthier, sending it to him by the hand of a wounded French officer who had obtained his exchange.

I had also had time to have some clothes made to fit me,

when orders came for me to be sent to Ashby in Leicestershire. Without any previous warning a public coach was brought up to my door at Forton, and I was made to get into it after having been told to sign a paper in English, which I was not allowed time to read, with my full name and rank. I was not even permitted to go and bid farewell to Captain Garat, but I had to get into the coach in all haste. In fact, every one was in such a hurry that my not having signed the paper after all was never noticed. As it was probably a form giving my word of honour to remain in England till I was exchanged, I thought this oversight very lucky, and I determined to turn it to account the very first time I got a chance.

I found myself now quite alone in the coach with a very pretty young girl, and like a true French cavalier I of course began to talk to her. She answered me brightly and gaily. It was a very long time since I had enjoyed any feminine society, and this meeting delighted me. I could not make out, however, why the girl remained so motionless, but I concluded that English etiquette demanded a rigid demeanour, and I was thinking that I would make a note of the fact in my account of my journey, when about a dozen miles from Forton the coach stopped, and four men got in who laid the girl down on a mattress and carried her to her relations, who were awaiting her arrival near by. Before they left, the good people thanked me in a manner I certainly did not deserve for the attention I had shown the young lady during the drive.

Near Andover I saw the residence of the exiled Bourbon princes. I little thought I should so soon see them again in Paris, and during my stay in England I collected many details about them which were very interesting to me, who as a child had known them at Versailles. I went to Blenheim, near Woodstock, and saw the residence of the Duke of Marlborough, erected by the people of England as a reward for the victorious general. The vast park in which the fine castle is situated is laid out on the plan of the battle field of Malplaquet, the clumps of trees representing the battalions and squadrons which took part in that terrible conflict, whilst statues of the various commanders are placed here and there. The trees which once stood for soldiers have now grown to such a height, and the swaying green foliage which once represented the plumes worn by the combatants, and the flags they carried, has spread out so widely, that it is difficult to make out the original purpose of the grouping or to read the lesson it was intended to teach to posterity. Nevertheless, I could not help admiring the national spirit of gratitude which had led to the working out of this singular and ingenious idea.

After a very pleasant journey, occupying a good many days, during which I visited various manufactories, picture galleries, collections of curiosities, and even several theatres in different towns, I arrived at Ashby-de-la-Zouch, where I was to reside. There were already about a hundred French prisoners in the town, some of whom had been there for fifteen years. I went to report myself to the agent in charge of the prisoners, who was a wholesale grocer of the name of Farnell, certainly the tallest, thinnest, most cadaverous looking seller of dry goods in the world. This worthy man, who seemed to move by clockwork, bowed politely, and proceeded to explain to me the routine to be followed by the prisoners. He gave me lease to lodge where I liked, and I was free to walk out of the town for one mile in any direction, but no further. Amongst the prisoners I found several distinguished naval officers, including Captain Hulliac, brother of a friend of mine, Captain Kergrise, with M. Boulan and Colonel Stoffel, who had been his brother's second in the duel at Astorga related above, with many others. I determined to lose no time in mastering English, and I was working very hard at it when I received an invitation to form one of a party of guests at the residence of General Hastings, about a mile from Ashby. General Hastings was the brother of Lord Moira, the intimate friend of the Prince of Wales. General and Lady Hastings had given a home to Miss Moore, daughter of the celebrated General Sir John Moore, who was killed in Spain at the battle of Corunna. The young orphan, who was a very bright, interesting, and charming girl, was quite the life of the circle which her host and hostess gathered about them. The courtesy and kindness with which I was received did much to cheer my spirits, prisoner though I still was. Lord Moira was even good enough to say he would try and get me permission to live in London, and I was about to profit by this generous concession, when an unexpected circumstance changed all my plans.

A man came to me one morning and said to me privately, 'The Duke of Rovigo, Minister of Police in France, authorised by the Emperor, has sent me to propose to you that you should let me arrange for you to get out of England and back to France.' The proposal he proceeded to make sounded most tempting, but it would mean a very great risk, and I mistrusted the fellow. Without actually refusing to do as he suggested, I replied that I expected to be exchanged, and begged him to see Colonel Stoffel first, and come back to me in a few days. I told Colonel Stoffel about it, and he made the inquiries necessary to assure us that the man was not a spy trying to find out my plans. After a few days' delay, the Colonel came to me and said, 'It is a *bona fide* offer, but the emissary has brought no money with him, and it will probably cost a couple of hundred guineas.' We had between us only a very small portion of that sum, and we must manage to get it somehow. So I went to a merchant named Baudins, who had been very civil to me, and whose frank ingenuous countenance had inspired me with confidence. I said to him straight out, 'I have come to show you how I trust you.' 'And what might that mean?' was his reply. 'There is a plan afoot for taking me back to France.' 'But that would be a great risk; there are a thousand dangers in the way.' 'Yes, I know, but I have decided to brave them, only I have not enough money. Can you lend me some?' 'How much do you want?' 'Five thousand francs!' With a frown he replied, 'I have not the whole of that sum by me, but come to me to-morrow morning, and perhaps I shall be able to let you have it.' I took my leave, and after saying good-bye, I added, 'You have my secret, but I feel quite easy in my mind.'

There was a ball that same evening, at which my friend Mr. Baudins and his daughter were present. When he caught sight of me, he nodded his head twice as if to say, 'Yes, yes,' and I answered him by signs only, for fear of compromising him. For the same reason I did not go and speak to him all the evening. But I danced with his daughter. Mr. Farnell the grocer was there too, and never did I see anything more comic than the appearance this provincial dancer presented, with the air of proud reserve suitable to a man who had charge of the French prisoners. It was really quite worth a journey to England only to watch him.

I was very punctual at the rendezvous the next morning, and Mr. Baudins gave me two hundred guineas, saying as he handed them to me, 'I have given them to you in gold to avoid the delay of changing paper.' I begged him to name the rate of interest I was to pay him, but he would not do so, assuring me that he lent me the money to oblige me, not with any idea of profit. The day and hour were now arranged with the emissary of the Duc de Rovigo, and Colonel Stoffel saw to everything without my appearing at all. I was invited to a grand dinner by General Hastings the very evening we were to start, and I duly appeared at it. The evening passed by very brightly, and at dessert, after the ladies had retired, the men remained behind to drink wine together, beginning with a toast to the ladies. As a matter of taste as well as by design, I kept my head clear, and when my companions were sufficiently exhilarated by the fumes of the claret they had drunk, they returned with somewhat unsteady steps to the drawing-room, where tea had been prepared by the ladies. The light-hearted way in which I answered the thousand questions put to me about the customs of Paris, and the entertainments given there, would never have led any one to guess the serious undercurrent of my thoughts at a moment when I was about to risk my life on the faith of an unknown emissary. Every one, in fact, was so pleased with the French Colonel, that when I took my leave at the time required by the regulations the prisoners had to comply with, every one begged me to come again the next day.

It was eleven o'clock at night and very dark, so that I found it difficult to make my way through the park to the place where I was to find Colonel Stoffel and the emissary. There was no one there, and I was afraid I had mistaken the way. I dared not make the least noise to betray my presence to them if they were in hiding. An hour passed in terrible suspense, and my heart was beating very quickly, when I at last heard a rustling amongst the leaves near me. I hid myself behind a bush, and waited till I recognised Stoffel and the guide. The latter led us to the first posting stage, and two minutes later we were in a good carriage, rapidly dashing along over the first of the hundred miles between us and the sea. We passed through Northamptonshire, the north of Middlesex, London, and Reigate, arriving at Hythe in Kent, five miles from Folke-stone, at night. The coast was guarded here by troops and cus-tom-house officers, and our guide told us we must pretend we were invalids come to take sea baths. Whilst the horses were being changed, he carried first one and then the other of us in his arms to place us in the fresh carriage, calling to the cus-tom-house officers to come and help him. Just imagine the dangerous position of two French officers in perfect health imitating fretful invalids in the arms of English custom-house officers, who, fortunately for us, never dreamt of asking for the passports of such sufferers. A little further on our guide dismissed the posting carriage, and had tea served for us in a public-house, whilst he went to make inquiries about how to get to Folkestone. He came back a few minutes afterwards with a terror-stricken look in his face, and unable to get out a word, he wrote on the slate belonging to the inn, 'Pay at once, and let us be off!' His gestures were so alarming that I gave the girl in attendance a guinea, saying, 'You can keep the change.' This generosity astonished her so much that she thought we must be criminals running away from justice, and looked ready to denounce us. There was no time to be lost, for we had to get through the village, which was full of troops. The guide made me a sign to lay aside the erect bearing of a French soldier, and stoop as much as I could. Thanks to our energy and to our round backs, we escaped without attracting notice; but as the country outside Hythe was very open, we should have been clearly seen from a long distance, and I thought it safer for us to hide amongst the wheat for the rest of the day. The guide went on alone to Folkestone, after noting our bearings, so that he could find us again in the evening.

He did not return for seventeen hours, and the night was over when he at last appeared and gave the signal agreed on, to which we replied. He then took us to Folkestone, and introduced us to a man named Brick, a surly, ferocious-looking smuggler, who was to take us over to France. The door of the room in which Brick awaited us was hidden by tapestry, and when we entered a woman was pouring out a glass of porter for him. The sinister appearance of the couple made our hearts sink, and we dreaded placing ourselves at the mercy of such people. Brick with a villainous smile accosted us with the words, 'Let's see the money you have brought!' I had paid for the post carriage, and still had the two hundred guineas. He insisted on taking the whole, though the price agreed on was rather less. It was of no use trying to beat him down, so I let him have it all. He then searched us to make sure that we were hiding nothing, looked if we had any rings on our fingers, and when he had quite made up his mind that we had neither money nor anything of value left, he said to us, 'The wind is contrary this evening; I will lodge you in a safe place, and to-morrow night I will fetch you to take you to Boulogne.' The delay was dreadfully trying, but we were in the man's hands, and had to submit. Our emissary now took us to the house of a woman who gave us a decent room and fed us well. She showed us a trapdoor under our beds, through which we could escape at the least alarm. For thirteen days in succession Brick came to say, 'The wind is contrary, and I cannot take you.' But the wind had been blowing our curtains about in every direction. My patience was at an end, and unable to endure waiting longer, I begged Brick so earnestly to take us that very night, that he at last said with a forbidding and treacherous smile, 'Well, follow me,' and as he left the room he added with an air of ferocity to the sailor with him, 'Like the others!' At these terrible words the woman who had looked after us for the last thirteen days began to tremble, and seeing me about to follow Brick, she flung herself before me and whispered with a timid glance after him, 'Don't go with him!' Colonel Stoffel and I, however, insisted, and the poor woman then, catching hold of our clothes to detain us, repeated in accents of the greatest terror, 'Do not go with him!' Surprised at her behaviour, I guessed there was some danger in our embarking that night, and Colonel Stoffel said to me, 'This is very extraordinary; let us wait.' We therefore allowed Brick to go on with the sailor, who was evidently his accomplice, and remained with the woman.

The men had hardly disappeared when the poor creature, almost insensible with fright, exclaimed as she drew us towards her, 'O my God! what are you going to do?' We pressed her with questions, but terror prevented her from answering, though we guessed there was some terrible mystery behind. We learnt later that Brick had already taken prisoners on board his boat some twenty times, promising to land them in France. He hid them under nets to evade the vigilance of the coastguards, and as soon as they were in the offing he murdered them and flung their bodies into the sea with stones tied round their necks. If he had been caught aiding in the escape of prisoners, he would have been himself condemned to the galleys. He never had any intention of saving the poor fellows who bribed him to help them, and many French officers, whose love of their country made them foolhardy and who were less fortunate than we were in finding a friend to warn them, fell victims to his atrocious mode of evading a great responsibility.

When our hostess had recovered a little from her emotion, we begged her to try and find some other means for us to get to France. We had no more money, but for all that she did find a sailor willing to take us without even naming a price. Seeing what a good fellow he was, I said to him, 'I will give you fifty louis at Boulogne.' On the evening of the fourteenth day of our detention at Folkestone the man brought us some sailors' clothes, which he made us put on, and took us some distance along the beach, replying to every challenge from the sentinels of 'Who goes there?' with the one word, 'Fishermen!' We came at last to a little boat drawn up on the sand. It was shoved off, and we jumped in, but three times the waves flung it and us back on the shore, wetting us to the skin. It was really impossible to get to the fishing smack which was awaiting us a few yards from the beach, so that we were compelled reluctantly to return to our hostess. She was very much put out, too, for she was running a great risk in harbouring us, especially now that our escape was known, and a reward of thirty pounds had been offered by the Government for our recovery. She was, however, loyal to us to the end, and the next night she brought the good sailor to us again. The sea was no longer so rough, and we were able to get off in the little boat which quickly brought us to the smack, a bark some four feet long, in which two fishermen with their nets were waiting for us. We passed under the very bowsprit of the police boat, those on board her taking us all for fishermen. To avoid exciting suspicion, however, for those on the brig might have watched us through their glasses, we manoeuvred with the nets as if we were about to fling them overboard. In this way we managed to get out into the offing, and when there we unfurled a little sail, for the sea was now quite calm. Five or six hours later we were in sight of Boulogne with nothing more to fear than being sunk by balls from the cannon of the advanced battery of the fort, which, we were warned through a speaking trumpet, would open fire on us if we came any nearer. Colonel Stoffel and I therefore hastened to wave our handkerchiefs as we advanced straight upon the mouths of the cannon. So near the French shore, we would rather have been killed than go back. The battery did not, however, fire on us, and we happily ran our little bark ashore on the beloved soil of our native land, where we were soon actors in a charming little episode.

At this time the English sent many smugglers over to France, and the country was simply inundated with incendiary pamphlets brought over by them, which the coast-guards had orders to seize. We no sooner touched land, therefore, than we were surrounded by some sixty men of various ranks, including custom-house officers, gendarmes, soldiers of the line, &c., who, crossing bayonets, made a perfect circle around us, in the centre of which we had to walk as if we were plague-stricken, and it would be dangerous to touch us. We were marched in this way before the various authorities coming at last to General Vandamme and the Chief Commissioner of Police, M. de Villier du Terrage, now a peer of France, who was a friend of mine and had fought side by side with me in our first campaigns. These two gentlemen welcomed me most heartily and placed their purses at my disposal, so I bade farewell to my sailor, giving him the fifty louis I had promised.

I then booked for Paris, arriving there at much the same time as the telegraphic despatch which had announced my return. It was only just five months since I left Paris, but the many vicissitudes which had been crowded into the time made it appear twice or three times as long, though I had been far more fortunate than thousands of my fellow countrymen, for I had soon cut short my time as a prisoner, whilst many of them had been exiled for fifteen years.

I alighted at the residence of the Prince of Neuchâtel (Prince Berthier), and he at once took me in his carriage to the Emperor, who was just then engaged with the Duke of Bassano, but he left him and took me out in the park. After he had asked me how I had managed to get back to France, the Emperor inquired if I had seen any of the Bourbon family when I was in England, in what style they lived, in what kind of consideration they were held, &c. He seemed very much interested in everything connected with them, and they were evidently a good deal in his thoughts. It really seemed as if their being so near to France made him distrustful, but he spoke of them all with the greatest respect. He was also very much exercised in his mind about the bitter feeling against him in England, and asked me if I could explain the insulting invectives in the press, which seemed to him to be the outcome of the personal rather than the political hatred of John Bull. He seemed both flattered and surprised when I told him that John Bull was very far from hating or despising him, as asserted in the newspapers. I added, 'I did not enter a single cottage or mansion in England without finding at least one portrait of "Bony" as they call you, Bony being short for Bonaparte. These portraits of your Majesty, moreover, are not caricatures, for every one wants to know the very features of the extraordinary man who is changing the face of Europe. At Lord Moira's, for instance, I saw a life-size likeness of your Majesty on foot, copied from Gerard's picture. Lord Moira gave two hundred pounds for that copy three months ago.' 'But,' was the reply, 'if that is how the English feel, why does the press inveigh against me so implacably?' 'Sire,' I said, 'the English find it difficult to get troops to fight against you, and this kind of thing seems to them quite fair in war.' 'Did you see my brother Lucien?' 'No, sire, he is in Wales, many miles from where I was. I was promised permission to go and see him, but the chance of escape, which I owe to your goodness, prevented me from having time to do so. I know, however, that he is allowed considerable liberty. He has a whole county as a prison, and he is eagerly working at his poem on Charlemagne, the first cantos of which are finished.' 'How could he be so stupid as to risk being taken prisoner for the sake of romancing about Charlemagne, when he might have been a Charles XII. himself, and have remained with me to second my efforts?' The Emperor was very fond of his brother Lucien, and wished him to employ his brilliant talents in the service of France. 'And did you see Lefebvre-Desnouettes?' 'No, sire, but I wrote to him. He is intensely anxious to get back to you, and is beginning to lose hope of being exchanged. He would do as I have done if he were not afraid of your Majesty's displeasure.' 'Oh, let him come, let him come! I shall be very glad to see him.' 'Does your Majesty give me leave to tell him so in your name?' 'Yes, yes; don't lose any time.'

I may as well add here that I told Mme. Lefebvre-Desnouettes of what had passed. The young wife at once went to get her passport, and left Paris to rejoin her husband. Her presence did much to distract the attention of the officer in charge of the prisoners, and made the escape comparatively easy. She shared all the dangers of the journey with heroic courage, and three months after my return she and her husband were both back in Paris.

The Emperor asked me a great many questions about the condition of the French prisoners in England, and a little later the appearance of Colonel Pelet's book confirmed the terrible description I gave. I made several efforts in this same interview to turn the conversation on to the necessities of Spain, and was told that King Joseph himself had been in Paris, but had returned to Madrid a few days before I got back. I noticed with regret that the Emperor no longer took much interest in the affairs of the Peninsula, and that he left them entirely in the hands of subordinates. I concluded that the state of things had improved since I left Spain, or else that the country was to be evacuated; but neither of these suppositions was correct, for far greater schemes than the amelioration of the condition of that unhappy country were now absorbing the thoughts of the Emperor. The woes of Spain, the neglect of which was to have such tragic results for the whole of Europe, were made no more of than some slight ailment which can easily be cured. My urgent report on the state of the French army in Spain had been duly handed to Prince Berthier. He thought my strictures on the generals in command, who were most of them friends of his, too severe. He knew that the Emperor's mind was full of other schemes, and he sent my report back to me without making any use of the information it contained. I could not help regretting having lost so much to gain absolutely nothing.

When after my talk with the Emperor in the gardens we returned to the palace, I offered him my congratulations on the birth of the King of Rome. He looked pleased, and took me to see the infant prince in his cradle. He was a very fine little fellow, and was already surrounded by a court of ladies of honour, governesses, chamberlains, &c., and had a grand equerry of his own in the person of the Count of Canisy.

Major-General Prince Berthier was good enough to drive me back to Paris, and the next day I went with him to join a hunting party at Grosbois, where he and his family were just then staying. This journey of six or seven leagues with the Prince was of deep interest to me, for in it I really got to know something about the General's kind heart, which I should perhaps never otherwise have done, for he made a point of always appearing grave and severe with his young officers. He looked at me now again and again with a happy, almost eager expression of affection, such as a father would wear who had regained a beloved son whose loss he had mourned. He maintained, however, the dignified silence of a commander, only breaking it now and then with an eager question, showing how great was his interest in what I was saying, and how much he felt for the sufferings I had gone through. Prince Berthier was very different in this respect from the Emperor, who was always very free and easy when he wanted to get information, and only put on a solemn manner when dismissing those he received. The Prince maintained, on the other hand, a dignified reserve with those under him, concealing with difficulty the promptings of his generous nature, and never yielding to the gaiety which really was part of his character, except with those over whom he had no authority. Prince Berthier's career had really been more brilliant than that of any of the officers immediately surrounding our Caesar, but he never assumed any special distinction, for he was always simple, modest, polite, and natural in his manner. He was never known to utter a word which could wound the self-respect of his subalterns, but, on the contrary, he tried to the utmost of his power to increase the dignity of their position. Only once did I see him out of temper, and that was with his young brother, whom he overheard asking me very politely to hold his horse for him for a minute. 'For whom do you take my aides-de-camp?' he cried with an angry gesture. His ordinary expression was one of benevolence; he was very generous, and he often secretly gave me from twenty-five to fifty *louis d'or* for emigrants who had returned home in poverty. Later, after the Restoration, I often heard the very people he had helped speak of him as M. Berthier without any title. He really was also the most indefatigable person I knew, and when I one day congratulated Count Daru on his wonderful power of sustaining fatigue and doing without sleep, he said to me, 'The Prince of Neuchâtel is even stronger than I am; I never spent more than nine days and nights without going to bed, but Berthier has been in the saddle for thirteen days and nights at a stretch.' The Prince had never given much time to the study of literature, as his way of expressing himself sometimes betrayed, but he was a very good geometrician, and had worked hard at mathematics when a boy, and his orders, whether verbal or written, were always couched in terms so lucid and simple that a very few words sufficed to describe the most complicated manoeuvres of an army. If circumstances had not made General Berthier a great warrior and a model chief of the staff, he would certainly have distinguished himself as an engineer. He was also a very good draughtsman, and several things he showed me proved that he had considerable talent for the graphic arts.

Few men had been more fortunate throughout their military careers than Prince Berthier. I often heard him congratulate himself on having served France in all four quarters of the globe. He made his début in the War of Independence in America, and returned home with very pleasant memories, for he became the personal friend of Rochambeau and Lafayette, under whom he served with the French contingent. He told me that of all the decorations he had received during his successful career, he had been most flattered at getting the little Cross of the Order of the Cincinnati. It was given to him by Washington and the American Senate when he was but thirty years old, a short time before he received from the King of France the Cross of St. Louis for the same services. As I have already related, I was with the Army of the North during Napoleon's brilliant campaign in Italy, which went far to eclipse our successes on the Rhine, and I often heard the marvellous feats of arms of Bonaparte attributed to the initiative of the young General Berthier. Whether it were jealousy or genuine conviction which led to the spreading of this report I do not know, but I fully shared in the opinion expressed when in 1800 Berthier, then Minister of War, took me as his aide-de-camp. I soon changed my mind on the subject after seeing the two men together, both so richly but so differently gifted, aiding each other with their counsel. It was the First Consul who inaugurated every plan, improvised the means for carrying it out, and by imbuing all with his own zeal made everything possible. It was General Berthier who, the plan of the chief once conceived, identified himself thoroughly with it, divided and subdivided the work to be done, assigning to each one the particular task by fulfilling which he was to cooperate with every other member of the army, smoothing down difficulties, providing for every contingency. His anxious solicitude, which kept him ever on the alert, his undaunted co-operation, were never relaxed until success was achieved. The glory which accrued to Berthier, though secondary, was yet considerable, but he was so modest that his aim was always rather to detract from his own merits, and to get the Commander-in-Chief to bestow his rewards on his comrades in arms. Of course, however, his fellow officers were too often jealous of him, and tried as hard to bring themselves into notice as he did to avoid calling attention to himself. Many of them were indeed ungrateful enough to accuse him of incapacity, because in 1809 he was not imprudent enough, as were so many of his fellow officers, to risk the loss of everything and to act in opposition to the wishes of Napoleon. But he was nobly avenged, for, in spite of all that his detractors could say, he was fully appreciated by the Emperor, and on the fatal field of Waterloo, when waiting in vain for Grouchy's corps to come up, Napoleon exclaimed, 'If Berthier were here, my orders would have been carried out, and I should have escaped this misfortune.' But I am anticipating dates, and must return to my subject.

No one served the Emperor with more loyal devotion from 1795 to 1814 than the Prince of Wagram, and whilst I was with him not a day passed without my noting some fresh proof of his devotion to his master, which was indeed a perfect religion with him. He was entirely without self-seeking, and yielded to his chief an affectionate and unfailing obedience often most touching in its patience and resignation. Though of medium height only, Berthier had a well-formed athletic figure, and his hair was thick and curly. He was an ardent lover of the chase, as eager in it as in war, and the Emperor, who knew how to appreciate all his good qualities, made him his Master of the Hounds. Such was the warrior under whom I was fortunate enough to serve for twelve years, going to him as a captain and leaving him as a general with many a decoration, a well-filled purse, a heart full of gratitude to him, and, what I valued far more than all my honours, many happy memories of the time I had been with him. These memories are still a delight to me in my old age, and give me strength to look forward to the future. May they also enable me to finish the story of my military career by telling of my experiences between 1811 and 1814, those most deeply interesting years of a century in which took place such extraordinary revolutions and wars, when empires were founded and overturned, when dynasties were changed, when so many men of eloquence and of genius rose into fame, and when such great discoveries were made, and the human race made such strides in progress.

I have now to relate my experiences in the two terrible campaigns of 1812 and 1813 in Russia, Saxony, and Prussia, from which I returned wounded in 1814.

As I have already related, I had gone through some very painful experiences in Spain and England, without any good results either for France or for myself. I was now back in Paris, and had the disappointment of finding that I had been again forgotten; for when on the occasion of the birth of the King of Rome the Emperor had showered rewards on the army and given promotion to many officers, my earlier services, which had given me a right to expect special recognition, had been quite overlooked. The favourable moment had gone by, but fortunately for me I was less sensible to the claims of ambition than to those of family and friends, and I soon consoled myself with the affection of my father, my relations, and others dear to me. I hastened also to remit to Captain Garat and my good friend Mr. Baudins the sums of money they had so kindly let me have.

When I got back to Paris, I resumed my duties on the staff of Major-General Prince Berthier. I had to mark on his maps the position of the different corps of the armies massed together in Germany, and the extraordinary gathering of troops seemed to me to justify the vague rumours of approaching war which were circulating in the capital. Neither the Russian Ambassador nor the representatives of the other Powers had, however, yet left Paris, and there was no sign of any ostensible cause of disagreement, nor anything to indicate which country would be the scene of hostilities, when on February 1st I received orders to go and collect as many horses as possible at Frankfort on the Oder, and to have a grand travelling carriage got ready.

All manner of guesses as to the meaning of these orders were hazarded, but no one was in the secret, and feeling very uncertain about the future we made most luxurious preparations for the campaign. I gave ten thousand francs to Martin, a very intelligent *valet de chambre*, who had replaced my poor Williams, and told him to go to Frankfort and Strasburg to buy horses for me. I ordered some brilliant uniforms for myself and comfortable suits of livery for my servants, and on March 5 I received orders to go and examine every detail of that part of the army which was assembled on the Oder and the Vistula and at Danzig, so as to be able to inform the Emperor of all that was still wanting to complete the equipment and organisation of the troops.

In the report I drew up on this occasion I included the complaint made to me by several officers in command, of the recruits sent to them being too weak for service. I also spoke of the serious inconvenience which resulted from this weakness to General Dejean, who had just organised a corps of cavalry 40,000 strong, and he transmitted to me the verbal reply the Emperor had made to a protest from him on the same subject: 'When I came back from Alsace after organising the cavalry,' said the General to me, 'I complained to the Emperor that one-third of the horses bought were not strong enough to carry their riders, and that half the men newly levied were too weak to wield a sword."But for your Majesty's precise orders to the contrary," I added, "I should have sent them back to the depots."'"You would have done very wrong if you had," replied the Emperor. "When I mount 40,000 men, I know well enough that I cannot expect to have that number of good horsemen, but I affect the morale of the enemy, whose spies hear it said and read in the newspapers that my cavalry is 40,000 strong. As the numbers pass from mouth to mouth they grow rather than decrease, and the 40,000 cavalry are supposed to be all of the same seasoned valour as the rest of my regiments have the character of being; so that when the campaign opens my army will be preceded by a rumour which will give a moral strength making up for the absence of the real forces I have been unable to procure."' Dejean was struck with fresh admiration for the man of genius who could thus turn everything to account, and who was quite unmoved by considerations which would have completely upset any plans but his own.

CHAPTER 5

To Russia

I returned to Paris on May 13th, gave a report of my mission, and on the 14th started again to join the Grand Army without knowing where it was. The gloomy forebodings of others affected me but little, and when my carriage was overturned and broken just outside Meaux, instead of being put out I rejoiced at the chance the accident gave me of spending the time necessary for repair with my sister and some of my friends.

On May 26th I found myself at Posen, where I gave news to many noble Polish parents of their sons, whom I had seen at Sedan a few days before. The Boyars, as the Polish nobles were still erroneously called, some of whom had long hair, whilst others were bald-headed, wore the Oriental costume and had grave dignified manners. They received us with the greatest enthusiasm, for they thought our arrival meant the restoration of Poland as an independent kingdom. Many fêtes were given in our honour, and the only rest we got after our long journey was in dancing!

On May 30th I reached Thorn on the Vistula, where I found my servants and horses. I had three days left to buy all that was still needed to complete my travelling equipment before the arrival of the Emperor on June 2nd.

Now began much hard work and hurrying to and fro for me; but I will spare the reader an account of my goings and comings, only adding that I was ordered to push on all the preparations for the advance of the army, and specially to report on the condition of the corps of Marshal Macdonald, who had under him two Prussian divisions, which, very much to my regret, we found placed in line with us as amongst our allies. The Commander-in-chief of this Prussian contingent was General York, who had with him Generals Von Kleist, Massenbach, and Grauwerth, and the forces under them were splendidly equipped and in first-rate condition. Both wings of our army were, in fact, composed of troops of the two nations who were most interested in the failure of our schemes, whether pacific or warlike. With Prussia on our left and Austria on our right, we were hampered by the fact that if we did restore the kingdom of Poland, Prussia would lose the province of Posen, and Austria that of Galicia. Moreover, Austria and Prussia were both unwilling to fight Russia, who was their natural ally against us, and with whom they had concurred in the dismemberment of Poland. To compel Prussians and Austrians to march with us against their will and against their own interests, was to provoke the result which we ought to have had sense enough to fear and to avoid. The sequel proved how terrible had been our mistake.

In my various journeyings to and fro I several times returned to the same town, and I was at Warsaw on June 14 and 15, working with the Emperor's youngest brother, King Jérôme of Westphalia, then at the head of a well-armed and well-equipped body of his subjects. I passed two days in examining the condition of his troops, and on the 16th I reached Pultusk, then occupied by Prince Poniatowski and his army of Poles, whom I had also instructions to see. On the 18th I was at Friedland, and on the 19th at Gumbinnen, worn out with fatigue after travelling day and night for so long, hampered by the difficulty of getting fresh horses in a poverty-stricken country full of troops, and with thousands of couriers hastening about on their various errands. The Emperor halted at Gumbinnen, and I made my reports to him there. It was only then that I learnt the true object of the campaign just opening, which was to compel the King of Prussia to join us in maintaining the continental blockade which was to ruin England.

So many historians have already given more or less truthful accounts of this memorable and tragic campaign in Russia, that I shall content myself with enlarging on the daily record of my own experiences in the notebook, not as big as my hand, which I carried with me next my heart wherever I went. This little book is not only much torn, but soaked with rain and with my own perspiration, for I suffered greatly from the intense heat in Russia in the earlier portion of the campaign, that country being as much too hot in the summer as it is too cold in the winter. The great variations of temperature were terribly trying to us all, and many who had everywhere vanquished their human enemies fell victims to the rigours of a climate which sapped their strength and frustrated all their hopes. The leaves of my little notebook, though the writing on them is much blurred, are still intact, and I will just jot down here succinctly what happened to me from day to day in the course of the alternating glorious and terrible drama. Some day, perhaps, a writer younger and more skilled in wielding the pen than I, will use what I have written, with the accounts of the other few survivors of the awful experiences of our disastrous campaign, to piece together a consecutive and faithful narrative.

To resume, then. The Emperor had sent a great many officers to the different corps of the Grand Army to perform duties similar to mine, and although, as already related, he made most formidable preparations for war, it was very evident that he still hoped to achieve his object by diplomacy. It was, I think, with deep regret that he found himself reduced to the necessity of endeavouring to obtain by fighting what he could not get by persuasion. It was during the short halt at Gumbinnen that Napoleon received the final refusal of the Czar to meet the wishes he had urged by every pacific means in his power. His mind was therefore very soon made up. The allied forces were already close to the Niemen, and the Emperor himself was but forty leagues from it. It was decided that the river should be crossed. We did the distance between Gumbinnen and it on horseback in two days, and after bivouacking for a few hours' rest we arrived at noon on June 23rd on the heights overlooking the Niemen.

Here the most extraordinary and magnificent spectacle awaited us, and one which could not but have an intoxicating effect on a conqueror by giving to him an exaggerated idea of the extent of his moral and material power. It is said that our army was 500,000 strong, and it was made up of nearly every nation of Europe. Many reigning princes, including the Kings of Naples and Westphalia, were at the head of their troops. King Murat in full-dress uniform rode with his cavalry. All the handsomest men of the day, in their most gorgeous martial costumes, mounted on the finest horses to be obtained in Europe, all alike richly caparisoned, were gathered about the central group of which we formed part. The sunbeams gleamed upon the bronze cannon ready to belch forth an all-destroying fire, and glinted back from the brass breastplates and scarlet-crested helmets of the gallant carabineers, and from the gilded, silvered, and burnished steel helmets, breastplates, weapons, and decorations of the soldiers and officers. The glittering bayonets of the masses of battalions covering the plain resembled from a distance the quivering scintillations in the sunshine of the waters of some lake or river when ruffled by a passing breeze. The crash of thousands of trumpets and drums mingled with the enthusiastic shouts of the vast multitude as the Emperor came in sight, and the spectacle of all this devotion on the part of the vast assembly of disciplined troops, which extended as far as the eye could reach on either side, the weapons shining like stars, impressed us all with a sense of the invincibility of a force of elements so mixed, united in obedience to a single chief. Our confidence in that chief became yet more assured than ever; not one amongst us had the slightest doubt of his success in this fresh enterprise, and when we looked round upon all the forces his mighty will had gathered together our hearts beat high with joy and with exultant pride. We already saw ourselves sharing in his approaching triumph, and no foreboding crossed our minds of the awful scene which was to be enacted on this very spot but a few short months later, when all the pomp and glory of our army marching to victory should be exchanged for the horrors of the retreat of men wasted by famine, fatigue, and misery, fleeing not only from their implacable enemies, but from the fire and ice, which claimed almost as many victims as the sword. Alas! how many young warriors lost their lives or all that made those lives worth having in this terrible campaign, how quickly were all these legions, now thirsting for fresh glory, to be dispersed! But a truce to these melancholy, these tragic memories. Let us rather rejoice in the last laurels God permitted us to gather, and with them let us crown the banners of the Empire before we finally succumb beneath the cruel reverse of fortune awaiting us.

June 23rd was a lovely day; the sky was clear, the heat not too great, and hostilities had not yet commenced. The Emperor and General Haxo, both disguised in the caps and cloaks of Polish guards, turned the quiet pause to account by going down to the river bank to decide on the best points for the snaking of the bridges necessary for the crossing of the army. The night was, of course, very short in this latitude, and it was really scarcely dark at all. Two hours, however, sufficed to throw over several bridges, and a few companies of skirmishers were sent over in advance in light boats, to drive off the Cossacks on watch on the further bank; these, contenting themselves with firing a few shots, rode off without offering any serious resistance to us.

The sun rose at two o'clock in the morning, and the army at once began the crossing of the river by the three bridges, advancing upon the road to Wilna opposite to them, and bearing on the left towards the little town of Kovno, built at the confluence of the Wilia and Niemen.

The enemy's squadrons, which were pretty numerous, withdrew at our approach almost without fighting, as if to mark the fact that we were the aggressors. The heat was stifling and almost insupportable when our advanced guard entered Kovno a little after noon. A tremendous storm now came up, and with a rapidity to which we were totally unaccustomed the air became completely charged with electricity. The thunder and lightning were terrific, and at about three o'clock two men and three horses were killed by lightning. The rain poured down in torrents for two hours, and we were soon drenched to the skin. The people of the town and the monks of the numerous convents, seeing the dilapidated and exhausted condition to which we were reduced, brought out a plentiful supply of refreshments. Their favourite beverages were mead and beer, which they were

125

very successful in making and drank iced. But heated and dripping as all the men were, the cold drinks made many of them ill, and this with the deaths from lightning seemed an ominous beginning of our march through an enemy's country.

The storm had swollen the waters of the Wilia, and the Russians had burnt the bridge over it before they retired. A Polish regiment of light cavalry managed, however, to cross it, the horses swimming all the way. They were followed by the 26th French light cavalry regiment, commanded by young Guéhéneuc, who was nearly drowned; and the right bank of the Wilia was soon connected with the town by a bridge of boats which the Emperor had flung across the stream so that our troops might pursue the Russians. The Emperor, who was as wet as we were, aided in the work, pushing on the construction of the bridge and imbuing every one with something of his own extraordinary energy. In the terrible storm which was still raging, some two hundred men of the engineer corps, finding themselves much hampered by their saturated clothes, took them all off and worked in a perfectly nude condition. As an artist I felt a real delight in watching their supple figures as they bent at their toil, and I was reminded of the fine compositions of Michael Angelo, Raphael, and Poussin, such as the *Bathers* and the *Deluge*, in which those great artists represented the human figure in every variety of attitude.

The Emperor still hesitated to begin actual hostilities, and we halted for three days in the little town of Kovno to allow the rest of the army to come up and deploy. During the delay we fortified ourselves by drinking a good deal of tea, the astringent quantities of which braced us up after our dunking. We learnt from the country people that the Russian army was also very numerous, mustering 250,000 infantry and 90,000 cavalry, under General Prince Bagration and General Barclay de Tolly.

During the nights of the 27th-28th, I went with the Desaix and Bourdesoulle divisions to Novitroki, which after a feeble defence by the Russians was taken by us. We pursued the enemy and entered Wilna in the evening. Marshal the Duke of Reggio came in by another gate at about the same time, and the Emperor arrived there on the 29th. Deputations of Polish noblemen arrived in rapid succession, eager to persuade him to decree the restoration of the Kingdom of Poland, and promising him if he would the loyal co-operation of the whole Polish nation, with a plentiful supply of money, men, and horses. In fact, they made many engagements which they were soon quite unable to carry out.

There is little doubt that Napoleon would gladly have met their wishes immediately, for an independent Poland would have been a steadfast ally to France, and have protected us from an invasion from the North. There were two princes ready to hand, to either of whom the crown might fitly have been given, and public opinion wavered between the two. Prince Poniatowski, nephew of the last King of Poland, was, by virtue of his birth, his character, and his proved courage, the man the Poles and our army would have chosen as the King, whilst failing him the votes would have been given for Marshal Davout, Prince of Eckmühl, one of Napoleon's most loyally devoted followers, who had administered the affairs of the districts of Poland occupied by our troops with consummate tact and ability, and who was quite accustomed to hearing himself spoken of as the future king. It must, however, be remembered that the Emperor was terribly hampered in any decision as to Poland by the fact that he would not only have to dispose of that portion of the dismembered kingdom still in the grasp of Russia, but also of the provinces of Posen and Galicia, assigned by treaty to Prussia and Austria respectively. Now Prussian and Austrian battalions were marching in line with ours, and were nominally our allies, but there was no doubt that at the slightest hint of the Emperor's intentions to take from their princes their portion of the spoils of the old kingdom of Poland, every Austrian and Prussian would have left our ranks to join those of the Russians. Napoleon had no intention, therefore, of accepting the Polish proposal of co-operation with him, and he needed all his diplomatic skill when at Wilna to evade destroying the hopes of the Poles or making any definite promise to them. Such was the strained state of affairs when on July 1st an aide-de-camp arrived from the Emperor of Russia, bringing with him that monarch's final refusal to consent to any pacific arrangement of the points at issue, which he proposed submitting to the arbitrament of war.

Whilst the difficulties of our position were thus increasing, we began to experience something of the rigours of the Russian climate, the changes in which are far more rapid and extreme than in France. The army, which was thoroughly well organised, had brought with it provisions for thirty or forty days, but one storm after another, notably those of June 24th and 30th, with that of July 2nd, which was the worst of all, had made all the draught horses ill, one-third at least had died, and we had to overload the wagons of those still remaining alive, for it would not have done to leave any of our provisions behind. Of course, thus terribly weighted the wagons made but very slow progress, and were often far behind the army, which began to suffer from scarcity of food for the men and fodder for the horses. We had to feed the latter on hay and on rye cut whilst still green, which were in their turn soon exhausted. The men, whose courage and habitual abstinence kept them from giving way, managed to fend for themselves somehow, and suffered less than the poor beasts. The long downpour of bitter cold rain which lasted the whole of the day and night of July 2nd was a veritable disaster to our troops, but they marched steadily on through it all after having stopped for several days on the rising ground beyond Wilna.

At this time we French officers were really in the position of protectors to the many petty princes from Germany who had brought their contingents to swell our ranks. Little accustomed to the vicissitudes and privations of war, the young scions of royalty from Sigmaringen, Darmstadt, Hesse Homburg, Bartenstein, Salm, and elsewhere, assiduously cultivated our friendship so as to share the luxuries enjoyed by the members of the staff. At Wilna I was quartered in the residence of one of the richest Polish nobles of the place, and I often had quite a number of youthful Serene Highnesses about me. Martin, my head valet, served us with ices as delicate and punch as well mixed as we could have got at Naples or at the Café Tortoni. One of my princely guests told me he hoped to receive me at home on our return from the campaign, and I replied, 'Yes, Prince, on our way back we will come and ask you to give us a breakfast.' This put him into a regular fright, and he said in a trembling voice, 'Yes, but don't bring the army; my principality could not afford a quarter of a breakfast for all your men!'

At this time I was the happy owner of a cow, which was attached to my provision wagon, and I was able to give my guests iced cream flavoured in different ways, for in Russia the humblest hut always contained a refrigerator for keeping provisions good in the great heat. As time went on, however, the enemy adopted the tactics of destroying everything they could not use, and our advanced guard cleared off any small remnants of food, so that we found nothing left but a little ice in the cellars and a few wisps of thatch on the roofs.

The army pressed on slowly. Marshal Davout was now at Minsk, and Macdonald was entering Courland. The Emperor left Wilna at eight o'clock in the evening on July 9th, and bivouacked in the midst of his Guard at Nemenchin, whence he intended to push on towards Witebsk, so as to separate as much as possible the two great Russian armies, and fight each in turn with all his own forces collected between them. Our wings and advanced guard had already had a good many tussles with the enemy, in which they lost a good many men, but these struggles had hitherto always ended in the retreat of the Russians. Few days passed without our being able to bivouac several leagues in advance of the point reached the night before. We found all the villages deserted, and most of them burnt to ashes. Here and there, however, the larger buildings had escaped destruction, and on the 10th, when we were camping amongst the still smouldering remains of the village of Zorokpoly, I noticed a big château some distance off well away from the road. Thinking I should find good accommodation there, I had a horse saddled and galloped off alone to reconnoitre. It had been a fine place, but it now presented a most desolate appearance with all the doors and windows broken and the very out-buildings empty. Despairing of finding any living thing there or any provisions, I was leaving the deserted spot to return to our camp, when, as

I turned into an avenue of the park, I saw lying almost under the feet of my horse a pretty little boy of three or four years old, with nothing on but a shirt, who smiled happily up into my face. I sprang to the ground, took the child in my arms, and as I caressed him asked him a number of questions he did not understand. In the hope of being heard by the parents of the child, whom I imagined to be hiding near, I kept caressing the little creature so as to inspire any one within sight of us with confidence, and asked questions in a loud voice in Polish and in German, but the only answer was the echo of my own words. Compelled, therefore, to give up hope of finding any one belonging to the child, I remounted, placed him before me on the saddle, and rode back to camp, where my comrades were very much surprised at the sight of the little companion I had brought to them. During my absence a *pope*, as a Greek priest is called, had come to the camp to beg for hospitality, telling our people that his house and the whole village had been burnt. He added that he had had no food for ten days but roots, which he had had hard work to dig up and which were very bitter. He asked for nothing to take away with him but a little salt, which we gladly gave him. He questioned in the Russian patois the child I had found, and we discovered that the little fellow had been deserted five or six days before, and had lived on wild strawberries and the small black fruits the Germans are so fond of, which they call Waldbeeren. We made a little collection amongst us of twelve louis d'or, which we gave to the unfortunate priest; and, in spite of his own misery, he promised to take care of the child till he could restore it to its parents.

As we were pushing on the next day, we came upon two poor creatures at a turn in the road whose condition tore our hearts. They were a handsome well-built man of about forty and a woman of about thirty, also with a fine figure, both stark naked. They approached us and said to us in very good French, 'Our home has been sacked by Cossacks, who stripped us of everything and left us as you see us. For pity's sake help us.' We could do nothing for them but give them a little food, and we felt very wretched as we turned away. The next day at a bivouac some distance off a fresh irresistible demand was made upon our pity, and our stock of provisions was so much reduced that I don't know what we should have done but that some German peasants brought us a few sheep, with which we replenished our larder.

The Emperor halted at Vizoy on July 14th, and on the 15th I was sent to the King of Naples to tell him that the cavalry under him were to co-operate with the slower movements of the infantry. King Murat had been for some days at the Castle of Belmont belonging to Count Mamerchi, then Ambassador for Russia at the Bavarian Court. There was something very attractive about this castle, and it presented a considerable contrast to an ordinary Muscovite residence. It overlooked a fine lake dotted with islands, on the highest point of one of which was a rotunda consisting of a hundred Corinthian columns, which were evidently adorned with draperies on fête days.

On the 21st I left the King of Naples to return to the Emperor, who was now advancing with the whole of his Guard, which formed a very strong picked corps of infantry and cavalry. After travelling for ten leagues in the direction of Beschenkovitz, I halted at Ostrovno at the residence of Count Zaboulon, a Polish lieutenant-general and senator. His house had been left uninjured, and he still retained a menagerie of living animals, including a remarkable camel and several gigantic bears, which were chained up at the entrance of a huge circular court. One of the bears acted as sentinel, standing erect, and armed with a formidable club, with which he nearly killed a young Polish officer of lancers who approached too near in spite of warnings, and did not make allowance enough for the length of the chain or the strength of the brute. He received a tremendous blow on the chest which felled him to the ground, and but for us he might have been killed. The Count specially called my attention to a courtyard covered in with a net, where some hundred birds were kept. I don't know exactly what they were, but they were rather like snipes with long legs and a kind of deep ruff of plumage round their necks. The Count called them *batailleurs*, or fighters, and to prove the justice of the name he flung them a handful of oats. A fearful fight at once began amongst the birds, which went on till every grain was gone. The Count seemed to be very fond of watching fighting, and was always making his bears, dogs, and wolves struggle together for his amusement. He was now, however, going to see men fighting rather nearer him than he cared for, and he begged me earnestly to leave him a few soldiers as a guard.

I pushed on and reached the isolated farm occupied by the Emperor at nightfall. I joined the bivouac of the staff and the Guard. The next day, the 24th, we reached Beschenkovitz, where we were in sight of the enemy.

On the 26th the Viceroy's corps, marching in advance of the main body, came upon the rearguard of the army a little beyond Ostrovno. This rearguard consisted of some 30,000 men, and a fierce struggle ensued, in which the Russians at first got the best of it. The enemy's left was coming up to the support of the rearguard, when King Murat, noticing how things were going, ordered his cavalry to charge the approaching auxiliaries, throwing them into disorder. Fresh bodies of the enemy, however, continued to hurry up, and we had been fighting without success for some hours, when the Emperor, impatient at the delay, and thinking the right moment had come, ordered the Viceroy to make a vigorous attack upon a wood occupied by the enemy. It was successful. The Russians were driven out and retreated all along the line. The Emperor took up his head-quarters that same evening (the 26th) about three leagues beyond the field of battle, which was covered with dead and wounded horses left by the enemy.

At daybreak on the 27th the two armies approached each other near Witebsk. Swarms of Cossacks flung themselves upon our cavalry, and for a moment threw our movements into disorder, even carrying away several of our guns. In the mêlée one of our comrades named Emmanuel le Couteulx cut his way through the Cossacks with his sword, and succeeded in recovering one of the pieces of artillery which the enemy were dragging away. In pursuing this body of Cossacks after the struggle with it beyond a deep and wide ravine, we came upon the main body of the Russian army drawn up in order of battle.

On our left the light infantry of the 9th Regiment of the Line, all Parisians, advanced too fearlessly, and were soon surrounded by masses of cavalry. We were still too far off to support them, but we loudly applauded their resistance, which lasted more than an hour, giving us time to come up to their rescue. The infantry under the Viceroy, formed in squares in divisions, suffered greatly as they marched, for they were exposed to a hail of grape shot and bullets from a numerous body of Russian artillery posted in a most favourable position flanked by a wood. Here again the gallant King Murat came up in the nick of time, and flinging himself like a mere trooper into the midst of the Cossacks he was followed by his cavalry. The Russian lines were broken, some of their artillery was taken, and they were compelled to retire beyond the deep ravine of a little stream, a tributary of the Dwina, which served as a protection to Witebsk. Night put a stop to the struggle, but we already occupied the outskirts of a group of burnt houses which we concluded to have formed part of a suburb of Witebsk. I passed the night there to look after Colonel Liédot, of the engineers, who had been mortally wounded towards the close of the day. The Russians remained on the other side of the stream, which was very deep and would be difficult to cross. We were not thirty paces from each other, but the night passed over quietly, for we were preparing and expecting to renew the struggle at daybreak.

General Barclay de Tolly now received a message that Prince Bagration could not join him at Witebsk, but would try and do so at Smolensk, where he hoped to arrive in time. On hearing this Barclay de Tolly broke up his camp during the night with an order and promptitude which were as extraordinary as the silence with which everything was done; and when in the twilight before daybreak I went to reconnoitre the enemy, there was no one to prevent my crossing the stream by any of the little bridges, not one of which had been destroyed. When the Emperor was told of this very unexpected event, he sent scouts in every direction beyond Witebsk to ascertain which way the Russian army had gone. That army was, however, marching straight across the plain, and its lines were so extended and the order maintained so complete that it was impossible to make out which direction it would take or to secure any prisoners to question. The Emperor was, therefore, obliged to resort to guessing, and he ordered our army to pass through Witebsk and advance six leagues along the road to Moscow by way of Smolensk, bivouacking himself at Agaponovitzy on the 28th. No definite news having yet been obtained of the Russian army, we were allowed to rest here for a few days.

When I got back to Witebsk on the 29th, I was struck with the picturesque situation of that town, rising as it does from the banks of the pretty river Dwina. I had seen it before through flame and smoke, which gave it a certain gloomy grandeur; but now the beauty of the day added to the charms of line and colour, which became of rarer and rarer occurrence the further we advanced in these remote districts of the North. I went every day to look after my poor friend Liédot, but my duties soon called me elsewhere.

On August 4th the Emperor learnt the results of the brilliant actions on July 30th and 31st and August 1st, in which the corps under the Duke of Reggio had been engaged with the enemy's extreme left under the Count of Wittgenstein. Unable to understand why the Duke should have decided to retreat after beating the enemy three times, taking fourteen guns and 3,000 prisoners, Napoleon told me to go and ascertain the exact state of affairs and to order Marshal Oudinot to pursue the Russians. I left Witebsk at nightfall on the 5th, and on the 6th reached a ford of the Dwina, which I was able to cross, thus avoiding a long détour. I entered Polotsk the same evening, after a tiring ride of forty-two leagues over difficult country. I was most courteously received in a Jesuit monastery, where I found the Duke, who explained to me the reasons for his retreat. He had been vigorously attacked by the Russians, and had not been able to obtain any provisions for three days. He told me that the Russians had purposely allowed themselves to be repulsed, hoping to entice the French in pursuit of them into desert districts, where they would perish of famine. The Marshal, however, declined to fall into the trap, and not having wagons enough to take the provisions he had left at Polotsk with him, he thought it best to collect all his forces there so as to distribute rations to them. They would thus be ready to recommence hostilities without delay.

As a matter of fact, all preparations were now completed, and on the 7th the troops, well rested and carrying with them provisions for several days, marched again in good spirits. The Duke himself, with the Legrand and Verdier divisions, the Bavarian corps under Von Wrede and Deroy, returned to Bieloe, and the next day bivouacked at Golositzy, having driven the Russians before them in the direction of Valentzy, Osveya, and Sebedzy, and accompanied the Marshal for four days, during which nothing remarkable occurred, the only difficulty being that of provisioning the army in the sandy plains diversified only by a few forests and lakes. The Duke of Reggio was joined before I left him by Marshal Gouvion Saint-Cyr at the head of the 6th Army Corps, and, leaving the two commanders together, I started on the 11th to take to the Emperor the information he required. After crossing the Dwina at the ford we lost our way in the darkness in the Oulla forest, where we had to wait for daylight at the foot of a tree to which we had fastened our horses. Fortunately when crossing these all but desert districts our cavalry had left a few outposts echeloned at short distances from each other, so as to maintain communications between the various corps. Some of these troops let us change horses with them, so that I was able to get to Witebsk late in the evening of the 12th. I was at once admitted to see the Emperor, and had a long interview with him. He disapproved altogether of the retreat of the Duke of Reggio, and said he ought to have pursued the Count of Wittgenstein much more hotly, for he was quite sure that if the French had pushed on to Opotscka and Novorjev the Marshal would have been able to find means of provisioning his army. Having explained to me his own plan of marching on Smolensk, the Emperor sent me back on the 13th to the Duke of Reggio to insist on his advancing into the enemy's country, and keeping his forces at the same level as those he was himself about to lead forward. He also wished me to tell the Marshal of the advantages gained over the enemy under General Lewis by Marshal

Macdonald, Duke of Taranto, at the head of the Prussians, who occupied Mittau, Jacobstadt, and Dunabourg, and were about to besiege Riga. On the 14th I supped yet again with the Jesuits at Polotsk, and on the 15th I was with the Duke of Reggio when he was attacked by the Count of Wittgenstein, who had received reinforcements. The unfortunate Marshal, still always hampered by the want of provisions, had again approached Polotsk. The troops were most devoted to him, and in spite of all they endured from famine, they fought with the greatest courage. The Bavarians seemed to have suffered more from scarcity of food than any of the troops with the Duke. Some of them made me look at their tongues and mouths, all inflamed with what they had to endure, and told me the heat was as trying to bear as their hunger. Yet they too fought well, and took some prisoners. On the 16th there was hot fighting all along the line. On the 17th the Russians brought up and deployed a vast number of troops and were driven back, but unfortunately Marshal Oudinot, who had gone forward in the midst of his skirmishers to prevent them from retiring, was seriously wounded in the shoulder, and General Gouvion Saint-Cyr took the command in his place. I now had a rare chance of seeing how a man of genius can turn everything to account, even under the most adverse and unexpected circumstances.

Our line had already begun to waver and we were losing ground, for the hail of grapeshot seemed likely completely to crush us, when General Saint-Cyr with the greatest sang-froid ordered all the troops to advance. The enemy, fearing the loss of their artillery, with which they had ventured rather too far, withdrew at once, and resumed their former positions. Night put an end to the struggle, but before it became quite dark Saint-Cyr had admirably disposed all his forces, availing himself of every accident of the ground, placing his men on the hills and between the lakes, &c. When day returned, the enemy, seeing how strong was our position, did not venture to attack us. General Saint-Cyr, however, who was determined to mark his assumption of the command and to withdraw with *éclat* from the very disagreeable position in which he had been left, decided to simulate a retreat, and ordered preparations for it to be made wherever we were overlooked by the enemy. The morning of the 13th was therefore spent in taking all the wagons and other impedimenta collected at Polotsk across the Dwina by the bridge. Several regiments of cavalry were also ordered to go over slowly. The Russians were completely taken in; they believed us to be in full retreat, and relaxed their vigilance, thinking they were not likely to be attacked that day. At five o'clock in the evening, however, at a signal agreed on, all our batteries opened a tremendous fire on the Russian lines. The four divisions of infantry, under Generals Legrand, Verdier, Von Wrede, and Peroy, advanced at the double, whilst the fifth under General Merle came up as a reserve. Before night the Russian General, driven back at every point, abandoned his positions and withdrew beyond the Dwina, leaving Saint-Cyr in peace at Polotsk for some time. This three days' struggle cost the Russians twenty pieces of cannon, two generals killed, three or four thousand men killed and wounded, and 1,000 taken prisoners. Our loss, though much less, was still considerable. Amongst our generals put *hors de combat* were the Duke of Reggio, General Verdier, General Von Wrede, and General Raglovich, whilst we had also to mourn the loss of Generals Deroy and Sierbein, who were killed. A young Colonel, Alexander Lebrun by name, second son of the Chief Treasurer of the Empire, was also killed by a bullet, and was deeply regretted by us all. I left Polotsk on the evening of the battle to take the sad news of these deaths to the Emperor, and I had a good deal of difficulty in making my way through the forests extending for more than a hundred leagues between my starting-point and Smolensk. The life of an officer travelling alone is exposed to many more dangers, and is much more tiring, than when he is at the head of a corps of troops.

In spite of my utmost diligence in this arduous journey, I was not able to reach Smolensk until the evening of the 20th. I found the Emperor on the battle field of Valutina-Gora distributing rewards to those who had distinguished themselves in the battle of the three preceding days. I heard Napoleon congratulating the men on the fact that in the struggle three Russians to one Frenchman had fallen. General Gudin, from whose admirable character as a commander so much might have been hoped, was killed in this battle. He was buried on the 21st, and I received orders to superintend his obsequies. The suburb on the right bank of the Dnieper was completely destroyed by fire; two-thirds of the town of Smolensk itself were still in flames, and whilst efforts were being made to save the great quantities of provisions left behind by the Russians, and my fellow engineers were at work restoring the big bridge which had been burnt, I led the funeral procession to the large bastion on the south-east of the town, thinking that it would form a fitting mausoleum for the illustrious warrior. I ordered a tomb to be dug out in the bastion, and above the corpse, arranged in the form of stars, were laid a number of muskets which had been broken in the struggle, for I thought to myself that some day perhaps Time, the all-destroyer, might expose the remains of the hero, and this trophy of arms might win for him the same attention and respect as we ourselves pay to the bones of brave Gauls when the ancient tumuli concealing them are opened.

The success at Valutina-Gora, dearly bought by the loss of from 10,000 to 12,000 French killed and wounded, left the Emperor full of regret for the fact that the army under General Barclay de Tolly had again escaped him. The fact was, Napoleon had counted on the arrival of the corps of the Duke d'Abrantes (Marshal Junot), which was to have fought in line with the rest of the army. The malady from which the Duke was suffering was not yet suspected, and whilst waiting for the belated arrival of the expected corps Napoleon lost the advantages he had hoped to gain by the co-operation of all his forces, for which co-operation he had sent reiterated orders.

During the few days' rest at Smolensk which Napoleon allowed to his troops, the news was brought to him that our right wing under the Prince von Schwarzenberg, and especially the Saxon corps under General Reynier, had obtained more successes over Prince Bagration, but at the same time he also heard that the Austrians were co-operating in a lukewarm manner only, and in fact behaving in a very suspicious manner. The Emperor, however, relying far too much on the promises of his father-in-law, did not share, or did not choose to show that he shared, in our forebodings.

The one pleasure we were able to enjoy in our short stay at Smolensk, nearly destroyed by fire though it was, was an occasional plunge in the waters of the Dnieper. These baths refreshed us greatly, after our arduous and fatiguing march, and did much to strengthen us for the exhausting work still before us as an invading army.

Many amongst us thought it would have been wise not to go beyond Smolensk in this preliminary campaign, and hoped that the Emperor would make it his headquarters. He could then have organised a kingdom of Poland friendly to him in the rear of his army, and all the resources of that country would have been at his command during the struggle.

Amongst our numerous Russian prisoners were many officers, all of whom often said, 'We fully expect you to get as far as Moscow, but you will most certainly return by way of Pultowa.' None of our Poles who acted as interpreters ventured to repeat these prophetic words to the Emperor, so that the ominous hint they contained did nothing to change his resolution.

On the 24th Napoleon ordered the whole line to advance, the Viceroy Prince Eugène on the left, the first corps, the cavalry, and the Guard in the centre, and the Poles flanking the right at a considerable distance. Thus far the Polish army had traversed districts which had been not nearly so completely laid waste as those which had fallen to our share, and as they had of course not suffered at all from famine they were still in splendid condition. The further we advanced, the more desolate became the country. Every village had been burnt, and there was no longer even the thatch from the cottages for the horses to eat; everything that could be destroyed was reduced to ashes. The men suffered no less than the animals; the heat was intense, and the sand rose in masses of white dust as our columns advanced, choking us and completing our exhaustion. Our misery was intensified by the want of water in these never-ending plains. The excessive heat was presently changed for a cold downpour of rain, which lasted several days. The army was beginning to show signs of discouragement, and Major-General Prince Berthier, though always very chary of expressing his opinion, ventured to advise the Emperor to retreat. But Napoleon, whose mind was full of his idea of dictating terms of peace at Moscow, received the suggestion very unfavourably, and told the Prince that if he were tired he could go back himself. The Prince, who was deeply hurt and offended, replied with dignity in these noble words, 'Before the enemy the Vice-Constable does not leave the army, but takes a musket and becomes a mere soldier himself.' Although they continued to work together, there was a coldness between the Emperor and the Prince for some days after this. The Emperor, however, did promise to retire if the rain continued, but it became fine again, and I was sent to King Murat to urge him to press on the advance of his troops.

The forces of the enemy were now united, Prince Bagration and General Barclay de Tolly having at last succeeded in meeting. They were now both under the orders of Field-Marshal Kutusoff, Commander-in-Chief, and the whole army retired before us in admirable order, making a feint, however, of defending every position which appeared at all tenable. Our advanced cavalry was, therefore, compelled to be always in attacking order supported by the artillery, and gained no ground without many an exchange of grapeshot and many a charge with drawn swords. It took us a very long time to advance a short distance, and we were still a hundred leagues from Moscow. We passed the whole day on horseback under fire and bivouacked at nightfall, but there was no appetising odour of roast meat from our camp fires to cheer our drooping spirits with the prospect of a hearty meal to fill our empty stomachs. Life with the advanced guard was not, however, altogether without charm, and I remember especially the night of August 28th-29th. We had noted in the distance a fine château, which looked as if it would be quite a royal resting-place for King Murat to sleep in, but when we got near we found only smoking ruins, and decided to camp at the foot of the château in the prettiest birch wood I ever saw. The birches, with their gleaming trunks here and there as white as alabaster, and their drooping foliage, were mixed with stately upright pines and firs, the various trees forming charming groves. The Polish lancers camped round the staff on the undulating ground, and stuck all their spears upright beneath the birches, so that the effect was very pretty when the wind played amongst the thousands of tricoloured streamers with which the weapons were decorated. The floating pennons, the ascending flames from the bivouac fires, the smoke from the impromptu kitchens, the huge braziers – containing, alas! all too little for our needs – and the merry groups of young officers tightening their belts with a laugh after an insufficient meal, combined to produce a picture alike charming and pathetic. I was not the only one to appreciate its beauty.

On August 29th we entered the pretty town of Wiasma, which was completely wrapt in flames, the very churches being on fire. Although the quarters assigned to me were in the courtyard of one of the finest hotels in the town, I had to pass the night in my carriage. On the 30th the Emperor arrived at Wiasma, leaving again on the 31st, and on September 1 we entered Giatz, forty leagues from Moscow. The town, which was of wood, was burnt to the ground, but some cellars were still undestroyed, and in them we found a few stores of cucumbers, cabbages, and beetroots, which are used by the Russians in making a fermented beverage. My horses and carriages occupied the courtyard of a fine house which had been burnt. I wanted my people to do something for me, and called them several times without obtaining an answer. I had begun to get impatient and was shouting out their names angrily, when I suddenly heard several voices crying in a stifled sepulchral kind of way, 'Monsieur! Monsieur!' The sound seemed to come from the centre of the courtyard, but I could see no one there. In my surprise and anxiety I called to them again, receiving only the same muffled answers. I rushed to the spot and found myself at the edge of a deep well, in which the skilful foragers, having let themselves down by a knotted rope, had discovered a number of valuable objects placed for security at the bottom of the water. The plucky fellows now climbed up one by one, each carrying under his arm

141

some treasures, such as rolls of gold or silver brocade, headdresses and bodices adorned with pearls and gold ornaments, which had belonged to the Jewish women of the community, all of whom had fled. I scolded the men for pillaging, and forbade them to take anything more.

Early in the morning of the 5th our advanced guard came up with the Russian army, drawn up in a strong position. King Murat had, therefore, to deploy his cavalry so as to cover the advance of our army, and the Emperor, foreseeing that a serious engagement would soon take place, made his Guard come up and posted them on the high ground near the Kolotskoy Convent.

CHAPTER 6

Moscow

The Emperor, having arrived about noon on the heights in front of the Monastery of Kolotskoy, saw the numerous columns of the enemy apparently taking up their positions in order of battle, and he ordered the cavalry to push forward a close reconnaissance. Whilst this operation was going on, our left wing, commanded by the Viceroy, was advancing by way of the Mojaisk road towards Borodino, whilst our centre, consisting of the corps under the Prince of Eckmühl (Marshal Davout), Marshal Ney, and the King of Naples, was marching towards Golowino, and the right, under Prince Poniatowski, was following the old road leading from Smolensk to Moscow. The smoke of the villages set fire to by the enemy as we approached, prevented us from being able to make out clearly the position of the Russian forces. We were able, however, to see that the Russian lines in front of Borodino were defended by a great redoubt, armed with from twelve to twenty pieces of artillery. The Emperor ordered the Compans division to attack this redoubt at once.

The enemy perceiving this movement sent considerable forces to defend the approaches to the redoubt. General Compans began his attack by ordering all his artillery to bombard the redoubt with a view to breaking down as far as possible the earthworks and palisades of the entrenchment; and when he thought them sufficiently injured for an assault to be practicable, he ordered that assault to be made by the 57th Regiment, led by Colonel Charrière, and sent two other regiments to its support. The first attack was repulsed, and General Compans was himself wounded in the left arm. He had, however, scarcely had his wound dressed, before he ordered a second assault. This too was repulsed, and Compans, irritated at his second failure and determined to succeed, now ordered a vigorous onslaught to be made on the rear of the redoubt, whilst he and Colonel Charrière at the head of the 57th Regiment scaled the breach side by side. This time the redoubt was won, and at nine o'clock the enemy's firing ceased, leaving the French in possession of the outwork. It had already been dark for two hours, and we had all been very anxious as to the result of the attack, the fury of the combatants seeming to increase with the difficulties to be surmounted, but at last we knew that all was well for our side. That same night Colonel Charrière was made a General. He had taken seven guns, but his fine regiment had lost many men, whilst the 61st lost an entire battalion. The next day the Emperor, who wished to reward all the brave fellows who had taken part in the assault, asked the Colonel of the 61st, 'But where is your third battalion?' 'Sire,' was the melancholy reply, 'it is in the redoubt.'

The tents of the Emperor and Major-General Prince Berthier had been pitched on the plateau from which we had looked down on the struggle, and we passed the night there in the centre of the square formed by the encampment of the Imperial Guard.

At the first gleam of dawn on the 6th the Emperor started on horseback with Prince Berthier, Prince Eugène, and myself, but without further escort, to reconnoitre the enemy's position, and we rode all along the front lines, drawn up on high ground at right angles with the Moscow road and separated from us only by the winding stream of the Kaluga, with its muddy banks, which flows into the Moskwa at Borodino. Everywhere our vedettes were barely a pistol-shot distance from those of the enemy, but neither fired on the other, both sides being probably too exhausted by the struggle of the evening before to feel any further irritation against each other. The Emperor availed himself of this fact to examine in detail the best way of getting at the Russians, and I was not without anxiety on account of his exposing himself as he did, for he might easily have been carried off by a few men hiding at the entrance to a ravine at the base of some fortified height, or even by some of the pickets of the centre of the enemy's line. Once, indeed, Napoleon, who was marching in front, came suddenly upon a patrol of twenty Cossacks some four paces only from our party. Thinking themselves surprised, they were already turning their horses to escape, when seeing our small numbers galloping away from them they pursued us for some hundred yards. Fortunately the fleetness of our horses and the protection of some fences saved us from the embarrassing predicament. Before returning to camp after this reconnaissance, the Emperor ordered me to ride carefully along the enemy's lines once more, to make a sketch of them, and to bring him also a few views of the ground occupied. I passed the rest of the day in performing this honourable task, which led to my making a very exact study of the locality. The Emperor duly received my sketches, examined them, and seemed satisfied with them. When he got back to headquarters he had told Bacler d'Albe, chief of the topographical engineers, to do the same thing as I had done, and his survey of the Russian positions was made before the evening.

The enemy's line was protected by well-chosen and formidable positions, supplemented by redoubts and redans, the firing from which would cross each other. The village of Gorka above the mill of Borodino was entrenched throughout, and immense abattis of forest trees, presenting their sharp points to the cavalry, stretched far beyond Gorka along the Moscow road. This strongly fortified position must have greatly encouraged the Russians; but what added yet more to their confidence, and gave them an immense moral advantage over us, was the fact that they had plenty of provisions and fodder, and neither men nor horses had suffered from famine. Moreover, as they were always falling back upon their reserves, their numbers daily increased. Only twenty-six leagues from Moscow, they were sure of reinforcements and help of every kind, and their General, knowing the superstitious piety of his soldiers, took care to rouse their fanaticism by making the war appear to be one in defence of their religion. He had the image of a certain canonised bishop, which it was said had been miraculously rescued from the impious hands of the French, carried through the ranks with all the pomp due to some sacred relic. It excited the greatest enthusiasm wherever it appeared, and we could hear the shouts of joy with which its passage was greeted by the 160,000 Russians making up the army.

Very different were the sentiments of the French. Not nearly so numerous as the Russians, they were yet full of confidence in the genius of the great man commanding them, and thought of nothing but the joy of entering as conquerors the ancient city of the Czars, where their labours were to end and they were to reap the reward of all their toil. Imbued with this idea, they one and all donned their best uniforms to take part in the battle which was to be the crown of their glory.

About seven o'clock on the morning of the 7th the signal for the attack was at last given, and immediately 300 pieces of cannon on our side opened fire on an equal number of Russian howitzers and guns, the projectiles from which ploughed through our ranks with a hissing noise such as it is impossible to describe. As ill luck would have it, our reserves at the beginning of the struggle, even those of the cavalry, were rather too near the fighting, and, either from vainglory or more likely from fear of giving a false impression to the enemy, they would not retire the few hundred paces needed to place them in a position less exposed to useless danger, so that we had the grief of seeing thousands of gallant cavaliers and fine horses struck down, though it was of the utmost importance to us to preserve them.

The Emperor had announced that he would establish his head-quarters on the redoubt taken the evening before, and as a matter of fact he passed a great part of the day on that elevated position, sitting on the steep bank of the exterior slope, and following all the movements of the troops with the glass he kept in his hand. His Guard was posted behind him on the amphitheatre formed by the redoubt and its surroundings, and all these picked men, curbing with difficulty their eager desire to take part in the fighting and help to secure the victory, presented a most imposing appearance.

General Compans had the honour of being the first to lead his infantry to exchange fire with the Russians. He was ordered to attack the enemy's centre on the left of the Passavero wood, and to reach it he had to scale the heights and take the redoubts which barred his passage. The 57th Regiment led the way with a dash, carrying all before it, the battalions charging the first redoubt at the double, where a hand-to-hand conflict lasted for nearly an hour. The rest of the division supported the movement, and the enemy returning with considerable reinforcements to try to retake the redoubt, the ditches were in a few minutes choked up with thousands of killed or wounded Russians. The Gérard and Friant divisions, meanwhile, supported by the cavalry, had attacked other redoubts on the right of that assailed by General Compans.

All this time the formidable artillery of the redoubts in the centre of the enemy's line was working such fearful havoc in our ranks, that it became of the utmost importance to take the largest of these redoubts and spike its guns. The sappers of the engineers, therefore, beneath a hail of grapeshot, flung several little trestle bridges across the Kaluga stream protecting the base of the ridge, and the Morand division crossed the ravine with their aid and managed to get at the enemy. The first brigade of this division, led by General Bonamy, scaled the height and the entrenchments, deployed successfully in the redoubt, and killed the artillerymen at their guns. But the Russians came to the rescue in great force, and General Bonamy, after receiving seventeen bayonet wounds, fell disabled, and as he was taken prisoner he had the grief of seeing all his men either killed or driven back. The remainder of the Morand division was only able to protect the retreat of the few who escaped in disorder.

The Delzons division, belonging to the Viceroy's corps, which was on our left, meanwhile vigorously attacked and took possession of the fortified village of Borodino. Prince Eugène, who had, of course, not foreseen that this attack would succeed beyond his hopes, had ordered nothing more than the taking of Borodino; but the 106th Regiment, carried away by success, was able to cross the Kaluga by the mill bridge as the Russians had done before it, and pursued the enemy to the heights beyond, scaling them as rapidly as did the retreating forces.

General Plauzonne, however, seeing that the intrepid soldiers of the 106th Regiment were allowing themselves to be separated and were not waiting for the rear of their column to come up, ordered them to halt so as to offer a combined resistance to a Russian column which was corning down to crush them. At that very moment, however, General Plauzonne was killed, and in the momentary confusion into which his death threw his men, the Russians swept down on them and very few of the brave fellows escaped. The 92nd Regiment hastened up to their aid, and in spite of our great loss and of every effort made by the Russians to retake Borodino, it remained in our hands.

Marshal Ney, meanwhile, was gaining ground on the heights above the village, bristling though they were with redoubts and batteries, the artillery fire from which mowed down our ranks. It was grand to see Marshal Ney standing quietly on the parapet of one of these redoubts directing the combatants who were hurrying up below him, and never losing sight of them except when he was enveloped in clouds of smoke. A few paces from where Marshal Ney was standing, the gallant General Montbrun, of the cavalry, was carried off by a ball.

Marshal Davout, Prince of Eckmühl, continued to defend the redoubts which he had taken, and which the enemy never ceased to try to regain. I was ordered to take the distressing news to him that Prince Poniatowski, who was manoeuvring on the right, had met with such terrible obstacles in the form of dense woods and swampy marshes that he could not, as arranged, fall upon the rear of the Russian left, and so harass it as to aid the first French corps by a powerful diversion. At this moment, in fact, the Marshal's position was most critical; for although the cavalry under King Murat occupied the whole of the plain before him, and made a series of charges on that of the enemy with the happiest results, the fire from the Russian artillery was making Davout's post all but untenable. He had just been wounded in the arm, but he remained in command of his division. His chief of the staff, General Romoeuf, was pierced by a ball as he was speaking to us. The Marshal, greatly put out at having to make an isolated assault in front on a position which he thought ought to be attacked simultaneously on three sides, said to me angrily, 'It's a confounded shame to make me take the bull by the horns.' I hastened to go and tell King Murat of the critical position of Davout, and he at once ordered several masses of cavalry to unite for the support of General Friant, to whom I carried the order to take Seminskoë. All of a sudden I now saw the plain covered with masses of cavalry, Russian, Cossack, French, and that of our allies, engaged in a desperate mêlée, and after half an hour's struggle our side remained masters of the ground.

It was about three o'clock in the afternoon when I took this good news to the Emperor.

The Russian artillery from the big central redoubt continued, however, to work terrible havoc in our ranks, which had advanced so boldly within range of it, and the Emperor saw the great importance of getting possession of it. Orders were therefore sent to General Gérard, whose infantry was at the base of the height on which was the redoubt, to take it by assault, whilst King Murat was instructed to support Gérard's attack with a numerous body of cavalry. The manoeuvre was admirably executed, and our infantry, supported by Caulaincourt's cuirassiers and pontonniers, penetrated into the entrenchments.

General Kutusoff, however, who looked upon this redoubt as the key of his position, immediately pointed 100 pieces of cannon upon us, hoping by that means to drive us back, whilst a considerable column of picked Russian grenadiers, who had been hidden at the bottom of a ravine behind the redoubt, advanced to attack us. In the struggle the wind, which was blowing strongly, raised clouds of dust, which mingled with the smoke from the guns was whirled up in dense masses, enveloping and almost suffocating men and horses. When at last the thick clouds, augmented every moment by the fury of the combat raging on every side, rolled away, we found that the column of Russian grenadiers had been driven back into the ravine, and that we were masters of the redoubt, where the artillerymen had been cut down at their guns. Thirty pieces of cannon also remained in our hands, the violence and rapidity of our cavalry charge having been such that the enemy had not had time to drag them away. Our victory had, however, been dearly bought, for Caulaincourt had been killed at the gorge of the redoubt, as he led the charge.

The Emperor, satisfied with all that had already been accomplished by General Friant and the other divisions under Davout, now thought the right moment had come to send his whole Guard to complete the victory, as yet only begun, when a timid counsellor remarked to him, 'Allow me to point out that your Majesty is at the present moment 700 leagues from Paris, and at the gates of Moscow.' The reflection that he was so near Moscow seems to have greatly cheered the Emperor by calling up a picture in his mind of his entry into that town with all the pomp of a conqueror, and, turning to me, he said, 'Go and find Sorbier, and tell him to take all the artillery of my Guard to the position occupied by General Friant, to which you will guide him. He is to extend sixty guns at right angles with the enemy's line, so as to crush him by a flank lire; Murat will support him.'

I galloped off to General Sorbier, who was a very hasty man, and he, incredulous of my message, did not give me time to explain it, but broke in on what I was saying impatiently with the words, 'We ought to have done that an hour ago!' He then ordered the artillery to follow him at a trot. The imposing mass of the artillery at once rolled away with a resounding clank of chains into the valley, crossed it, and ascended the gentle slope covered with the entrenchments we had taken from the enemy, where they broke into a gallop to gain the space necessary for extension by the left flank. In the distance I could see King Murat caracoling about in the midst of the mounted skirmishers well in advance of his own cavalry, and paying far less attention to them than to the numerous Cossacks who, recognising him by his bravado, as well as by his plumed helmet, and a short Cossack mantle made of a goat's skin with long hair resembling their own, surrounded him in the hope of taking him prisoner, shouting, '*Houra! houra! Murat!*' But none of them dared even venture within lance's length of him, for they all knew that the King's sword would skilfully turn aside every weapon, and with the speed of lightning pierce to the heart the boldest amongst his enemies. I galloped up to Murat to give him the Emperor's instructions, and he left the skirmishers to make his dispositions for supporting General Sorbier. The Cossacks took his withdrawal for retreat or flight, and followed us. My horse, which was not so fleet as that of the King, for he was mounted on a beautiful fawn-coloured Arab, caught its feet in the drag-rope of a gun which was making its wheel of a quarter circle at a gallop. The animal, though hurt and shaken by the shock and fall, struggled up again at once without throwing me, and galloped furiously to where General Sorbier was standing in the centre of the terrible battery, now beginning to pour out volleys of grape-shot, shells, and balls on the enemy's lines, which it enfiladed, every discharge telling.

The enemy's cavalry made many useless efforts to destroy our line of guns. We remained masters of the fortified position, which the Russians had looked upon as impregnable, and I went to the Emperor to report on what had taken place.

The day was already far advanced. We had dearly bought the advantages we had gained, nor was there as yet anything to indicate that the struggle would not be renewed on the morrow. When I got back to the Emperor he had already been able to judge of the good results achieved by the artillery of his Guard, and he was still hesitating whether, as many amongst us wished, he should follow up this success with a grand charge from the whole of the brilliant cavalry of the Guard. Just at this moment a Russian lieutenant-general who had been taken prisoner was brought to the Emperor. After having talked to him very politely for a few minutes, the Emperor said to some one standing by, 'Give me his sword.' A Russian sword was at once brought, and the Emperor, taking it, graciously offered it to the Russian general with the words, 'I return your sword.' It so happened, however, that it was not the prisoner's own sword, and, not understanding the honour the Emperor meant to do him, the Russian general refused to receive the weapon. Napoleon, astonished at this want of tact in a general, shrugged his shoulders, and turning to us said, loud enough for the General to hear him, 'Take the fool away!'

The battle now seemed to be approaching its close. The noise of the firing was diminishing, and the sun was setting. The Viceroy had posted a large body of his troops on our left beyond the Kaluga stream, at the foot of the height on which was the big redoubt taken by our cavalry. The Prince was going about amongst his battalions, when the enemy, who had probably recognised him, ordered a considerable body of Cossacks to charge and try to carry him off. Fortunately the Prince noticed the masses of cavalry threatening our left, and in anticipation of their attack he at once formed his divisions in squares by regiments. The Viceroy had only just time to fling himself into the 84th Regiment, beside Colonel Pegot, and to order the Italian regiment to repulse the thousands of Cossacks advancing upon us with lowered spears, before the shock came. But the point-blank discharge from our infantry drove the mass of riders, always so clever at turning tail, back upon themselves. Our cavalry pursued them for a short distance, and then returned to the ranks. The night fell, and put an end to the exhausting struggle all along the lines of the rival hosts.

The tents of the Emperor and of Major-General Prince Berthier were pitched on the verge of the battle field, which in itself was doubtless a token of victory, but the enemy's army was still within gunshot of us; the Russians, too, were rejoicing over a victory, and on our side the leaders were all making preparations for the resumption of the struggle the next day. The night was very dark, and gradually the fires on both sides, all too numerous, warned us what we might expect on the morrow.

Whilst waiting for the frugal repast which was to restore our exhausted forces, I jotted down notes of what I had seen during the day, and compared this battle with those of Wagram, Essling, Eylau, and Friedland. I was surprised that the Emperor had shown so little of the eager activity which had before so often ensured success. On the present occasion he had not mounted except to reach the battle field, and had remained seated below his Guard on a sloping mound, from which he could see everything. Several balls had passed over his head. Whenever I returned from the numerous errands on which I was sent, I found him still seated in the same attitude, following every movement with the aid of his pocket field-glass, and giving his orders with imperturbable composure. But we did not see him now, as so often before, galloping from point to point, and with his presence inspiring our troops wherever the struggle was prolonged and the issue seemed doubtful. We all agreed in wondering what had become of the eager, active commander of Marengo, Austerlitz, and elsewhere. We none of us knew that Napoleon was ill and suffering, quite unable to take a personal part in the great drama unfolded before his eyes, the sole aim of which was to add to his glory. In this terrible drama had been engaged Tartars from the confines of Asia, with the elite of the troops of some hundred European nations, for from the east and from the west, from the north and from the south, men had flocked to fight with desperate courage for or against Napoleon. The blood of some 80,000 Russians and Frenchmen had been shed to consolidate or to overturn his power, and he looked on with an appearance of absolute *sang-froid* at the awful vicissitudes of the terrible tragedy. We were all anything but satisfied with the way in which our leader had behaved, and passed very severe strictures on his conduct. Supper interrupted our discussion, and after it we were soon all wrapped in heavy slumber, whilst the chief, whom we had been accusing so severely, was watching and studying how best to resume the conflict the next morning. Three hours before daybreak he sent for me and said, 'Go and find the Viceroy, and make a reconnaissance with him of the Russian line opposite to him; then come and tell me what is going on.' It was now September 8th.

A few minutes later I was riding stealthily along side by side with Prince Eugène at the base of the heights of Borodino, trying to find out something about the enemy's intentions. The darkness of the night protected us, and we reached the entrenchments of Borodino, still occupied by the Russians. Seen from below, the fortifications stood out black against a sky of a less sombre hue, and we were able to ascertain that the weapons of the sentinels pacing to and fro were lances, not muskets with fixed bayonets. Having made quite sure on this point, we concluded that the enemy was in retreat, for otherwise the defence of the fortifications would not have been left to Cossacks, and I hastened back with this news to the Emperor. The reports brought in from other reconnaissances tallied with mine, and he ordered that the enemy should be pursued without loss of time. It was only now that we were able to feel quite sure that the victory was ours.

The terrible struggle, so hotly contested, had won no results at all commensurate with the great losses sustained on both sides. The French had to mourn two generals of division, Montbrun and Caulaincourt, and eight other generals killed, thirty-eight generals wounded, ten colonels killed, and some 40,000 men killed or wounded. The Russians had lost sixty pieces of cannon, and had had thirty-five generals killed, wounded, or taken prisoners, with 45,000 men killed or disabled, and 5,000 taken prisoners.

After all our fatigues the pursuit was slack, and the Russians retired in perhaps even more admirable order than on the day preceding the battle. For several leagues their route was dotted with the wooden crosses they had hastily set up over the graves of the wounded officers who had died by the way. The numerous graves and crosses amongst their lines of abattis, in the rear of Gorka, made them look like a regular cemetery. We too spent a short time over the sacred duty of interring our dead, and when I climbed up into the big redoubt to examine the condition of the fortification which had given us so much trouble the day before, I found our troops digging graves for their many comrades and officers who had fallen. Caulaincourt was placed in the centre of the entrenchment, and I had the gallant Vasserot laid beside him. One side of that officer's face had been carried away, but without altering the expression of what remained, and he seemed to be still saying in accents of command, 'Follow me, my friends; we shall conquer!' As in the case of General Gudin, I made the men cover over these two bodies with quantities of broken armour and weapons.

Nothing could have been more melancholy than the appearance of the battle field covered with groups occupied in

154

carrying away the thousands of wounded, and in taking from the dead the few provisions remaining in their haversacks. Some of the wounded dragged themselves towards Kolotskoy, where Baron Larrey had set up an ambulance, whilst others were carried thither by their comrades in one way or another. Very soon an immense number were waiting attention, but, alas! everything needed for them was wanting, and hundreds perished of hunger, envying the happier lot of those who had been killed on the spot.

Our cavalry under Murat pursued the Russians with sufficient vigour to compel them to take up a position at Mojaisk, and I was sent to urge the Viceroy to second the efforts of the King of Naples. We came up with the Russians at Mojaisk, and had to give them battle to drive them out of it. They withdrew, leaving the place encumbered with dead and wounded. All the Russian horses which had been hurt in the battle of Borodino seemed to have come to Mojaisk to die. The action was well sustained, and General Belliard was seriously wounded.

It was on September 9th at Mojaisk that I first saw our troops use horseflesh as food. The court of a house I occupied, and the street it was in, were alike piled up with unfortunate horses, many still breathing, though too severely wounded to be able to rise. A report I had to draw up occupied me an hour, and when I came out with it, what was my surprise to find all the horses cut to pieces and the best part of the flesh carried away by our men! I was not yet reduced to eating the tough, yellow, tasteless meat, but ere long it was to be all we were to have to save us from the torments of famine!

It was here that the Prince of Wagram (Marshal Berthier) told me that the Prince of Eckmühl (Marshal Davout) wished to make me chief of his staff. This news, which would have flattered and delighted every one else, afflicted me greatly, and I begged Marshal Berliner not to take any notice of the request. That same evening, however, the Emperor sent me the appointment, signed by himself, and there was nothing for it but to submit.

This change to the position lately held by General Compans, which had contributed so greatly to his advancement and added so much to his wealth, filled me with the most lively regret. I had served so long under Prince Berthier, and my greatest desire was to remain with him. I went at once to the Prince of Eckmühl and begged him to make another choice, but he insisted on having me, and it was with tears in my eyes that I returned to bid farewell to the Prince of Wagram before I went to receive my instructions from my new chief, who was in his tent on the road to Moscow.

On the 12th and 13th we followed the Russians, and a little before nightfall on the 14th we came in sight of Moscow. King Murat's cavalry was in advance of us, and had not only already entered the town, but had penetrated at the same time as the infantry under Marshal Ney as far as the Kremlin.

The troops of the first corps, to which I now belonged, were posted to cover the occupation of the heights overlooking the town, and we spent the night with them. It was here that we discovered that the Russians had just set fire to the town to prevent us front deriving any benefit from the resources it contained.

Many amongst us thought our advance on Moscow most imprudent, and General Haxo said to me, 'This will lead to our having to defend Paris before long.'

When King Murat entered the town on the 14th at the head of his cavalry, he advanced with considerable caution, fearing that the ease with which he was allowed to advance meant that some trap had been laid for us. It was not until he reached the foot of the Kremlin that he met with any resistance at all. This resistance was easily overcome, and he entered the Kremlin or citadel itself, that lofty fortress within which are the palaces of the Czars.

The Emperor entered Moscow on the 15th, and took up his quarters in the Kremlin. On the 16th the spread of the fire drove him to take refuge in the Château of Peterskoe, but he returned to the citadel on the 18th, when the conflagration was beginning to subside.

The first corps from its post of observation outside the town was able to watch the immediate results of the fire, which appeared to us to have begun near the Kremlin. The reports of our foragers who went to look for provisions in the houses of Moscow all confirmed our idea that the fire was the prearranged work of incendiaries, for the breaking open of a door often fired a train of gunpowder, which set light to piles of tow shavings or faggots, so that the house was soon in flames. Many doors were also found armed with gunlocks, the triggers of which fell at the first shock, setting fire to the inside of the house, so that our men had hard work to snatch from the flames the few sacks of flour, sugar, loaves, and other provisions which the owners had stored up against the approaching winter. The wind fanned the conflagration, and it soon embraced the whole city, which resembled the crater of some huge volcano, over which hung dense masses of smoke, dashed here and there at times by silvery light from the moon. The Emperor's first care was to prevent pillage, but presently he ordered it to be encouraged, so as to save as much as possible from destruction and snatch from the flames the provisions which were being reduced to ashes.

The first corps did not leave its position outside the town till the 19th, when it went to take up its quarters in a suburb which had escaped the fire. To reach it we had to pass through the burning streets, and march beneath a perfect vault of flames, which made the passage of the artillery very dangerous. We reached the suburb, however, without accident, and found there some twenty palatial residences. One of these was set apart for Marshal Davout and another for me, but we had scarcely installed ourselves in them when they were found to be on fire, though how it came about we could not tell. We had to go elsewhere, and I entered a very handsome building, which appeared to have belonged to a merchant, for the rooms were all encumbered with quantities of bottles of scent labelled in French, medicines, rolls of opodeldoc, &c., probably sold for the amelioration of the chronic rheumatism of the Russians. I had scarcely written a page of the orders I had to give, when I was nearly suffocated by smoke, and had once more to beat a retreat. Three times in that one morning did a similar accident happen, and it was not until I had told my men to fire on every one who looked at all like a Russian that I succeeded in getting a house I could stop in. Marshals Davout and Mortier had experienced similar difficulties. My sister, who had been living in Russia for twenty years, and now joined me, told me all about what happened to Marshal Mortier. I must, however, explain my sister's presence in Moscow. She had suffered much from an affection of the eyes, and had come to that city to consult a great oculist, under whose treatment her sight was restored. She had been about to return to St. Petersburg when the French army arrived at the gates of Moscow. Hearing from some French officers who had teen taken prisoners that I was with the army, she was most anxious to find me, more especially as the evacuation of Moscow by the Russians left her in a very terrible position. Marshal Mortier was the first person to whom she applied for news of me; he received her kindly, and she remained with him till she found me. She was, therefore, amongst those who had to flee with the Marshal from the houses in which he endeavoured to establish himself. Five times they were driven out by the flames before they finally settled down in a building from which the incendiaries had been ousted without being able to complete their work. Many of these wretches passed themselves off as patients from the hospitals, who had come to beg us to aid then.

The sentinels in the quarter we now occupied having, as already stated, received orders to fire on all the Russians loitering about in the streets, the conflagration gradually burnt itself out. At the end of nine days it was practically extinct, though the incendiaries, anxious to prevent us from being able to build barracks in which to spend the winter at Moscow, had begun to set fire to a huge timber yard containing some thirty million beams for building. I sent the guard to put out the beginnings of what would have been another great conflagration, and a few well-aimed shots brought down the Russians at their evil work. By this apparently cruel order to our sentinels I was fortunate enough to save for the unlucky people of Moscow the materials for erecting, when they returned, shelters above the ashes of their homes in which to take refuge from the rigours of the winter so fatal to ourselves. But for this charitable precaution, which I rejoice at having taken, they would have had to withdraw to distant forests, and would have suffered far more than they did, whilst I should not have had the consolation of knowing that I had done at least a little to mitigate the horrors of war.

Like every one else who had stopped in Moscow with a view to separating himself from the Russians, my sister had been robbed of everything belonging to her, and she remained some days at Marshal Mortier's before she was able to join me. Even when we did at last find ourselves under the same roof, and one which was not on fire, I had little time to spare for her, or to talk over family affairs, for I was very much occupied. To keep her company, however, she had two young Russian prisoners, Colonel Sokoreff and Colonel Desapour by name, who both spoke French like Parisians, the latter an Indian prince, both of whom had been brought to me some days before, and shared my meals. The exchange of courtesies between my guests under circumstances so extraordinary, and in the midst of the barbarous surroundings of such a war as this, was certainly most interesting.

As chief of the staff, I had from twenty to twenty-five people to provide for and superintend every day. These included five or six secretaries, several aides-de-camp on various missions, and ten or twelve assistant officers. The men told off to supply our needs had no means of doing so but by pillage. Every day their task became more difficult and dangerous, as they had to go further and further afield. Often they did not return, for they had been taken prisoners or killed. Our position was, indeed, all but unbearable, and we could not maintain it many days longer. Our one hope was that the enemy would sue for peace. The Russians took pains to encourage this hope, and the leaders of the advanced guard, ready to believe what they so ardently wished, were far too easily deceived. The reports they sent to the Emperor confirmed him in his error, and he shared with them the hope of extricating his army from its critical position by a favourable treaty of peace. Hoping to smooth away difficulties, he even wrote to the Emperor Alexander to the effect that he was willing to grant generous terms in such a treaty. Of course this was a positive proof to the Russians of the great difficulty of our position, and an additional reason for prolonging our uncertainty until the time of year when the climate would become their most powerful ally against the French.

Our outposts extended scarcely two days' journey beyond Moscow, and the Emperor found it extremely difficult to get any certain information as to the position of the Russian army. The Russians, on the other hand, were fully *au courant* of all our movements, and few days passed without our receiving the melancholy news that this or that battalion or squadron, sent to protect our foragers in their search for food, had fallen into the hands of the enemy.

At one time the bold project was even discussed of getting out of our painful situation by making a dash for St. Petersburg, but to do this we should have to abandon our wounded and our lines of communication, to go and make war as mere isolated bodies of adventurers, cut off from their supporting points. This new invasion might lead to the rising *en masse* of the whole population of Russia, whom the proclamations of the Emperor Alexander were already calling to arms. Hitherto the peasants had shown great patience with us; but now they too were beginning to be hostile, and simple as the march on St. Petersburg might appear, it would probably launch us on an enterprise far beyond our strength in the cold and rainy season about to commence. For all that we were eager for it, and we had already begun to withdraw our prisoners, such of the wounded as could be moved, and much of the impedimenta of the army towards Smolensk. I took advantage of this chance of starting my sister for France, installing her in one of my carriages drawn by three good horses under a first-rate driver. I took care to pack the carriage with plenty of provisions and furs, commending her to the care of several of our wounded generals, and, better still, to the protection of Providence.

The army, thus to a certain extent relieved of the non-combatants, who left Moscow on the 13th and 14th, was now far more manageable and awaited with impatience the decision of

Napoleon. These last few days were very trying. Our purveyors were no longer able to bring back anything either for the men or for the horses. The accounts they gave of the dangers they had incurred were appalling, and, according to them, we were hemmed in by a perfect network of Cossacks and armed peasants, who would kill any isolated parties of French, and from whom we ourselves might find it difficult to escape.

All this, of course, added greatly to our perplexities, and the generals in command and their chief staff officers found the task of the reorganisation of the army most arduous. The days and nights were all too short to overcome the many obstacles in our way, and I had scarcely time to see anything of Moscow except the long street leading from our suburb to the Kremlin, which passed the tower for which a bell had been cast some two centuries before, so big that as yet no means had been found for hoisting it to its place. In our dreams of glory – for in dreams all things seem possible – we fancied ourselves carrying off this huge bell as a trophy to Paris. Other treasures, including the big cross from Ivan's Tower, were already packed on carriages for removal, and in placing them there a vision rose up before us of Paris as the capital of the whole world, with her museums, other public buildings and squares already so full of objects of value, yet further enriched with the spoils of foreign countries.

The weather was still fairly fine, and there was yet no hint of the bitter winter approaching, so that, in spite of the evident change for the worse in the health of the Emperor, and the consequent decrease in his activity, in spite of our uncertainty as to the future, and the many privations we had to endure, we cherished the most delightful illusions, and all sorts of grand things seemed possible, when on October 18th we were roughly awakened from our dreams by the noise of a brisk cannonade in the distance. The news soon reached us that our outposts had been suddenly attacked at Vinkowo, and, being taken by surprise, had been routed. General Kutusoff had turned the delays skilfully to account to repair the losses he had sustained, to receive new levies of troops, and in a word to get his army into first-rate condition. On October 18th he ordered considerable forces to make sudden simultaneous attacks all along our lines of outposts.

General Sebastiani lost in this attack, which took him completely by surprise, no fewer than thirty pieces of cannon and all his baggage, whilst 5,000 of his men were killed and many others taken prisoners. King Murat himself was all but carried off, only escaping by charging and overturning at the head of his carabineers a whole Russian corps which attempted to bar his passage.

From this day our position was completely changed. Our flag had been torn down from the proud position won by our many victories, and Napoleon, disappointed in his hopes of peace, had to hasten his retreat, lest the enemy should render escape impossible. Fortunately the Russians still stood to some extent in awe of the well-known energy of the French, and their fear that we might resume the offensive if we were rendered desperate made them cautious, preventing them from securing the full success which their position and the superiority of their numbers could not have failed to win.

On October 18th we received orders to leave Moscow, and to march by way of the Kalouga road on the 19th. Thus, after a month's delay at Moscow, which had been of no special advantage to us, during which our army had received few reinforcements and our troops had been worn out hunting for provisions, we left that city and sadly began our retreat towards France. We were fortunate in having beautiful autumn weather, and the first few days' march was peaceful enough, for we only had to drive off a few Cossacks who hovered on the flank of our columns. But, as on our advance, we were everywhere harassed by the Russian plan of burning everything on our approach, and we could do nothing to prevent it. About ten leagues from Moscow the first corps halted at the base of a fine castle, the foundations and first floor of which were of hewn stone. I had several orders to write, and I went up a grand staircase into a suite of rooms which seemed to have been but recently deserted, for they still contained a piano, a harp, and a good many chairs, on which lay a guitar, several violins, some music, drawings, embroideries, and lady's unfinished needlework. I had scarcely been writing ten minutes, when we all noticed a smell of smoke. This smoke quickly filled the place, becoming so dense that we were obliged to give up work to try and find out whence it came. It seemed to issue chiefly from the wooden framework of one door. I had it broken in, and thick smoke at once poured through the aperture. I then went down into the cellars to see if the fire originated there, but I could discover nothing. I tried having a few buckets of water flung into the opening we had made, but even as my orders were obeyed such masses of flames rushed out upon us that we had only just time to collect our papers and escape. We had scarcely got downstairs when we heard the windows breaking with a crash, and as we looked back on our way to join the bivouac of our corps we saw volumes of flames issuing from all the windows of the castle, which fell at last, bearing witness by its destruction to the patriotic fury with which the Russians, torch in hand, were determined to pursue us.

Of course other fires occurred accidentally, with which the Russians had nothing to do. The little grain or flour found by our soldiers was made into cakes and put in the ovens with which all the peasants' huts were provided. Scarcely was one batch of cakes done before other troops came up, and the oven was heated again till the chimney would suddenly catch fire. This was how most of the fires which were to light up our passage from Moscow to the Niemen came about.

My courage almost fails me when I try to relate the horrors of those awful days and nights of suffering. But in spite of that, I shall put down here all that I find in my notes, for I think that the lessons taught by the past should be brought forcibly before the eyes of those whose genius leads to their being called to command armies.

Kutusoff justly felt that the best way to make war on us was to cut off our communications, so as to isolate us in the midst of a hostile population to whom our loss would be gain. He therefore took up a position at Vinkowo commanding the Kalouga road, by which he thought it probable that we should retire. The success he had achieved on the 18th confirmed his belief that the course he had adopted was the best, and the aim of his later manoeuvres was to bar our passage.

Under these circumstances it was important that we should push on as rapidly as possible during the first days of our retreat, so as to gain a couple of days' march on the enemy and get possession, without fighting, of the principal passes. But, alas! this was just what we did not do. Although much of the impedimenta of the French army had been sent on some days before, we were still encumbered with a great number of wagons and carriages laden with provisions for the prisoners, and with the booty we had taken, which included warm garments to protect us from the cold we should have to encounter. The amount of baggage was really enormous, and to give some idea of it I will just mention what I, an officer, who realised as much as any one the importance of getting rid of encumbrances, was trying to take with me. I still had 1. Five saddle horses; 2. a barouche, drawn by three horses, containing my personal effects and the furs in which I meant to wrap myself when bivouacking in the open; 3. the wagon, drawn by four horses, in which were all the papers of the staff, the maps, and the cooking utensils for the officers and their servants; 4. three smaller wagons, each drawn by three little Russian horses, in which rode our servants and the cook, under whose care were the stores of oats, a few precious trusses of hay, with the sugar, coffee, and flour belonging to the staff; 5. my secretary's horse; 6. the three horses I had lent to my sister, which had gone on in front, making altogether six carriages and twenty-five horses, to take along little more than bare necessaries. The traces of the carriages were constantly breaking, the march was retarded whilst they were mended, there were perpetual blocks in the sand, the marshes, or in the passes, and it often took our troops twelve hours to do a distance which a single carriage could have accomplished in two.

The Emperor, who was very much concerned at these delays, ordered that all the carriages not absolutely necessary for the transport of the few provisions we had with us were to be burnt and the horses used to help drag the artillery. So many were, however, interested in eluding this stern but wise sentence, that it was very insufficiently carried out. To set an example the Emperor had one of his own carriages burnt, but no one felt drawn towards imitating him, and the army, which still numbered between 105,000 and 106,000 combatants, and had 500 pieces of cannon, took six days to cover some thirty leagues. Further precious time was lost in getting across country by difficult roads, from the main Kalouga route, which was very bad, to a better one, and the Emperor leaving only Murat's cavalry and Marshal Ney's infantry on the old road to cover us from the attacks of the army under Kutusoff.

The Viceroy's corps marched at the head of the column on the new road, whilst the Delzons division, as advanced guard, occupied Malo-Jaroslavitz, the passage through which was extremely difficult.

Malo-Jaroslavitz was a little town of wooden houses, with tortuous streets, built on the steep sides of a lofty hill, at the base of which wound the little river Luya in a deep valley it had hollowed out for itself. A narrow bridge spanned the river below the only road by which the town could be reached from Moscow, and this road was here bounded on either side by impassable ravines, down which flowed the rapid torrents of such frequent occurrence in Russia during the rainy season. On the evening of the 23rd the town was occupied without resistance by the first of our battalions to arrive, the inhabitants having all fled at their approach.

That same evening the Emperor halted at the post-house of Malo-Jaroslavitz, a mere peasant's hut, where he passed the night after having sent out officers bearing his orders to the corps echeloned on the road from Moscow to Smolensk, telling them to meet him at the latter town.

On October 24th the Emperor was riding with the first corps and his Guard, as he thought, in perfect security, when a considerable body of cavalry appeared on the right, which we all took at first to be Murat's troops. We were not long left in our error. It appeared that a certain Platoff, a celebrated Cossack hetman or general, had promised Kutusoff to carry off Napoleon, and now with several thousands of his men he suddenly flung himself upon that part of the French army which he fancied included the Imperial staff. He had guessed rightly, and in the twinkling of an eye Napoleon was surrounded by Cossacks and compelled to draw his sword in his own defence. Fortunately, however, his escort was made up of men devoted to his person, and they pressed round him, breaking the shock of the barbarian charge. General Rapp, as he was engaged in trying to get the Emperor away, was overthrown in the mêlée, whilst his horse was pierced by a lance. Several officers near the Emperor were wounded. The mounted grenadiers and chasseurs of the Guard, however, recovering from the momentary surprise caused by the bold attack and wild cries of the hordes of Cossacks, dashed into their midst and put them to rout. In this struggle Emmanuel Lecouteulx, one of Prince Berthier's aides-de-camp, having broken his sword in the body of a Cossack, seized his lance and brandishing it above his head pursued his other enemies with it. A green furred pelisse, rather like those often worn by Russian officers, hid his uniform, and a French grenadier, taking him for a Cossack, plunged his long sabre into his shoulder, the point coming out through his breast. We all thought this terrible wound would lose us a favourite comrade, but God preserved him, and he is still alive. After being thus quickly dispersed, the Cossacks, leaving many of their numbers behind, dashed away, but they were stopped in their flight by a Dutch battalion, which flung itself upon them and greeted them with volleys of musketry.

Soon after this skirmish news was brought to the Emperor that our advanced guard had been vigorously attacked at Malo-Jaroslavitz, and the army quickened its march to go to the rescue. General Kutusoff, informed of our change of route, had at once sent a body of infantry and artillery more than 60,000 strong, under command of General Doctoroff, with orders to take possession of Malo-Jaroslavitz. These troops easily turned out the few French battalions under General Delzons, and occupied the town in their place. General Delzons, it is true, drove the Russians back to the centre of the town, but a ball fractured his skull, killing him and his brother, who was beside him, on the spot.

The French began to give way, and the Russians recovered the ground they had lost. General Guilleminot was sent to replace Delzons, and Prince Eugène supported him with the Broussier division. Again and again Guilleminot drove the Russians beyond the principal square, but fresh efforts on the part of the enemy forced him in his turn to retreat. The formidable Russian artillery placed on the heights overlooking the town and in its gardens poured a murderous fire down upon the road on which the French were coming up, whilst we were unable to reply with an effective fire from below, as we could only get our guns into position in the meadows by the Luya. Everything had therefore to be done by us with the bayonet in a space so limited that any flank manoeuvres were impossible. The enemy had all the advantages alike of the ground and of superiority of numbers. During the thick of the struggle, Prince Eugène had a second bridge flung across the river beside the first, so as to facilitate the passage of his troops.

Ten times at least we drove the Russians back, only in our turn to lose the ground we had gained; but at last the united efforts of Guilleminot and Broussier, supplemented later by the gallant charge of the Italian grenadiers under Pino, compelled the enemy to retire, leaving us masters of the town, which was now in flames. Our artillery was at last able to scale the hill so as to debouch in the plain, and dashing through the burning streets, crushing the wounded, the burnt, and the dead as they went, they succeeded in getting through the town and taking up their position on the hills, to pour down in their turn a hot cannonade upon the Russian troops posted within range across and behind the road to Kalouga.

The first corps seconded this operation, and spent the evening actually amongst the bodies of the dead all kneaded up by the wheels of the guns. A dark night fortunately shrouded the horrors from our sight, and we were able in the end to take up our position on the plain beyond the mangled remains of our comrades.

In this battle, in which our numbers were but one to four of our adversaries, we lost many men, and we were threatened with a similar struggle at every pass.

167

The Emperor went over the scene of the awful combat, over-whelmed Prince Eugène and his generals with praise, and then withdrew to a distant hut, where he passed the night. I was told afterwards that he held a council of war with several of the Marshals and King Murat, and that, after having the maps spread out and discussing them, he seemed to be for some time plunged in the greatest uncertainty. He finally dismissed every one at midnight without having come to any decision. This must have been indeed a cruel night for the great man, who now saw his star beginning to set, his power crumbling away, and who must already have begun to wonder if he could ever re-establish it, or even if he would get back to France.

On the morning of the 25th, Marshal Davout, Colonel Kobilinski, and I went the round of our outposts and saw with regret that the Russian army was drawn up in good order not far off, completely blocking the road to Kalouga, which we hoped to take. We made our dispositions for forcing a passage, and as we stood in a close group, bending over our maps, we offered an excellent mark for a Russian artilleryman. A ball from a twelve-pounder passed between the Marshal and me, and carried away one of Colonel Kobilinski's legs. The unfortunate officer fell against me, and we thought he was killed, but he recovered miraculously, and I shall speak of him again later.

The Marshal and I, with hearts torn by this catastrophe, impatiently awaited the signal to advance, when a very different order filled us with surprise and dismay.

I must explain that Kalouga, whither we thought we were bound, was a town of great importance to the Russians, as it was their emporium of provisions and weapons. Built as it was beside a river divided into several branches, it could easily be fortified, and afforded an admirably defended position for the Russian army, which had arrived before us. The Emperor doubted whether we were strong enough to force a passage through it, and he had lost so much time hesitating that he was now reduced to the necessity of ordering the army to abandon the Kalouga road for the one leading to Mojaisk, by which we had come. This was to fling us back upon the desert without provisions, to make us tramp once more over the ashes we had left behind us on our way to Moscow; in a word, it was to deprive us of all hope of finding a scrap of food. Needless to say that this decision afflicted us all most cruelly. The Emperor with his Guard went first, followed by the various corps of the army with all their terrible encumbrances, whilst henceforth Marshal Davout's corps, which of course was also my own, formed the rear-guard.

Chapter 7
Retreat

It became momentarily more difficult to reassure our soldiers on the subject of this loss of time and retrograde movement. On the second day of our retreat for the Mojaisk road, that is to say on October 26th, a fine cold rain set in, which damped every one's spirits yet more, and greatly increased the difficulties of the march. Once more we saw a fine castle, which looked as if it would provide us with a comfortable shelter, but we had no sooner entered it than fire broke out, and that before our people had lit a match. We found the incendiary apparatus, which had been left in position by the owner, but too late to extinguish the flames. Our troops were already beginning to suffer from dysentery through insufficient and badly cooked food, a few cakes and a little poor soup being all they had even now. The sick who were unable to march with the rest were abandoned on the road. Meanwhile Marshal Mortier rejoined us at Verea with the two divisions of the Young Guard; he had accomplished the melancholy task assigned to him of blowing up the Kremlin, against which his noble soul had revolted. Before leaving Moscow some of Mortier's troops took prisoner one of our bitterest enemies, the Russian Lieutenant-General Vintzingerode, and he was being taken to the Emperor, when he had the good fortune to make his escape.

On the 27th the advanced guard of the army re-entered Mojaisk, still encumbered with the wounded left behind after the battle of Borodino, and on the 28th the rearguard arrived. How painful and touching was the meeting with our unfortunate wounded, to whom we now returned with none of the comforts or the cheering news which they expected us to bring them! All we could offer them was an exhortation to resignation; we dared not tell them that we were about to abandon them once more, this time finally, and we were ourselves slowly beginning to face the fact that their terrible lot would most probably soon be our own. Wherever we passed, every refuge still left standing was crowded with wounded, and at Kolinskoy alone there were more than 2,000. Hitherto we had only been pursued by a few Cossacks, but every day their numbers increased, and they became more aggressive. Just before we left Kolinskoy on the 30th, wishing to reconnoitre the enemy on the plain, I was walking along the terrace of a convent, when I suddenly found myself in the presence of about a hundred Cossacks, who were like myself approaching to reconnoitre. When they caught sight of me they at first took to flight; but seeing that I was alone, they returned, and I had only just time to mount and gallop off to rejoin our troops, who had started and were already some distance off. Here and there we passed carriages left on the road because the starved horses, exhausted with fatigue, had fallen down. The few which could be made to get up again were at once harnessed to the wagons containing some of the wounded, but they all died after dragging their new burdens for a few steps only. Then the wounded were in their turn abandoned, and as we rode away we turned aside our heads that we might not see their despairing gestures, whilst our hearts were torn by their terrible cries, to which we tried in vain to shut our ears. If our own condition was pitiable, how much more so was theirs with nothing before them but death from starvation, from cold, or from the weapons of the Russians! The 30th was a sad and terribly long day, for we had to march nearly all night in intense cold, the severest we had yet had to encounter, it being important that we should arrive at Giatz before the enemy, who were pushing on rapidly by cross roads in the hope of getting there first.

The first corps arrived at Giatz on the 31st, and a few hours afterwards the Russians appeared in great force. The next day, November 1st, they tried to force a passage through our troops, and having failed they had to be content with hotly cannonading one of our big convoys which had been considerably delayed, and was defiling near the entrance to the town just in front of the enemy's guns. The balls wrought terrible havoc in this convoy of ours, and amongst the carriages was that in which I had sent my sister on in advance. I was fortunate enough to be able to save her. The coachman assured me that the three horses were still fresh and in first-rate condition, so I said to my sister, 'Dare you face the guns?' She replied trembling, 'I will do what you tell me.' I at once turned to the coachman with the words, 'Cross that meadow at a gallop; the balls will go over your head, and you will succeed in getting in front of the rest of the convoy. You will then be able to push on without stopping.' He followed my advice and with the best results, for my sister got off unhurt. The convoy consisted of some hundreds of badly harnessed carriages, containing many wounded, with the wives and children of several French merchants of Moscow, who were flying the country after having been robbed of their all by the Russians. The company of the Theatre Français of Moscow had also joined this party, the unlucky actors little dreaming of the terrible tragedy in which they were to play their part through placing themselves under our protection, so soon, alas! to avail them nothing.

On November 2nd snow began to fall, and there were already eight or nine degrees of frost. The various divisions of the first corps took it in turns to act as rearguard, and on that day it was the turn of the Gérard division, with which we had passed the night in a wood beneath the snowflakes. The effects of the great cold were already disastrous; many men were so benumbed at the moment for departure as to be unable to rise, and we were obliged to abandon them.

We reached Viasma on November 3rd at the same time as the Russians, whose advanced guard was checked by Marshal Ney's troops drawn up in front of them. It was evident that a battle must take place here, and every preparation was made on both sides. The French troops in a position to take part in it numbered about 30,000 or 40,000, whilst the Russians had two corps consisting together of more than 60,000 men.

Marshal Davout's and the Viceroy's corps, with the Poles under Prince Poniatowski, were successively engaged, and for a long time exposed to an overwhelming fire from a strong body of artillery with horses better harnessed and in far better condition than ours, which were too worn out for manoeuvring. The first corps and that under Prince Eugène became separated from each other twice, and were both for a time in very critical positions. Fortunately Marshal Ney was able to send a regiment to the rear of the Russian army, which threw it into confusion, and Generals Kutusoff, Miloradowich, Platoff, and Suvoroff, who had hoped to make us lay down our arms, stopped the pursuit, though fifty pieces of cannon still poured out their fire upon our luckless convoys, which were defiling past during the battle. Many men were lost on both sides here as elsewhere, for our soldiers were still undaunted, and nearly every shot from us told in the Russian ranks, which were more numerous and more closely serried than ours.

Marshal Ney, whose turn it was to act as rearguard, now protected the Viasma pass, and the French army marched towards Dorogobouj. After having passed the night of the 3rd and the day of the 4th on the road, we halted in the evening in a pine forest on the borders of a frozen lake not far from the Castle of Czarkovo, where the Emperor had been for two days. On the 5th the first corps took up its position at Semlevo, so as to let that of Marshal Ney pass on, it being our turn now to be rearguard. The Cossacks harassed us greatly, and many of our stragglers, whose numbers increased every day, fell into their hands. We now also made out on our flanks numerous columns of Russian cavalry and artillery, which were trying to pass us so as to await us at the entrance to the pass on this side of Dorogobouj. Marshal Ney foresaw this danger, and instead of going through the pass he halted near it for us to come up. Thanks to his forethought and support, we only suffered from a slack cannonade and reached Dorogobouj safely.

Leaving that place on the 6th we made a long march, and at nightfall we camped in a large wood, where General Jouffroy had been obliged to halt with the badly harnessed and damaged artillery under his care. We spent the night in packing the wagons which were still in a fit state to proceed, blowing up those we had to abandon, and burning the gun-carriages we could not take with us. These explosions, which were now of very frequent occurrence, were signals of our misfortunes, and affected us much as the tolling of the bell at her child's funeral would some bereaved mother.

General Jouffroy had had a tent pitched, and invited me to share its shelter and his supper. A supper! Good heavens! what a luxurious treat in the midst of our misery!

I had a new experience at that supper. Hitherto a few cows had still remained to the staff, and I had not been reduced to eating horseflesh. But now the General had nothing to offer me but a repast of horseflesh so highly spiced that in spite of its toughness and the coarse veins, which resisted the efforts of the sharpest teeth to masticate them, it really tasted not unlike what the French call *bœuf à la mode*. Generally horseflesh is so black, and its gravy is so yellow and insipid, so very like liquid sulphur, that it looks most repulsive, but we quite enjoyed our meal, washed down as it was by a flask of good wine which had belonged to some great man of Moscow.

For a long time the only meat our soldiers ever tasted had been horseflesh, and the poor fellows were so brutalised by misery and famine that they often did not wait till an animal was dead to cut it up and carry off the fleshy portions. When a horse stumbled and fell, no one tried to help it up, but numbers of soldiers at once flung themselves upon it, and cut open its side to get at the liver, which is the least repulsive part. They would not even put it out of its misery first, and I have actually seen them angry at the poor beast's last struggles to escape its butchers, and heard them cry, 'Keep quiet, will you, you rogue?'

The numbers of the stragglers increased in a perfectly appalling way; they stopped in crowds to roast a few shreds of horseflesh, and the French, who must always have their joke whatever their misery, called the tattered wretches the *fricoteurs* or revellers.

During the night of the 6th and the day of the 7th, a heavy

fall of snow drifting before a strong wind rendered our march extremely arduous. We were often unable to see two paces before us, but all the time the balls from the enemy were ploughing up the ground, and every now and then a few victims fell. No one had the heart to stop to help those who were struck, for the most selfish egotism crushed all kindly feeling in almost every breast. It was in a state of bodily and mental torpor that we reached Pnevo on one of the tributaries of the Dnieper, a very difficult river to cross. To protect its passage during our occupation of the country, we had had a big log hut built surrounded by a weak earthwork. This little redoubt was the only shelter which had not been burnt on the long road we were traversing, and the first corps halted there to pass the night. It was built in the same way as the huts of the peasants, with big squared trunks of trees laid horizontally on each other, forming walls almost impervious to balls, but not more than fifty people could get inside, so that the rest of the troops had to camp around it. The heavy snow and the bitter wind prevented us from going to get fuel, for there were no trees near, and every one suffered terribly from cold during the night.

In our halts we always faced the north. The Viceroy, who was marching on our left, met with the greatest difficulties, for he had counted on finding a bridge over the Wop, but this bridge was broken, so that he had to cross by the ford, and the water was all frozen over. His artillery and baggage stuck fast in the mud on the banks, and he was compelled to abandon them.

General Rapp and several other officers came to share our small quarters, where we were all very closely packed together. At nine o'clock the next morning when we left our shelter we found the ground near the wretched little redoubt encumbered with poor fellows, who, after having with infinite trouble managed to light fires, had been overcome with the cold, and burnt by flying sparks though covered with snow. Many of them were never to rise again from the spot on which they had fallen. Before we left we had the log hut burnt down.

The coating of ice on the roads made them so slippery that men and horses could scarcely keep their feet. My horse fell with me, and I was so much hurt that I could not remount, and I went to share Marshal Davout's *wurst* or ambulance wagon, drawn by a very strong pair of cobs, which galloped along on the ice as easily as others would on turf.

Having burnt the bridge behind us, we imagined ourselves to be in security for the rest of the day. But when we halted for the first time about noon, we heard a brisk firing a short distance off, which evidently came from the twelve-pounders of our own park of artillery. This made the Marshal both uneasy and angry, and he sent for the officer in command of the artillery. He came hurrying up with a smile on his face, as if he were the bearer of good news. Davout, however, frowning at him from his *wurst*, accosted him roughly with the words, 'So it's you, you scoundrel, who have dared to fire my reserve guns without orders from me!' Greatly surprised at this address, the officer had the presence of mind to pretend not to know to whom Davout was speaking, and after looking about him, he said as he set spurs to his horse to return to his post, 'Surely that language cannot be addressed to me!' A few minutes later we learnt that some 1,200 Cossacks had flung themselves upon the big park of artillery, but when the commanding officer halted he had prudently prepared his guns for action and formed squares to guard against a cavalry charge, so that when that charge was made a volley of grapeshot from thirty guns overthrew one half of the assailants and put the other half to flight. I now once more entreated the Marshal, as I had so often done before, to choose another chief of the staff, pointing out to him that half our aides-de-camp and commissaries were already killed or taken prisoners, and that I really could not do all the work he required alone. He, however, begged me to remain, with a politeness which was so truly remarkable from him, that General Haxo maliciously asked me, 'Whatever have you done to the Marshal? He must be very fond of you, for I never saw him pet any one as he does you.'

On this same eventful 9th of November we re-entered Smolensk, where the Emperor received news of the Malet and Lahorie conspiracy at Paris, and of the check received by the corps which he had ordered to debouch on his flanks. The tidings from Spain were not of a kind to afford him any consolation, for there was no unity of purpose or of action amongst the French Generals there, a fact by which the enemy was not slow to profit. The Emperor, fearing lest discouragement should spread through the ranks of our retreating army, pretended to be quite unmoved by all this distressing news. He wanted to appear superior to every adversity and ready to face calmly every event, however untoward, but his assumed indifference was misinterpreted and had a bad effect.

We no longer had a smithy for rough-shoeing our horses, so that they nearly all fell and were too weak to get up again. Our cavalry was thus completely destroyed, and the dismounted men even flung away their weapons, which their fingers were too frozen to hold. Some 300 officers, who had lost all their men, then proposed forming themselves into a kind of picked corps, ready to fight together on every emergency; but with them, as with the common soldiers, strength and discipline soon gave way, and what might have been a noble band, bound together by misfortune, fell to pieces in a few days without having rendered the slightest service to any one.

We camped for the night of the 10th on the banks of the Dnieper, beside the bridge where General Gudin had been killed. Our bivouac fires were soon surrounded by those of the numerous stragglers who had met here. Their appearance would have torn our hearts if we had not already been reduced to the level of the brutes, without the power of feeling compassion. Many of the poor wretches, who were all without weapons, were wearing silk pelisses trimmed with fur, or women's clothes of all manner of colours, which they had snatched from the flames of Moscow or taken from carriages abandoned by the way. These garments, which were fuller and looser than those of men, were a better protection from the cold. Some also wore the clothes of their comrades who had died on the road.

Numbed with cold and famishing with hunger, those who had been unable to make a fire would creep up to their more fortunate comrades and plead for a little share in the warmth, but no one dreamt of sacrificing any of the hardly won heat for the sake of another. The new arrivals would remain standing behind those seated for a little while, and then, too weak to support themselves longer, they would stagger and fall. Some would sink on to their knees, others into a sitting posture, and this was always the beginning of the end. The next moment they would stretch out their weary limbs, raise their dim and faded eyes to heaven, and as froth issued from their mouths their lips would quiver with a happy smile, as if some divine consolation had soothed their dying agony. Often before the last breath was drawn, and even as the failing limbs stretched themselves out with an appearance of heavenly calm, some other poor wretch, who had been standing by, would seat himself upon the still heaving breast of his dying comrade, to remain resting upon the corpse with his living weight until, generally very little later, his own turn should come, and he also, finding himself too weak to rise, should yield up his breath. The horror of it all was but slightly shrouded by the falling snow, and we had to witness this kind of thing for yet another thirty days!

The first corps entered Smolensk on the 11th, and remained there till the 16th. The interval was employed in distributing to the troops the few provisions and clothes which had been collected in the storehouses by order of the Emperor, and in seeing off for Wilna all the convoys which could still be supplied with horses.

The Imperial Guard, which was always held in reserve, had fought very little and lost fewer men than any of the other corps. The Emperor still owned in that Guard a force of from 3,000 to 4,000 men in good fighting condition, but these troops, though the discipline to which they had to submit was much less severe than that enforced in the rest of the army, really suffered quite as much as we did. The Emperor had their affection for him very much at heart, and in the friendly familiar way which he knew would please them he used sometimes to go amongst them, and pulling the long moustaches, all stiff with ice, of one or another, he would say, 'Ah, old Grognards, you may count on me as I count on my Guard to fulfil the high destiny to which they are called.' These few words would at once restore the confidence of the brave fellows in their chief, and to the end of the journey the Emperor was always surrounded by them.

We had still more than 120 leagues to cross between Smolensk and the Niemen. There were already from 12 to 15 degrees of frost, and the cold was still increasing. The roads grew worse every day, and there was too little of everything at Smolensk for the four days' halt to have done much to recruit the exhausted strength of the troops, or to restore anything like order in the disorganised army. My chief, the Prince of Eckmühl (Marshal Davout), who, as the Emperor justly remarked, was a man of iron constitution, was very exacting, and expected the Staff accounts to be written up every day just as in times of peace. Now all my assistants but one had disappeared, and I therefore again tendered my resignation. Just as we were leaving Smolensk, the Emperor consented to my leaving Davout, and named Charpentier, a general of division just removed from the Government of Smolensk, to take my place. That general, however, being not at all anxious to take up a task of which he knew the difficulties, evaded appearing at his post for ten or twelve days, so that I had to go on doing the work of the chief of the Staff without the title or pay.

Before he left Smolensk the Emperor ordered Marshal Ney to remain there until the 17th, when he was to blow up the fortifications. He also told him that his corps was to act as rearguard after the departure of the 1st corps, which was to precede him by one day and await him at the Krasnoe ravine. This ravine, which was a very difficult pass, had been encumbered for nine days with carriages, many of which were being burnt to clear the way.

The Viceroy's corps, now reduced to 1,200 or 1,500 men, which was marching in advance of ours, had been greatly harassed ever since leaving Smolensk by some 12,000 or 14,000 Russians, with a strong force of artillery mounted on sledges. The Emperor and his Guard had waited at the entrance to the terrible defile for the Viceroy to come up with his corps and protect his passage through it, and he now determined not to enter it until the arrival of the first corps also, which had not been able to leave Smolensk until two o'clock in the morning of Monday, the 16th. During this halt Napoleon learnt that the enemy was advancing in force upon Orcha to intercept the passage of the Dnieper, and had massed a large number of troops in the village of Kourkovo, not far from us. The Young Guard, commanded by General Roguet, whose gallant audacity was well known to the Emperor, had joined him during the day, and Napoleon now sent him to create a diversion in the night by attacking the enemy's corps which was causing us so much uneasiness.

The 1st corps, which had been the 4th under the Viceroy, was terribly harassed all through the march on the 16th by numerous Cossacks with artillery. When darkness fell the attacks lessened, and we availed ourselves of the reprieve by marching all night towards the Krasnoe pass. With the first gleams of light on the 17th, however, we found ourselves threatened by great masses of Russian infantry and cavalry struggling to surround us and make us lay down our arms; and though they did not venture actually to attack us, the fire from their guns wrought great havoc amongst us. Again and again our little army, reduced to 4,000 men bearing arms, but hampered by numerous stragglers, halted to face the enemy and await Marshal Ney, who was to cover our retreat. On this occasion I had a fresh opportunity of admiring the courage and sang-froid of General Compans. Severely wounded in the shoulder, and suffering greatly, he was compelled, like most of us, to march on foot. This, however, did not prevent him from facing the enemy with a smiling face and as unruffled a calm as if he were walking about in his own garden at home. The sight of his happy face and composed demeanour had the best results on his soldiers, giving them a sense of security, and leading them to imitate their general's stoicism.

Our position at Krasnoe was, however, anything but pleasant. Surrounded by enemies ten times as numerous as ourselves, we could not imagine how it was that Marshal Ney, whom we supposed to be just behind us, had not managed to beat off at least some of them. We fought steadily, hoping every moment to see him appear. But the enemy's cannonade became hotter and hotter, making terrible gaps in our ranks, and the snow, which had been falling heavily ever since the evening before, added to our difficulties, rendering our situation all but desperate. The Emperor, who was becoming very anxious about our fate, generously turned back and came to meet us, cutting a passage through our assailants at the head of the Old Guard, and meeting Marshal Davout's advanced guard beyond Krasnoe.

Meanwhile nothing had been heard of Ney and the rearguard with him, but it turned out afterwards that on leaving Smolensk the Marshal, with the few troops still remaining to him, had been immediately pursued by thousands of the enemy, who poured such a hot fire into his already diminished ranks from every side, that after three days' continuous struggle he was compelled to abandon the attempt to cut through the enemy's forces, and to deviate from the main road to Krasnoe, where we were so anxiously awaiting him. When darkness was beginning he found himself far away from us, with the Dnieper between him and safety. He took up a position parallel with the river, and allowed his troops to light their bivouac fires. Kutusoff, who had followed Ney, now looked upon him as his certain prey, for he could see no way of escape for him, and sent an officer with a flag of truce to summon him to surrender.

The envoy, who performed his mission with the greatest politeness, was received with assumed courtesy, and detained on various pretexts whilst the Marshal was having the depth of the river sounded, and the strength of the ice on it tested. He was told that several men had gone over to the other bank and returned safely. He then ordered the throwing of fresh fuel on the fires, as if he had decided to remain where he was, and telling the envoy that he would have to accompany him, he gave the signal for crossing the river, instructing his subordinates to make the men go over in single file, and to keep well away from each other. Everything − artillery, baggage, even wounded − which would have hindered the safe crossing or broken the ice, was abandoned on the banks. The transit was accomplished without accident, and at daybreak on the 18th the Marshal was several leagues from the further bank, but he was now attacked by a considerable body of Cossacks under Platoff, but he managed to fight his way through them, though he had none but infantry with him, and after three days' march along the winding banks of the river, his rear harassed perpetually by Bashkirs and Tartars, who picked off and ill treated all stragglers, Ney at last rejoined the Emperor at Orcha.

In the struggle at Krasnoe, which lasted the whole day and in which we were exposed to a terrible artillery fire, my servant was wounded by grapeshot, and the two saddle horses he was leading were killed, whilst that on which he was mounted was very badly hurt. I thought the poor animal would certainly die of his awful wound, but, strange to say, he was the only one of all my horses to live to reach the Vistula. He was, in fact, quite well again when he was taken by the enemy at the gates of Thorn, and my poor servant was killed. With the horses I lost the furs they were carrying for my use, and nothing was left to me to protect me from the cold but a silk waterproof cloak, which turned out much more useful than I could have imagined, for it kept out the cold, and prevented my own animal heat, little as it was, from escaping.

As the day wore on at Krasnoe, and Ney did not appear, the anxiety of the Emperor and the army became more and more intense. Napoleon, fearing that his own retreat to Orcha would be cut off, dared not linger longer at Krasnoe, and he and his Guard left us an hour before nightfall, ordering us to wait for Marshal Ney. When the Emperor abandoned Krasnoe, the little town was full of those who had been wounded during the day. Nothing could have been more heart-rending than the sight of all the rooms in every house crowded with fine young fellows, their ages ranging from twenty to twenty-five years, who had but recently joined the army and had been under fire for the first time that day, but who within one short hour were to be left to their fate. Some few, who were able to march after their wounds had been dressed, were eager to be off again, but all the rest to the number of about 3,000 were left without surgeons or any necessaries.

The whole of the Guard was already gone, our much reduced first corps could no longer defend the heights beyond Krasnoe, and General Compans, who had remained till the very last, went down towards the town and crossed the ravine as night fell. He had scarcely done so, when, anxious to find out what the enemy were doing, I managed to creep along behind a hedge at the borders of the pass. The ravine was not more than thirty paces wide, and I very soon found myself almost face to face with a body of Russian artillery, which was being hastily put in position so as to riddle us with grapeshot. Beyond the ten or twelve guns of this battery I could see several considerable infantry corps advancing in line in our direction, leaving me no longer in any doubt of our being completely cut off from Marshal Ney. I hurried back with this distressing news to Marshal Davout, and recognising the hopelessness of waiting for Ney any longer, he did at once all that was left to us under the circumstances, by having a few guns placed in position to prevent the enemy from crossing the ravine, whilst the infantry was ordered to withdraw towards Lidoni, where we arrived a little before daybreak, our retreat having been facilitated by a very dark night. The Russians, thinking that we were still in force at Krasnoe, did not enter it till the next morning.

The army was still deeply grieved at the supposed loss of Marshal Ney, for we were all certain that if he were alive he had been taken prisoner. The thought of his fate caused general discouragement, and all we hoped was to escape captivity ourselves. The numbers of the stragglers, ever on the increase, had now become immense; at every pass or difficult bit of road there was a block of wagons and carriages, and many vehicles broke through the ice on the marshes and remained embedded in the mud beneath. This was how I myself in our march from Lidoni to Koziani lost my baggage wagon and a barouche, which were still properly harnessed, for both of them with their drivers and horses were swallowed up by the mud. Hundreds of others met with similar misfortunes, and as I was going through Dombrowa the day after my loss, I came upon a carriage belonging to a M. De Servan, in which sat my sister. She had lost her carriage in the same marshes as I had mine, and De Servan, who had been more fortunate than either of us, had been good enough to take her on with him. A few hours later, just at the entrance to Orcha, De Servan's carriage was smashed by a cannon-ball. M. Levasseur, however, whose carriage got through safely, was good enough to allow me to transfer my sister to it, and showed her every possible attention.

On the evening of the 20th, when the moon was shining brightly, our advanced posts on the right bank of the Dnieper saw an officer approaching, whom they at first mistook for a Russian. They soon saw, however, that he was French, and on questioning him they learnt to their great joy that Marshal Ney, who had miraculously escaped from the clutches of Kutusoff, was but a league away from us. It would be difficult to describe our delight at receiving this news, which did much to restore the tone of the army, so lowered by discouragement. The Viceroy and Marshal Mortier hurried off to meet Ney, and the next day he was welcomed by the Emperor, who received him with the greatest enthusiasm, greeting him with the words, 'I would have given everything rather than lose you.'

The first corps continued to cover the retreat, and we were aroused before daybreak after our arrival at Orcha by the coming up of the Russians in great force, who hoped to shut us into that town. Like every other place we passed through in our retreat, Orcha was encumbered with carriages crowded, as were the houses, with sick and wounded. A young cousin of mine, Alexander Lejeune, had been left at Orcha as manager of a hospital. I saw him as I went through, and he stuffed my pockets full of sugar and coffee ready roasted and ground. I urged him to fly whilst he could, and advised him to start in advance of us. He said he would just go and fetch a cloak and his money, but I never saw him again. He was probably delayed, and perished in the crowd after we left. If blood shed in the service of one's country is a patent of nobility, our family escutcheon ought to receive ten or twelve new chevrons of honour! for many of my nearest relations were wounded or killed in the Emperor's service, including five first cousins, namely, one Gérard, killed in Egypt; one Vignaux, killed in Spain; one Lejeune, killed in Russia; my brother, wounded at Friedland; the husband of my eldest sister, Baron Plique (General), wounded several times, who died whilst on active service; the brave and witty General Clary, brother of my wife, also wounded several times; and her other brother, who died at the age of twenty-two, as colonel of a regiment he had himself got together in Spain, and who was mourned as a son by his uncle, King Joseph.

I feel very proud at leaving such memories as these behind for my son, and have already too long delayed recording them in my Memoirs.

At Orcha the Dnieper is very wide, and so rapid that the ice was not firm enough to allow of our crossing it easily, although there were twenty-five degrees of frost. The two bridges, which were all we had been able to construct, were very narrow and far from strong, whilst the approaches to them were so slippery as to be very dangerous. We had had a great many carriages burnt in the streets of Orcha, but we were still terribly encumbered with them; the enemy harassed our rear perpetually, and had already gained a position from which they could cannonade our bridges. As soon as our troops were across we were compelled to set fire to these bridges, leaving behind us all who were without arms, or were for any reason unable to follow our rapid march. It was a terrible moment for us when we had thus to abandon so many of our wounded.

We passed the night of Sunday the 22nd with the rearguard in a little wood on the road, and arrived in the evening of the 23rd at Kokonow, where we learnt, alas! that General Tchichakoff had taken possession with a large force of Borisow, so that we were cut off from that way of retreat. This news was distressing enough, but at three o'clock the next morning an event occurred which in its horror surpassed almost anything which had yet befallen us.

185

Opposite the house occupied by Marshal Davout and his officers, and not more than a couple of paces off, was a huge barn with four large doors, in which some five or six hundred persons, including officers, soldiers, stragglers, &c., had taken refuge as affording some shelter from the cold. Thirty or forty fires had been lighted, and the inmates of the barn, broken up into various groups, were all sleeping heavily in the warm air, which afforded such a contrast to the bitter cold of their usual bivouac, when the thatched roof caught fire, and in an instant the whole place was in flames. Suddenly, with a dull crash, the burning roof fell upon the sleepers, setting fire to the straw in which they lay, and to their clothes. Some few, who were near the doors, were able to escape; and with their clothes all singed they rushed to us screaming for help for their comrades. We were at the doors in a very few seconds; but what a terrible sight met our eyes! Masses of flames many yards thick rushed out from the doors to a distance of several yards, leaving only the narrow passage of exit some six feet high beneath a vault of fire which, fanned by the wind, spread with immense rapidity.

We could not, any of us, get near the poor creatures, whom we could see struggling wildly or flinging themselves face downwards on the ground so as to suffer a little less. We hastily tied ropes, our handkerchiefs, anything we could get hold of, together, to fling to them, so as to be able to drag some of them out; but fresh shrieks soon stopped our efforts, for as we pulled they fell upon and were stabbed by each other's bayonets. Captain d'Houdetot got nearer to them than any of the rest of us were able to, but his clothes caught fire and he had to draw back. The 500 or 600 victims made several last despairing efforts to rise, but their strength was soon all gone, and presently the building fell in upon them, their muskets became heated, the charges in there exploded, and their reports were the only funeral salute fired over the corpses of all the brave fellows. Very few escaped from the terrible conflagration, and those few had to tear off all their clothes. I saw one poor child of twelve or fourteen years old going about stark naked, but none of us could give him anything to put on, for we had lost our carriages, our horses, everything. There were now 13 degrees of frost, but we had to harden our hearts against the sufferers, for to help them was beyond our power.

On November 24th we passed the night at Tokotschin. The evening before Marshal Victor, pursued by Count von Wittgenstein, had joined the Emperor here, and would now protect his retreat. The Marshal had only just arrived from Germany, and had still 5,000 fresh troops in good order, whilst ours were thoroughly disorganised.

A singular episode occurred on the afternoon of the 24th, which had opened so tragically. I will just mention it here to give an idea of the vicissitudes we went through in our terrible retreat. Like the rest of us, I suffered very much from hunger, and for several days I had had nothing to eat but a little biscuit, whilst my only beverage was an occasional draught of cold coffee, which, however, kept me going somehow. I was marching sadly along, pondering on our woes, when an officer whom I scarcely knew by sight ran up to me, and with a pleasant smile asked me to do him a favour. 'My position,' I answered laughing, 'is not such as to enable me to serve any one. But what do you want?' His reply was to hand me a parcel carefully done up in paper, and about the size of my two fists, which he begged me to accept. 'But tell me what is in it,' I said. 'I entreat you not to refuse it.' 'But at least say what it is,' I urged, trying to push it away with my right hand; but he closed my fingers over it and ran off. A good deal puzzled by suddenly receiving a present from a stranger, and quite at a loss to imagine his motive, I smelt the packet to begin with, and the result encouraged me to open it, when lo! and behold! a delicious odour of truffles greeted my nostrils, and I found myself the happy possessor of a quarter of a *pâté de foie gras* from Toulouse or Strasburg. I never saw the officer again, but I think my fervent expressions of gratitude must have found an echo in his heart. May he have escaped the fate which overtook so many of us, and from which his timely gift preserved me for a few days!

Another bit of good fortune marked this same day. As I have already said, I had lost all my furs and winter clothes, and in these deserted districts money was of no avail to buy new ones. I was feeling the want of them dreadfully, when I came across Colonel L. shut up in his carriage, and quite ill from the excessive precautions he was taking against the cold. 'What do you want with all those furs?' I asked him. 'You will be suffocated in them. Give me one.' To which he replied, 'Not for all the gold in the world!' 'Bah!' I cried, 'you will give me that bearskin, which really is in your way, and here are fifty gold napoleons for it.' 'Go to the devil! go to the devil with your napoleons! you bother me! – but there, General, I can't refuse you anything.' He took the napoleons, and I hastily seized the bearskin, for fear he should think better of it. I went off with my treasure with indescribable joy, but the unlucky owner of so many sables and other furs was frozen to death a few days later.

The first corps passed the night of the 24th at Toloczin, and at daybreak the next morning the Russian firing recommenced, and we were pursued during the whole day by them, their balls mowing down our ranks. It was throughout our disastrous retreat the custom of the enemy to harass us all day, and when night fell to withdraw to distant villages, where they had a good rest and plenty of food, neither of which we were able to obtain, returning the next morning stronger than ever to attack its again with fresh vigour, whilst we were ever growing fewer and weaker.

On the same day we went through Borv, and the first corps halted for the night at Kroupski. A newly formed brigade of light Polish cavalry had just arrived in this village, and were heating the ovens in the cottages. An inn with stabling for twenty horses was assigned to Marshal Davout. In putting the horses which had followed – for, as I have said, we all went on foot now – in the stable, we found three children in a manger, one about a year old, the other two apparently only just born. They were very poorly dressed, and were so numbed with the cold that they were not even crying. I made my men seek their parents for an hour, but they could not be found; all the inhabitants had fled, and the three poor little things were left to our tender mercies. I begged the Marshal's cook to give them a little broth if he succeeded in making any, and thought no more about them. Presently, however, the warmth of the horses' breath woke the little creatures up, and their plaintive cries resounded for a long time in the rooms in which we were all crowded together. Our desire to do something to help them kept us awake for a long time, but at last we were overcome with sleep. At two o'clock in the morning we were roused by the news that the village was on fire; the overheating of the ovens had led to flames breaking out nearly everywhere. Our house, standing somewhat apart, was the only one to escape, and our three children were still crying. At daybreak, however, when we were starting, I could hear them no longer, and I asked the cook what he had done for them. He had, of course, suffered as much as we had, and he answered, with the satisfied air of a man who has done a good action, 'Their crying so tore my heart that I could not close an eye. I had no food to give them, so I took a hatchet, broke the ice in the horse trough, and drowned them, to put them out of their misery!' Thus does misfortune harden the heart of man!

During the retreat many of the French were drowned. The wells in the village were all open and level with the ground, so that when troops arrived in the dark several men often fell into them, and rarely did any of their comrades try to save them. I saw more than ten wells, none of them very deep, on the surface of which the dead bodies of such victims were floating. Overcome with misery, other poor fellows committed suicide, and we often heard the discharge of a musket close by, telling of the end of some unfortunate wretch. On the other hand, some of the men who were simply covered with wounds kept up their courage and marched steadily on. One day, weary of walking, I sat down to rest on the trunk of a tree beside a fine young artilleryman who had just been wounded. Two doctors happened to pass us, and I called out to them to come and look at the wound. They did so, and at the first glance exclaimed, 'The arm must be amputated!' I asked the soldier if he felt he could bear it. 'Anything you like,' he answered stoutly. 'But,' said the doctors, 'there are only two of us to do it; so you, General, will be good enough to help us perform the operation.' Seeing that I was anything but pleased at the idea, they hastened to add that it would be enough if I just let the artilleryman lean against me. 'Sit back to back with him, and you will see nothing of the operation.' I agreed, and placed myself in the required position. I think the operation seemed longer to me than it did to the patient. The doctors opened their cases of instruments; the artilleryman did not even heave a single sigh. I heard the slight noise made by the saw as it cut through the bone, and in a few seconds, or rather minutes, they said to me, 'It is over! it is a pity we have not a little wine to give him, to help him to rally.' I happened still to have half a bottle of Malaga with me, which I was hoarding up, only taking a drop at a time, but I gave it to the poor man, who was very pale, though he said nothing. His eyes brightened up, and he swallowed all my wine at a single gulp. Then, on returning the empty bottle with the words, 'It is still a long way to Carcassonne,' he walked off with a firm step at a pace I found it difficult to emulate.

Marshal Oudinot, who had recovered from his wound, was now sent forward to Borisoff to try and take possession of the bridge over the Beresina, which had already been for several days in the hands of the Russian forces under Tchichakoff. This general had only just come from Moldavia, and on seeing the boldness with which Oudinot's troops advanced he took it for granted that the whole of the French army was approaching, and thinking his own position with the river behind him a very disadvantageous one, he wished to avoid a regular battle. He therefore only made sufficient defence to cover the retreat of his army, and retired beyond the Beresina. Marshal Oudinot attacked Borisoff with his usual vigour, and entering it took 500 or 600 prisoners and all the baggage belonging to the Russian army. Tchichakoff had, however, burnt the bridge over the Beresina after crossing it, so that this victory gained us nothing.

The Emperor, who had no means of forcing the passage of the Beresina with an army of some 40,000 Russians opposing him, endeavoured to find a favourable point for throwing bridges across, and at the same time evading Wittgenstein, whom Marshal Victor was with infinite difficulty holding at bay, and Kutusoff, who was pursuing us. He was told that there was a ford at the village of Studzianka, which he could reach by ascending the left bank of the river, but though the water was at the most four or five feet deep the approaches were very marshy and would be difficult for our carriages and artillery. The river, which was very muddy, was covered with ice, but it broke beneath those who tried to walk across it.

The difficulties on the other side, if we succeeded in reaching it, would be even greater, for heights commanding the banks were occupied by a Russian division, and the approach to these heights was a marshy tract without any firm road whatever. The road from Borisoff to Molodetschno by way of Zembino, the only one we could hope to reach, was a very narrow causeway, with many bridges raised to a good height above the marsh, much of which was quite under water. If any one of these little bridges should break, the march of the whole army would be arrested; but the Emperor had really no choice, and was compelled to resign himself to attempting the passage at Studzianka.

The engineers, pontonniers, and artillerymen therefore set to work at once, all the wood found in the village, even that of which the houses were built, being quickly converted into trestles, beams, planks, &c., and on the evening of the 26th, all appearing ready for the throwing across of the bridge, an attempt was made to place it in position. But the bed of the river was so muddy that the supports sank too deeply in it. It was, moreover, wider than had been supposed, and all the work had to be done over again. Two bridges instead of one were now made, and the army began its march for Studzianka. On the 27th the first corps, now forming the rear guard, passed through Borisoff, and arrived at night at the ford chosen, where there was already a terrible block of carriages, those belonging to the corps of Marshal Oudinot and Marshal Victor, who had but recently rejoined us, being added to the others which had escaped from previous accidents, and whose owners had evaded the orders for burning them.

When we arrived at Studzianka about nine o'clock in the evening, the Emperor had already sent over in small rafts several hundred skirmishers to protect the bridges and those making them, whilst the corps of Marshals Ney and Oudinot with 500 or 600 cuirassiers of the Guard had crossed the river and taken up a position on the right in a wood beyond Studzianka. We passed the night in trying to bring something like order into our arrangements for crossing, sending the ammunition wagons first, and repairing the bridges where they had given way under the weight of the artillery. It was a very dark night, and many French, Dutch, Spanish, and Saxon soldiers fell into the wells of the village and were drowned. Their cries of distress reached us, but we had no ropes or ladders with which to rescue them, and they were left to their fate.

At daybreak the crossing of the river by the bridges went on without too much confusion, and I was able to go backwards and forwards several times, seeing to the safety of all that was of the greatest importance for the army; but at about eight o'clock in the morning, when the light revealed the immense crowds which had still to be got over, every one began to hasten to the bridges at once, and everything was soon thrown into the greatest disorder. Things became even worse when an hour later a combined attack was made on us by all the Russian forces, and we found ourselves between two fires. Truly our misfortunes had now reached their height.

Marshal Victor, who had taken up a position on the heights above Studzianka, was trying to beat off Wittgenstein, who had attacked him about ten o'clock with a large force of artillery, and although he had but very few troops with him, he managed to keep the Russians at a distance, but their balls, falling amongst the masses of carriages blocking the approaches to the bridges, flung their occupants and drivers into the most indescribable disorder, killing many and smashing up the vehicles. Some balls even rolled on to the bridges.

On the right bank meanwhile Tchichakoff was attacking the French all along the line with some 25,000 or 30,000 Russians, whilst Marshals Ney and Oudinot had to oppose them only 9,000 or 10,000 men, with what was left of the Imperial Guard behind them as a reserve. Their front was but half a league in length, and the ground was very much broken up by woods. The Russians came to the fight well fed and warmed up by plenty of brandy; the French were debilitated by privations, and had moreover a cutting wind driving the snow in their faces. But with the enemy before them, they seemed to regain all their old energy, and Tchichakoff tried in vain to break their ranks, though he flung upon them in succession all the forces under his command. Marshal Oudinot, always in the front amongst the skirmishers, was wounded at the beginning of the action, and Marshal Ney took the command. Seizing a favourable moment he ordered General Doumerc, who had just brought up some 500 cuirassiers, to make a charge. This threw a Russian column into disorder, and won the French 1,500 prisoners. It was during this brilliant charge that a young officer, whom I loved for his many engaging qualities, met his death. Alfred de Noailles, only son of the Duc de Noailles, was struck in the heart by a ball, and his face and body were so disfigured by being trampled beneath the feet of the horses, that he was only recognised by his height and by the mark on his fine white linen.

It was a melancholy consolation to his mourning widow and family to find his portrait in my album, in which I had collected likenesses of many young officers whom I numbered amongst my friends, and all of whom had been cut off in the flower of their age, before they had had time to fulfil the lofty destiny to which their noble names and exalted courage would have called them.

Towards three o'clock in the afternoon, when it was already beginning to get dark, for night falls very early in the winter in these latitudes, Tchichakoff drew back, and we soon saw the fires of his bivouac, marking the position he had taken up about a league away from us.

Whilst all this was going on, the most awful scenes were being enacted at the entrance to the bridges on the right bank of the Beresina, and we could do absolutely nothing to prevent them. Wittgenstein's artillery poured shells upon the struggling crowds, beneath whose weight the bridges were bending till they were under water. Those who could swim flung themselves into the river, trusting to their skill to save them, but they were overcome by the cold, and hardly any reached the further bank. On either side the hapless fugitives pressed on, driving others into the water, many clutching at the ropes of the bridges in the hope of being able to climb on to them. In the awful struggle none who fell ever rose again, for every one was immediately crushed to death by those behind, whilst all the while shells and balls rained upon the helpless masses. I was blessing God that my sister had escaped this terrible catastrophe, and had crossed some time before, when, to my horror, I saw M. Levasseurr carrying her in his arms and endeavouring to make his way up to me. He had managed to extricate her from the crowd, and now brought her to me. 'In what an awful moment do we meet again!' I exclaimed; 'and what in the world can I do with you in your exhausted condition, now that you have found me? But courage,' I added. 'I got General Vasserot safely over in his carriage; I will find him, and put you under his care.' This I managed to do, and two hours later my sister was kindly received by the General, to whom she said, 'Oh, General, you have saved me; now I will take care of you.'

The Beresina disaster was the Pultava with which the Russians had threatened us; it was not our only defeat or the last, but it was by far the most bloody of any which befell us. It involved the loss of the greater part of Marshal Victor's corps, which perished in defending our passage; and the loss of the whole of the Partouneaux division, which had to surrender. In a word, it cost the French and their allies some 20,000 or 30,000 men, killed, wounded, drowned, or taken prisoners. General Eblé, charged with the painful duty of burning the bridges after Marshal Victor's corps had passed over, had the greatest difficulty in cutting his way to them, and many of our own people were piteously struck down by the hatchets of his men before they were able to perform the task assigned to them. When at last the flames arose and the last hope of safety was cut off from those left on the other side, terrible were the cries of anguish which rent the air as thousands of poor wretches flung themselves into the water in a last despairing effort to escape. The ice broke beneath them; all was over, and the Cossacks swept down on the quarry, finding an immense amount of booty

On the evening of this terrible November 28th we halted at Zembino, a little town which had already been pillaged by our predecessors. Marshal Davout and I took up our quarters in a little house crowded with others, which was heated by a stove. By dint of very close packing we managed to be able to lie down on the ground, and most of us slept profoundly till the time came to start again, which was before daybreak. I had been roused a few minutes before the clock struck the hour for departure by hearing stifled sobs, and by the dying light of a lamp I now made out the form of a tall and beautiful woman leaning against the stove, her face hidden by her hands, whilst the tears trickled through her fingers. It was a long time since I had seen any human creatures who had not lost all pretensions to good looks through their privations, and I was struck by the graceful attitude of this weeping figure, with the masses of light hair shading her ideal features. She reminded me of Canova's *Muse leaning on a Sepulchral Urn, and lost in Meditation.* Whilst every one, wrapped in selfish egotism, left the room without taking any notice of the lady in distress, I approached her and asked her in a gentle voice what she was weeping about. She turned to me, revealing her beautiful face, wet with tears, and pointing to a pretty child asleep at her feet, she said, 'I am the wife of M. Lavaux, a Frenchman, who had a library at Moscow. The Governor Rostopschin has sent him to Siberia, and I took refuge with my boy in the French army. The Duc de Plaisance and two other generals let us share their carriages till they were destroyed, and I have carried my child from the Beresina here, but my strength is exhausted. I can go no further, and I am in despair.' 'Could you keep your seat on horseback?' I asked at once. 'I could try,' she replied. 'Well, do not lose courage; let us make haste. I will take your boy and place him on my sister's knee; she is in General Vasserot's carriage, and I will put you on a horse which a faithful servant shall lead. You will thus be able to follow your boy.'

A smile of hope lit up her expressive features. I fetched a wolf's skin, which was on the horse I meant to give her, and wrapped it about her to protect her from the intense cold which had now set in, took off several silk handkerchiefs I had about me, and tied them together to make sashes to fasten her on to her steed. I then placed her on her horse, put her under the care of one of my mounted servants, and they started together. I never saw lady, servant, or horses again; but Vasserot and my sister took care of the child, and gave him back to his mother, who came to claim him in the evening. I shall refer again to what I was able to learn of the adventurous career of this lady, who two years later was found by the Emperor Alexander I. teaching the Demoiselles of the Légion d'Honneur at St. Denis.

Beyond Zembino we had to cross a number of little bridges which the enemy had neglected to burn, and we felt that God had not entirely deserted us when He left us this means of getting over the marshes. We had not a scrap of food to give the 2,000 or 1,000 prisoners we were taking with us, and I purposely shut my eyes when they availed themselves of every chance of escape in the woods through which we passed. I could not bring myself to enforce their remaining with us by the cruel measures which alone could have availed, and I knew well enough that at any moment our fate might be worse than theirs.

Sunday, the 29th, was occupied by a dreary march to Kamen, which we reached about midnight. Our men, as tired out as ourselves, and longing for sleep, took a few bits of meat from the one wagon we still retained, in which tobacco and everything else were mixed together helter-skelter. They did not notice in the darkness that some tobacco was sticking to the meat, and put it all into the pot on the fire together. At four o'clock in the morning, just before we started, the soup was given out, but it tasted most horribly of tobacco, and nobody but myself would take any of it. I was so hungry that I was not so prudent as the others, and I swallowed the whole of my portion. I had not marched far before a terrible headache came on; I felt sick, and soon began to vomit. I fainted away, and it was easy to see that I was poisoned. The news spread; even the Emperor heard of it, and in his despatches for Paris of that day he mentioned the matter, so that every one there thought I was dead. When we halted during the day, General Haxo and others, who had still a little humanity left, made me some tea, and drinking it saved my life. I remained with Marshal Davout in his *wurst*, and we arrived at Kotovitchi in the evening, where we put up at the house of the priest, a good old man, who spoke French very well, and who had declined to leave with the rest of the inhabitants because, though he had nothing with which to supply our bodily needs, he hoped to be able to minister to our spiritual necessities. Under his affectionate care I completely recovered, and when we set off again at four o'clock the next morning we were full of real gratitude to him.

During the whole of December 1st we were marching through dense forests, in which at every turn we came to difficult passes. We lost nearly all our prisoners here.

On December 2nd we crossed the Ilia before daybreak, and entered yet other vast forests with no well-defined roads, and the snow added to the difficulties of our march, so that it was late before we got to Molodetschno. Whilst arranging for the camping of our troops in the dark, I fell into a swamp, and was only with great difficulty extricated. The cold was so intense that the mud froze about me immediately, so that it was hard work to get me out. On the very same day and at the same hour seven years before I had been seated on the snow beneath a tree, but it was after the battle of Austerlitz, and I was in a very happy frame of mind. The Emperor arrived at Molodetschno the same day, but instead of celebrating the anniversary of the greatest victory of his life, he had to dictate that terrible twenty-ninth bulletin describing succinctly the disasters his army had met with, though he disguised their true extent.

At four o'clock on the morning of the 3rd we started once more, without daring to count those who were unable to rise. Our route was strewn with the dead, and the wheels of the carriages, which were scarcely able to turn, went over the ice-covered corpses, often dragging them along for a little distance.

Haxo and I walked arm in arm, so as to save each other from

197

slipping, and a soldier and an officer were walking one on either side of us. Presently the soldier drew a hunk of black Russian bread about the size of a fist out of his pocket, and began to gnaw at it greedily. The officer, surprised to see such a thing as bread, offered the grenadier a five-franc piece for it. 'No, no!' said the man, tearing at his bread like a lion jealous of his prey. 'Oh, do sell it to me,' pleaded the officer; 'here are ten francs.' 'No, no, no, no!' and the bread rapidly disappeared, till quite half was gone. 'I am dying! I entreat you to save my life! Here are twenty francs!' Then with a savage look the grenadier bit off one more big mouthful, and, handing what was left to the officer, took the twenty francs, evidently feeling that he had made anything but a good bargain.

We were all covered with ice. Our breath, looking like thick smoke, froze as it left our mouths, and hung in icicles from our hair, eyebrows, moustaches, and beards, sometimes quite blinding us. Once Haxo, in breaking off the icicles which were bothering me, noticed that my cheeks and nose were discoloured. They looked like wax, and he informed me that they were frozen. He was right, for all sensation was gone from them. He at once began to rub them hard with snow, and a couple of minutes' friction restored circulation, but the pain was terrible, and it needed all my resolution not to resist having the rubbing continued. Colonel Emi, of the engineers, was frozen in exactly the same way a few minutes later, and in his despair he flung himself down and rolled about on the ground. We did not want to abandon him to his fate, but we had to strike him again and again before we could make him get up. Dysentery also worked terrible ravages amongst us, and its victims, with their dry and livid skin and emaciated limbs, looked like living skeletons. The poor creatures had had nothing to eat but a little crushed corn made into a kind of mash, for they had no means of grinding or of cooking it properly, and this indigestible food passed through the intestines without nourishing the body. Truly the unhappy wretches, many of them stark naked, presented, as they fell out by the way, a picture of death in its most revolting aspect.

Providence, however, had still a few moments in reserve for some of us, in which we found consolation for our woes, and gathered up fresh strength for the further trials awaiting us.

This was the case on December 4, as I will now relate. We had started before daybreak to escape a cannonade from some Cossacks, and we were already some distance from our bivouac when a second troop of Cossacks, bolder and more numerous than the first, flung itself across our path, and carried off two carriages belonging to the Commissary-General. Fortunately he was on foot, and managed to escape. A few miles beyond our party the same horde of Tartars drew up at the entrance to a ravine through which a body of some 300 or 400 Polish cavalry was endeavouring to pass so as to rejoin us. The Cossacks seemed likely to completely crush the Poles, when the noise of the firing attracted our attention, and we realised the danger of the brave fellows. General Gérard, with his usual chivalry, at once offered his services to Marshal Davout, and asked for volunteers to go to the aid of our allies. Though his men were worn out with fatigue, they were still full of confidence in him, and they one and all shouted, 'I am ready! I am ready!' General Gérard dashed across the plain at their head, and when the Cossacks saw the little body of infantry approaching, they feared they were about to be caught between two fires and galloped off. The Poles thus rescued soon joined us, and a bit of really good fortune rewarded us all for our mutual help.

Some carriages belonging to a convoy from Germany had succeeded in reaching Markovo, a little village we were just about to enter. These carriages were packed full of fresh provisions of many different kinds, and the delight of our brave soldiers may be imagined when they found awaiting them a good meal of bread and cheese and butter, with plenty of wine to wash them down. What a feast it seemed after forty days of such scanty and miserable diet as theirs had been! We of the first corps shared in this rare good fortune.

General Guilleminot with his division had been the first to arrive at Markovo, and he had taken care that the precious carriages should not be pillaged. He was at the window of a little *château* when we were passing, and he called to us to join him. After having taken the necessary precaution of rubbing our faces with snow, but for which we should certainly have lost some of our features, we went into a warm room, where a very unexpected sight awaited us. Tea services of beautiful china were set out on handsome mahogany tables, whilst here and there were great piles of white bread and hampers of Brittany butter. At the sight of this wonderful spread, after our many weeks of privations, our eyes brightened and our nostrils became expanded like those of some Arab steed at the sound of the trumpet. Needless to say how eagerly and gladly we accepted the invitation to share in this delightful breakfast. We each did the part not of four, but of ten – our appetites were simply insatiable. Never did any breakfast party do greater justice to the fare provided than we did to the great bowls of tea poured out, and the thick slices of bread and butter cut for its by our host. It was hard work to tear ourselves away from this warm room with all its comforts to go and camp beneath the cold light of the stars near Smorgoni, where there were twenty-five degrees of frost.

The name of Smorgoni roused our curiosity, for we knew that the inhabitants of that village, situated as it was in the Heart of a vast forest, devoted themselves to the chase of bears, selling the furs of the older animals, and training the young ones as gymnastic performers, often taking them the round of Europe to show off their tricks. The people of Smorgoni had not expected us, and took flight at our approach, carrying their furs and young bears with them, but for all that we expected to find the village interesting.

It was at Smorgoni on December 5th that the Emperor, yielding to the earnest entreaties of his most faithful servants, decided to leave the army and return to France, where his presence was most urgently needed. Before leaving, he signed the order for the promotion and reward of many officers and generals, which had been drawn up by Major-General Prince Berthier. He called his marshals together, frankly expressed to them his great regret at having lingered too long at Moscow, and announced to them his approaching departure, appointing King Murat of Naples to the command of the army.

It was eleven o'clock at night, and there were twenty-five degrees of frost when the Emperor left Smorgoni, accompanied by the Dukes of Vicenza and Friuli (Marshal Duroc) and the Count of Lobau (Marshal Mouton), and made his way to Osmiana, miraculously escaping from the 1,200 Cossacks whom he had to pass, and who would certainly have taken him prisoner if they had known he was so near them with an escort of scarcely 100 men. A little before dark these same Cossacks had been beaten by General Loison, and driven out of Osmiana, where they had hoped to arrest our retreat. Whilst waiting for daylight the enemy were sleeping a little distance from the road, and the Emperor passed them unnoticed. Napoleon's departure threw the whole army into the greatest discouragement.

General Charpentier still declined to take my place, and I was compelled as before to perform the duties of Chief of the Staff. Fortunately, Marshal Davout now seemed to understand my position better, and was no longer so exacting. This made me willing to remain with him a few days longer.

On December 6th we passed through the little village of Pletchinzy just as a very interesting scene was taking place in it. Marshal Oudinot and General Pino, both wounded, had passed the night there with twenty-five or thirty officers and men belonging to their suite. A Cossack officer had heard of their presence, and thinking to take a great prize, he with some 200 men had surrounded the house in which they were. Speaking in good French, he politely summoned them to surrender. 'We never surrender,' was the reply, and a few well-aimed shots struck down some of the Cossacks. The hovel, for it was little more, was now regularly besieged, the French firing at close quarters into the ranks of the assailants, which they thinned considerably. Marshal Oudinot himself, though suffering greatly from a ball in the loins and unable to rise from the pallet on which he lay, made some holes in the walls between the planks, and firing through them picked off a good many Cossacks, for he never once missed his aim. Meanwhile, however, the enemy received reinforcements, and a gun was brought up to their aid. Four balls had already made a breach in the hut, but no one had been hurt. The French, after the manner of the Spanish, at once turned the opening to account by firing through it at their besiegers. A fifth ball broke the pallet on which the Marshal lay, and at the same time brought down the side of an oven in which five or six little children belonging to the peasant who had owned the hut, were discovered huddled together. The poor little things rushed out into the smoke and confusion in a great state of terror, much to the surprise of our men. There was something very touching in the way the little creatures clung to each other in the midst of the struggle. Fortunately our party came up just when things were going hardly with the besieged, for we had quickened our pace when we heard the firing, and the Cossacks, who had lost some fifty men killed and wounded, took to flight at our approach. We escorted the Marshal to Osmiana, where we halted for the night.

Here we found a division, consisting of some 12,000 fine young recruits, who had just arrived from France as reserves, under General Loison. Alas! twenty-four hours of our temperature was enough to kill off half of them, for they were in summer clothing, and not yet acclimatised; and three days later, when we reached Wilna, not one survived of the poor fellows whose weeping mothers had watched them start so short a time ago. I have been told since by several Russians that if the wind had blown from the north with the temperature at from 25 to 30 degrees, not one of us would have escaped alive. When the murderous north wind is blowing, the Russians generally remain in doors all day and night in rooms heated by stoves, and if they ever do venture forth it is only after a good meal, cased in woollen garments and thick furs, with which in our inexperience few of us had provided ourselves. The French died off, but the Cossacks fared splendidly.

The nearer we got to Wilna the more intense was the cold, especially at night, and every morning those still capable of bearing arms became fewer and fewer. The first corps now numbered scarcely 300 men, and the colonels and generals had to carry the colours of their regiments themselves. The enemy continued to cannonade us without venturing to come to close quarters. At last on December 8th we arrived on the heights of Wilna, where the little remnant of General Loison's corps perished of cold whilst a brisk cannonade from the Russians was going on. The approach to Wilna by the Minsk gate was so blocked with carriages piled up on each other and inextricably locked together, that I gave up trying to get in that way, but made my entrance through a garden by means of two ladders conveniently placed one on each side of a wall.

The first object I noticed in the street I entered, which was also much encumbered by broken vehicles, was the overturned carriage of the paymaster of the army; the cash boxes had been broken open, and most of the contents stolen, but some 200,000 to 300,000 francs were scattered about on the ground for the first comer to pick up. The frozen metal, however, blistered the fingers of those who tried to carry it off, and the emaciated passers-by, scarcely able to drag themselves along, had not the courage to stoop or to burden themselves with heavy money.

What was my surprise at meeting in this street Colonel Kobilinski, who, as related above, had had his thigh smashed at Malo-Jaroslavitz and had fallen against me! He had been found by some soldiers, who carried him on their shoulders to a hospital. He slipped from their hold some twenty times in his insensibility, but, when his wound had been dressed for the first time, four Jews carried him to the house of a nobleman of Wilna, where he was kindly received. He had suffered greatly for no less than fifty days from cold, hunger, and dysentery, yet his iron constitution brought him safely through all, and he is now in the service of Russia as governor of a fortress.

As I hurried about the town trying to make arrangements for my return to France, I came upon General Vasserot's carriage, which had safely arrived the evening before with its owner and my sister in it. They had escaped all the dangers of the road, and were just about to start for Danzig, where they were to wait for me. They had still perhaps the most difficult and dangerous part of the journey to perform, for between

Wilna and Kovno were two very steep hills, now completely covered with ice. Always almost impassable, the presence of the enemy now added greatly to the difficulties of this part of the route, and here was left behind the last remnant of our war material. General Vasserot, however, who was a soldier to the backbone, managed to get safely over every obstacle, and was amongst the very few who did so.

I went back by way of my two ladders to tell Marshal Davout, Generals Haxo and Gérard, of this way of getting into the town, as they would probably not have discovered it for themselves. On my way to them I found a young artillery officer, who had had his arm amputated, exactly where I had left him some hours before. I had told him then that he had better follow me, as I could lend him a hand in climbing over impediments. He had thanked me, but said he had promised to wait at the entrance to the suburb for his servant. I said no more then, but when I came upon him again I represented to him the risk of remaining stationary in such murderous cold. 'I know all about that,' was his reply; 'but my faithful soldier George is my foster brother, and he has given me a thousand proofs of his devotion ever since I joined the army. My own mother could not have taken better care of me since I was wounded. He is ill and suffering, and I would rather die than break my word to him.' Touched by this devotion at a time when hardly any one had a thought but for his own preservation, I did not dare to suggest to him that his beloved foster brother might be dead of cold, or a prisoner in the hands of the Russians. I merely asked him his name, his age, and his country. 'My name is Arthur de Birassaye, I am twenty-two years old, and I come from Bayonne,' was the reply. I never saw the officer again, but when I was in Bayonne some years later, I made inquiries about him, and learnt that he had never returned thither.

The people of Wilna, who during our absence had received immense convoys of stores and provisions, which were collected in magazines, received us kindly, and were full of hospitality and pity for our sufferings; but gradually, as fresh crowds of starving, debilitated wretches arrived, and it became impossible to maintain order in the distribution of food, pillage set in, all discipline was at an end, and scarcely anybody profited by the supplies. Fortunately, however, when the town itself was about to be pillaged, a strong force of police was organised, and the destruction was arrested. Meanwhile Major-General Prince Berthier, the Duke of Bassano, and Count Daru, Commissary-General, did their best to restore order in the ranks of the army, but they could achieve little. King Murat recognised that the task the Emperor had left him was beyond his powers, and his efforts were restricted to escaping being taken alive by the Cossacks, whom he had so often defied and so many of whom he had cut down, or from falling into the hands of the dreaded Tchichakoff, of whom we all stood in great awe, though so far he had not done us very much harm.

The Emperor had left orders for us to hold Wilna, and General von Wrede, with the few troops remaining to him, had joined us there with a view to supporting us. He fought valiantly all day long under a ceaseless cannonade from the enemy, but it was hopeless to attempt to stop the movement of retreat now, and all idea of making a stand at Wilna was soon abandoned. King Murat was himself the first to leave for Kovno with the remainder of the Guard, for he was eager to place the Niemen between himself and the enemy, but that river was frozen hard, and could no longer be said to divide the districts on either side of its course.

I now held no post in the army, and had taken leave of Marshal Davout, so that I was free to get back to France as best I could. I bought a sledge, and as the Polish General Kovitzki offered to act as my guide and interpreter, we left Wilna together at three o'clock on the morning of December 10. We crossed the ice covering the Wilia, and took the least frequented route on the right bank of that river for Kovno. The next morning at Assanovo we met Prince Radzivil, said to be the richest nobleman in Poland. Several of his ancestors had been chosen to wear the crown, so long hereditary in the Jagellon family. The Prince joined us and was good enough to let us have some of the horses he had ordered for himself at every posting house, so that we reached Kovno at the same time as Marshal Davout, who had taken the shorter route.

The weather was very bad, and snow was falling so heavily on the day of our arrival that we could hardly see ten paces before us. Half of Kovno was on fire, whilst the other half had been given up to pillage, and the wagons containing the Imperial treasure had only with great difficulty been saved.

The King of Naples was preparing to leave, having heard that the Prince von Schwarzenberg, who had already withdrawn to Bialistock, was continuing his retreat towards Warsaw. Marshal Macdonald meanwhile, abandoned by the Prussian corps under General York, was retiring on Memel. Nothing could have exceeded the melancholy appearance presented by Kovno, with snow falling so thickly as to darken the air, and scarcely any light but that from the flames consuming the town. It was, indeed a gloomy augury for the future. The little remnant which had returned to Kovno represented to me the army whose fortunes I had shared so long; and when I turned my back on it, it was with feelings such as those of some brother abandoning the dead bodies of those belonging to him in a home smitten by the plague.

As I cautiously made my way across the bridge in my sledge, I could not keep back the tears at the thought of the contrast between the scene I gazed on now, on this melancholy 12th of December, and that I had so proudly looked down upon on June 24th. True, the storm which had broken upon us then might have warned us of what was in store for us. It had really been, though we did not realise it, premonitory of the disasters awaiting us, from which none but the strongest escaped, and I thanked God for having brought me safely through them all. I now took the shortest route to Königsberg, and was soon out of hearing of the cannonade from the Cossacks, and the yet more melancholy reports, so long of daily occurrence, of the blowing up of our ammunition wagons to save them from falling into the hands of the enemy. I did not stop at Königsberg, but pushed on for Danzig, where I arrived on December 10. My sister and General Vasserot joined me there the next day. The General still needed rest for his complete recovery from his wound, and we too were worn out, so we stopped quietly at Danzig for ten days, which we spent in providing ourselves with new clothes. As soon as I arrived I burnt the clothes I had travelled in, for they literally swarmed with vermin, and for the first time for two months and a half I enjoyed the luxury of a bath and a shave, for during our retreat I had never been able to give the slightest attention to my toilette, and my face was literally blackened with smoke and exposure. I now resumed my usual habits, and my spirits rose greatly.

On December 30th my sister and I took leave of our good friend General Vasserot, and we left Danzig together in my sledge. A tremendous storm overtook us by the way, and our vehicle was several times overturned. Each time we fell, we left the impression of our faces in the snow. If only that snow had been clay or some other enduring material, those impressions would have been preserved as curiosities by the people of the district, which is rich in fossils, many being embedded in the stones of which the houses are built. These small accidents, which were rather comic than tragic, only made us laugh, and restored to us the gaiety to which we had so long been strangers. The storm had melted the snow, and the sledge was no longer of any use, so we had to stop at Neustadt to buy a carriage. I got one of the little *chars à bancs* in Germany which are as light as they are pretty, and on the third day, the snow having disappeared, we were able to resume our route.

Nothing happened during the journey of 400 leagues between Danzig and Prussia of much importance to be related here; but one rather amusing episode is, perhaps, worth recording. I was sent at Labehn to the house of the Countess of Koëstoritz, who with her numerous family received us very kindly, and asked us to join them at the dinner just about to be served. During the meal she remarked that she was surprised to see us eat so little, adding that a General had been stopping in her house for three days who, though very ill, consumed such a quantity of food she could hardly keep pace with his needs. He was, moreover, particular in his choice of diet. 'What is his name?' I inquired. 'His people told me, but I have forgotten it,' was the reply. 'He is so ill that he was carried from his carriage to his room.'

After dinner was over, I went to ask the General's servants what his name was, and they replied haughtily, 'He is Count Baraguey d'Hilliers, General of Division.' 'I know him well; I should like to see him.' 'He is very ill; he receives no one.' I made a few further inquiries, but the replies were evasive, and suspecting mischief, I said I must see him. It was no good, the servants persisted in their refusal to let me in; so, feeling more sure than ever that something was wrong, I broke open the door, and passing through an antechamber found myself in a big, well-lighted room, in which was a table, where five or six people had evidently just dined. On four chairs behind the table lay what looked like a corpse wrapped up in its shroud. I asked angrily for the General, and was at once surrounded by a number of servants in his livery, who whispered an eager request that I would not denounce them. 'What do you mean?' I cried; and they answered in low voices, 'We were ordered to take the General's body back to France, and we have suffered so dreadfully from hunger all though the campaign, we thought we would pretend that the General was still alive, so as to get a good meal every day as if for him, and thus regain a little strength ourselves. Have pity on us, and do not betray us.' At first I did not like to promise, but they persuaded me, and I was so sorry for them that I said I would say nothing if they promised to leave before daybreak the next morning. I did not examine the corpse to identify it, but the carriage and liveries were certainly those of General Baraguey d'Hilliers. When I went back to the drawing room, I was rather embarrassed as to what I should say, but the Countess said with a smile, 'I suppose it really is his servants who eat all the food they ask for the General, if he himself is so ill?' I told her she was right, adding that they would leave very early the next day. This news evidently gave her the greatest pleasure. My sister and I took leave the same evening, as we, too, meant to start before daybreak. My light carriage amused the postilions very much wherever we stopped to change horses, and they all said as we started, 'You will never get to the next post;' to which I replied, 'We'll hold on as long as the carriage lasts.' The mischievous fellows would then try to keep the horses at a gallop so as to break my vehicle if they could; but all their efforts only cost me a little string to strengthen my wheels, and, thanks to their malice, I got to Paris two days sooner than I had hoped.

At St. Denis, near the gates of Paris, my sister left me to go to some old friends, and I gave my carriage to their children, whilst I took a cab for myself, and drove home, glad enough to have got back safe and sound. I tried to sleep, but was haunted by a long nightmare, in which one confused scene of the campaign succeeded another, whilst the noise of the cannonade still sounded in my ears, and the face of Tchichakoff as I imagined it – anything but a flattering likeness probably – continually stood out vividly from all others, even as the memory of the torments of hunger exceeded that of the various sufferings which disturbed my rest.

But after all I was in Paris at last! I hastened to let my friends know of my return, and was everywhere eagerly welcomed. I should soon have forgotten my woes, petted and made much of as I was in their society, but that they, of course, made me tell them all my adventures.

CHAPTER 8

The End of an Epoch

The Emperor had arrived at Paris on December 18th, 1812, whilst I did not get there till February 5th, 1813. The Emperor had every reason to dread the arrival in Paris of the witnesses of our disasters in Russia, for he knew that the relation of the sad details of our retreat would damp the ardour of those whom he relied on to aid him in raising fresh levies to be led against the enemy. I understood well enough the false position in which my return without leave had placed me, and I modestly kept aloof from court society, in spite of the many invitations I received, seeing no one but my father and my most intimate friends, whilst I tried to regain my health, and get my affairs into order. Still I felt that my case was an exceptional one, for I did not know another Frenchman who had in so short a time gone through such an immense number of perilous vicissitudes. When, therefore, I felt that the state of my finances would permit me to take the field once more, I wrote to the Duke of Feltre, Minister of War, in the following terms:

Paris, February 17th, 1813.

My Lord—The Emperor's goodness conferred on me, against my own desire, the honour of being chief of the staff to Marshal Davout, Prince of Eckmühl. I begged again and again to be replaced, and at Smolensk the Emperor gave his consent, naming General Charpentier as my successor, but he would not take up his post, and I continued to perform the duties without the pay of Chief of the Staff.

His Majesty is not ignorant of the dangers to which I have been exposed during the last eighteen months. In Spain my horse was killed under me, having been struck by more than thirty balls, whilst I was taken prisoner stripped naked, and, without exaggeration, all but shot, all but hanged, and finally taken to England, whence I escaped miraculously from the hands of smugglers, who had intended to murder me, so that I was able to join the Russian campaign, in which I endured the torments of famine, was poisoned and frozen, and, for the second time in less than twenty months, completely ruined by the loss of all my baggage and horses.

Finding myself without employment in the Grand Army, I left the Prince of Eckmühl at Kovno, and returned to Paris to collect the means for rejoining the army. I have achieved what I came for, and now have the honour of placing myself at the disposal of your Excellency, ready to continue to serve the Emperor and France with the same zeal as I have already done for twenty-five years. I have the honour to be, &c.'

The Duke of Feltre submitted my letter to the Emperor, but his Majesty was not in the least touched by the exceptional position in which I was placed. He merely observed, 'He owns his fault; he shall pay for the others;' and when on February 19 I presented myself to pay my respects to the Duke, I was told he could not receive me. Returning home, I found the letter he had just written to me, which contained the very unexpected words: 'General, the Emperor orders you to give yourself up as a prisoner at the Abbaye.' There could be no reply to so gracious an order! and the same day my good friend Colonel Bontemps went to see me placed under lock and key in a room where many men of much higher military rank than myself had been confined. My faithful friend even remained with me for the sixteen days my captivity lasted. Many ladies also called to see me, but I was very much mortified at the position in which I had been placed, and declined to allow any of them to stoop to enter my prison. In denying myself the pleasure of seeing them, I hoped to deprive the Emperor of some of the éclat he evidently hoped to gain by shutting me up, for if I had admitted them behind my bars, I should have been much talked of, many carriages would have driven up to the entrance to the Abbaye, and my name would have been in all the papers, which was just what I wanted to avoid.

On the sixteenth day I received orders to join the army in Germany. I at once bought a good travelling carriage, and on March 11th I quitted Paris once more. By the evening of the 19th I was at a little place called Hombourg, beyond Metz, where my cramped quarters contrasted greatly with those I was in on the same day the year before in a Moorish palace of Cordova, Andalusia, which was decorated in a fairylike manner in honour of the birthday of King Joseph.

I arrived at Mayence on March 21st, and there I found General Compans, whom I had not seen since we parted at Krasnoe. He was just the same as ever, as calm and smiling as he had been on the battle field. His costume alone was different. The thick furs needed as a protection against the bitter cold of the Russian winter were discarded, he no longer carried his arm in a sling, and his happy expression was not now the result of self-control in the midst of dangers, but the outcome of genuine content-ment, for his pretty young wife had come to join him with her parents M. and Mme. Lecoq, who were old friends of mine. They all pressed me to stay as long as I could with them, and when I left them it was only to go to Frankfort, where I was received by Marshal Mortier with equally touching proofs of his faithful friendship for me, which dated from the beginning of the campaign on the Rhine.

Napoleon had but quite recently raised Von Wrede to the rank of a Marshal of the Empire, and made him a Prince of Bavaria, his native land, which had just been converted into an independent kingdom. The defection of that General with his troops had made a great gap in our ranks, and Von Wrede hoped by turning against us his 20,000 Bavarians to cut off our retreat to France. Providence, however, did not permit him to succeed.

But we must not anticipate by referring in advance to the

events which were now rapidly to succeed each other. It will not do to speak too soon of the brilliant battle of Hanau, when the united Bavarian and Austrian troops under Von Wrede were defeated by our brave fellows, who, few though they were, surpassed themselves, and not only kept open the way back to their country, which Von Wrede endeavoured to close to them, but put to the blush their old comrades in arms, who must indeed have felt ashamed of having deserted the ranks of the noble allies with whom they had been for so long on such cordial terms.

My one desire now was to find out where I could get the horses and harness I needed for a new campaign, and I was hunting about, when I saw some one I thought I knew advancing towards me on a very fine steed. It was Captain de Vaux, and, roused to envy at seeing him so well mounted, I accosted him with the words, 'You are lucky to have been able to get such a good horse.' He drew rein for me to see its points. It was a young iron-grey animal, with a long white waving silky mane, falling over a swanlike neck, as glossy as satin. The thick hair partly hid the brilliant dark eyes and the wide-open nostrils, the edges of which were of a deep red colour. Whilst De Vaux was chatting to me about his travels, and showing off his horse, the beautiful creature was champing the bit, flecking us with foam, and raising clouds of dust as it fretted against the delay. The Captain told me, to my relief, that he had just bought his steed from the Prince of Sondershausen, whose palace was about four leagues off, adding, 'In his stables you will find 200 horses reared on his estates, and he will sell you as many as you like.' This news, of course, delighted me, and I ordered my postilion to take me to Sondershausen as quickly as possible. We soon reached it, and found it to be a pretty little town almost surrounded by woods.

I knew that I must go first to the Grand Equerry, a certain wealthy Jew, named Von Schleidnitz, whose house and office were on the chief square opposite the Palace. Having first inquired who I was, he received me with the most courtly politeness, and as soon as he knew the object of my visit, he said, 'I will go and ascertain the wishes of his Highness, who is now hunting about two miles off.' He had his horse saddled at once, and an hour later he came to the hotel at which I had put up, with a favourable reply. The Prince had given orders that the court stables should be shown to me by the equerries in gala attire, and the contents of those stables placed at my disposal. He added a gracious invitation to me to come to the Palace that evening to see the grand opera of *Tamerlane*, with music by Winter. A palace! Court stables! Equerries in gala attire! The grand opera of *Tamerlane* in the midst of the forest! This must be a Versailles in miniature. I felt as if I had fallen from the clouds, and arranged to go to the stables to see the wonderful horses at the time named by the Grand Equerry, who was good enough to come and fetch me. We soon arrived at the Palace, where the little garrison was under arms. The Prince, I found, had to furnish thirty men to the Confederation of the Rhine. A drum was beaten as a salute on our arrival, and this was also the signal of our approach to the equerries in charge of the court stables.

A vast sanded court surrounded by fine buildings still separated us from the manorial residence of the Prince. We entered on the right the principal corridor of the stables, which presented a most charming and striking *coup d'œil*. More than 100 young fellows of about eighteen or twenty were standing motionless, drawn up in long lines on the right and left at the entrance to the stalls, whip in hand, and wearing green jackets relieved, in English fashion, with a few silver ornaments, tight-fitting white leather breeches, riding boots, and jockey caps. Here and there stood a man in more richly decorated garments, who was apparently in command of the others. The silence was only interrupted by the noise made by the horses as they munched the hay which they pulled from the racks made of oak or polished walnut, the dark colour of which contrasted well with the white marble of the mangers. The corridor was full of the delicious scent of the hay. The horses, which were almost at liberty in their big stalls, appeared very happy, and quite indifferent to our praises of their graceful beauty, their colour, &c. They all seemed very gentle, and to expect us to caress them. I found that each horse had its own saddle, bridle, and harness, and that if I liked the Prince would sell them with the horse chosen. I was very glad to hear this, which would save me a lot of trouble, so I asked to have twenty horses, the age of which had been told me, led out for me to look at more closely. Twenty of the young equerries then left their ranks, and either leading the horses, or vaulting lightly on their backs, put them through their paces for my benefit. I chose twelve out of the twenty, six of a good and six of a moderate height. Then, my voice almost trembling with eagerness, I asked the Grand Equerry to speak to the Prince about the price. The thought of owning all these beautiful creatures filled me with delight, but I was dreadfully afraid that a sum beyond my means would be asked, for I well remembered the experience of one of my friends, who bought some horses from the Prince of Plesse, who had a very fine stud in Holstein, and was celebrated for his skill in breeding the finest races of horses. He did not want to make money, but he did want to cover the expenses involved in the keeping up of such an establishment as his. He never, therefore, allowed a horse bearing his brand to pass out of his hands under a sum considerably over 100 louis, and every animal bred by him was certainly well worth that on account of its beauty and noble qualities.

At every sale, therefore, the word 'hundred' was understood, and when a stranger asked the price of some steed to which he had a fancy, and the reply was twenty, fifty, or eighty louis as the case might be, he was often overjoyed at the idea of getting a fine animal for such a moderate sum; but when he offered his eighty louis he was asked for the other hundred for the brand on the horse chosen, and, surprised at the demand, he would often break off the bargain. In my case, however, the Prince of Sondershausen, fearing probably the chances of war, asked no more than fifty louis for each big horse, and forty for each small one. He was very moderate too in the prices he put on the saddles and harness, and I soon found myself the happy owner of twelve fine horses, which seemed to me more beautiful than ever now they belonged to me. Good strong horses mean everything to a general officer – courage, speed, life itself – and I was full of thankfulness. I gladly emptied my purse into the hands of Von Scheidnitz, who lent me some trusty fellows to take the horses to Magdeburg. I excused myself from waiting to pay my respects to the Prince, or to listen to the opera of *Tamerlane*, and set off again in my carriage in the evening.

I had scarcely gone a league through the pretty avenues of trees leading from the Prince's residence, when I heard a carriage drawn by eight horses gaining rapidly on us. My postilion had only just time to say to me, as he respectfully uncovered, 'The Princess Regent!' before the vehicle dashed past us. I followed his example, and saluted. A few minutes later two carriages, each with six horses, followed the first. 'The ladies of the Court!' cried the postilion, and we both saluted again with the same respect as for the Princess herself.

Whilst I was halting for a moment at Halberstadt, I saw my charming little troop of horses pass in good condition, and felt a fresh glow of pleasure in their possession. I reached Magdeburg on March 29th, and alighted at the residence of my friend General Haxo, who with General Rogniat had orders to put that stronghold into a good state of defence, as a base of operations in the approaching campaign. Prince Eugène, Viceroy of Italy, was also there, having collected the remnants of his army on the banks of the Elbe. Every day fresh reinforcements arrived from France, and all the troops of the new army, already of considerable strength, were eager to avenge the disasters of the Russian campaign. Marshal Davout, who was still pursued by Wittgenstein, had passed from the right to the left bank of the Elbe at Dresden. On March 29 he had blown up two piers of the big bridge and retired on Leipzig. It was, however, important to bar the approach of the enemy along the many open roads on the frontiers of Germany, so the Prince of Eckmühl with the reinforcements he had received went down the left bank of the Elbe, and took up a position beyond Magdeburg on the lower river on the left of the Viceroy's corps.

The Emperor joined the army again on April 17, just at the time of the arrival of the reinforcements from Italy, and on May our army took up its position at Œtch on the road to Lützen, a little to the south of the battle field where the great struggle of November 6th, 1632, took place, in which Gustavus Adolphus lost his life. The French now came into collision with the enemy for the first time in the new campaign, and in the shock of a brisk cannonade Marshal Bessières was killed by a ball. The Emperor and his Guard slept that night at Weissenfels.

On May 2nd took place the second great battle of Lützen. The Russian and Prussian forces advancing on to the plain were vigorously attacked by the Emperor, who won a great victory over them, and drove them back upon the Elbe.

On the evening of this great battle occurred one of those exciting episodes so frequent in war, in which General Compans behaved with a noble devotion, recalling that of the Chevalier d'Assas.

The General had achieved great successes during the day with the sturdy marines of the Guard forming the greater part of his fine division, and when night fell our men, finding themselves isolated in the midst of a vast plain, closed up in squares to guard against sudden attacks from the enemy's cavalry.

By ten o'clock all was quiet but for an occasional cannonshot fired just to keep us anxious and to show us that the enemy had not yet completely withdrawn.

We felt that this silence might mean the preparation of some surprise, and General Compans left the square of his division to creep along the plain and listen to what was going on in the distance. After an hour of silence, he fancied he detected the tramp of cavalry. He listened still more intently, and clearly made out the peculiar rumbling sound produced by horses approaching in numbers with muffled tread. The sound came nearer and nearer, leaving the General in no doubt as to the fact that a sudden cavalry charge was about to be made, and he set off in all haste to regain his division. But the sound of trotting was soon changed to that of galloping, and long before he could regain the ranks of his own men, Compans could hear the orders given by the enemy's officers. Running as fast as he could, though he had no longer any hope of escape for himself, the French General shouted at the top of his voice, 'Compans' division! Compans' division! To arms! to arms! Prepare to meet a cavalry charge!' Then, commending himself to God, he flung himself down on his face in a rut beside a number of dead, whose fate he expected soon to share.

His troops, recognising the voice of their chief, stood to arms, and with crossed bayonets awaited the shock. The General heard the clash of the steel, and awaited the event in agonised suspense. With the speed of lightning, but with no other sound than that of the tramp of the horses, which shook the ground on which Compans lay, the whole charge swept over him, to dash upon the compact body of the marines, who received it with a murderous fire at close quarters. The horses, terrified at finding themselves suddenly in the midst of the flashing and crashing of the fire from thousands of muskets, reared and whirled round. The whole body of cavalry was thrown into disorder, and instead of carrying all before it, as the leader of the charge had expected, it galloped off as rapidly as it had come.

Truly terrible was the position of General Compans during the few moments occupied by this attack and defence. He might have been hit by our balls, he might have been trampled under foot by the enemy's cavalry; but Providence, recognising, perhaps, that his devotion deserved a reward, turned aside our fire, and intensified for the nonce that instinct natural to horses to avoid stepping on to anything likely to give way under their feet. General Compans was not even wounded, but trembling with emotion, and covered with earth and dust, he rejoined his division, who received him with shouts of joy at seeing him come back safe and sound after an experience so terrible and extraordinary. The rest of the night passed over quietly; the enemy had discovered that we were on our guard, and we were all able to get a little rest.

The Emperor passed the night after the battle of Lützen at Eisfeld. A brisk, well-sustained cannonade went on for the whole of the next two days, during which we pursued the enemy, and on May 4 Napoleon slept in the château which had been occupied the night before by the Emperor Alexander and the King of Prussia. It was here that he appointed me General-in-Chief of the Staff of the 12th corps commanded by Marshal Oudinot.

I started that same evening (May 4th), marching all night by way of Weissenfels and Naumburg, to join the Marshal. Having come up with him, I now followed the 12th corps on its way to pass the night at Zeist. On the 6th and 7th we halted at Altenbourg; on the 8th, having passed through Kennitz, a pretty town of Saxony, we halted at Sederau, and marched thence by way of Zensperg, Freiburg, and Hetzeldorf, to the camp two leagues from Dresden, where we halted on the evening of the 10th, and remained for five days.

On May 16th my new corps left Dresden, and on the 20th General Belin, of the engineers, and I went to throw some bridges over the Spree by which to reach the enemy on the next day. Whilst we were at work on the 21st, the Russians and Prussians were advancing in the direction of Bautzen to cross the Spree and cut off our retreat. It was of the utmost importance to us to check this offensive movement, and our bridges over the Spree being fortunately finished, the 12th corps crossed the river on them at once, a brigade of 3,000 or 4,000 Neapolitans leading the way, deploying immediately in picturesque fashion on the heights beyond the right bank.

Just as the Italians had gained the heights, a gun was fired by the enemy, and I distinctly saw one ball whiz through the air more than 100 feet above their heads. Not a man was touched, but the whole brigade, taken by surprise, fell on their knees. We were marching behind them, and the sight of all these plumed grenadiers overcome with fear of a single ball made us laugh so loudly that they got up in a great hurry, and marching upon the enemy flung themselves furiously upon the advanced guard, doing it a good deal of mischief.

My corps was ordered to take up a position with the left wing resting on Bautzen, and the right on a very lofty plateau which was covered with entrenchments not visible from below, and surmounting the wooded hills sloping down from it towards the Spree.

The Pactod division was ordered to scale these heights, take the entrenchments, and establish themselves amongst them so as to check the enemy should they attempt to go down to the Spree by way of the hills to destroy our bridges and cut off our retreat.

The Lorencez division supporting the Pactod was posted in the plain behind a little wood and the plateau just mentioned.

The Emperor with his staff and Guard were at Bautzen.

Marshal Macdonald, commanding the 11th corps, supported our left, whilst the rest of the army stretched away on the left of Macdonald's corps, the corps under Marshal Ney, which formed the extreme left of the French army, taking up a position at right angles with our line of battle.

Such was the position occupied by the French and the disposition of their forces in the great battle of Bautzen between them and the combined Russian, Austrian, and Prussian forces.

I shall content myself with mentioning what fell under my own observation as attached to the 12th corps, the operations of which I was instructed to press on and to report.

Fire was opened on our right by the Pactod division, which drove back a considerable column of Prussians upon their entrenchments, erected on an elevated point to harass our march to the Spree.

The Pactod division maintained the struggle on the plateau with admirable courage and perseverance for no less than thirty-two hours under a continuous hail of cannon-balls, grapeshot, and bullets, whilst all along the line for several leagues an equally terrible conflict was going on.

The Russians, However, succeeded in gaining ground a little; their artillery dashed up at a gallop to take a position on a height dominating the plain occupied by us, and looking down upon us at their feet they poured forth such volleys of balls and grapeshot that the ranks of the Lorencez division were mown down by them. For an hour we were all in a very painful position, and Marshal Oudinot was compelled to send a message to Marshal Macdonald on his left asking for reinforcements. The Marshal at once sent the Gérard division, which came up to the support of General Lorencez just as that officer had his thigh shattered by a ball, whilst his troops were suffering cruelly. Almost at the same moment my horse was struck in the belly and horribly wounded. The poor creature in its agony flung me several feet in the air, and I fell heavily into a deep rut in the ground.

As soon as I recovered from the giddiness caused by this fall, I dragged myself to a stream to bathe my face, which had been a good deal bruised and cut. The cold fresh water fully revived my senses and strength, and I returned to seek my people, who gave me another horse. I then went to Marshal Oudinot, who did not at first recognise me, I was so much disfigured.

I soon left the Marshal again to go with his aide-de-camp, the brave Colonel de Cramayel, to rally the remnant of the Lorencez division and join it to that under Raglovitch, the united forces being ordered to go to the right to the support of Pictod, who had lost his position and nearly all his men.

After a few terrible moments of suspense, which seemed like hours, we suddenly had the joy of hearing a brisk cannonade in the distance behind the enemy, which led us to hope that we were about to be extricated from our critical position.

We were right; the firing came from Marshal Ney, who had flung himself with his usual vigour upon the Russian reserves. The Emperor, I heard later, had looked at his watch a hundred times before he gave the signal for this onslaught, so anxious was he that it should be delivered at exactly the right moment to ensure success.

We began to breathe once more, for the enemy drew back before us, gave up the attempt to drive us beyond the Spree, and the battle of Bautzen was won.

We remained two days in the position we had so dearly bought, and then the 12th corps received orders to march on Velau.

We arrived at Hojersverda on May 26th, and drove the Prussians out of it.

Marching through the little town of Hojersverda, surmounted as it was by lofty walls, was rather a difficult matter, but Marshal Oudinot knew that there was a wide meadow beyond in which he could deploy his troops, and he therefore pushed through and drew up in battle order face to face with the Prussians, by whom we had been pursued, and who had already taken up a position on the heights beyond.

The Marshal, who thought his position better than it really was, did not trouble to protect the narrow entrance to the town behind him, and, thinking that he had a good opportunity for successfully attacking Tauenzin's corps, he did not hesitate to advance.

The enemy, however, advantageously posted on slopes from which they could watch every movement of ours, placed a considerable force of artillery in position, and poured a murderous fire upon us, which mowed down our ranks, and soon compelled Marshal Oudinot himself to take refuge in one of the many squares into which he hastily formed his troops, and in which the grapeshot was working terrible havoc.

Most fortunately the Marshal had left behind at the entrance to the town, with two battalions, a brigade of Hessian cavalry, commanded by General Wolff (a Frenchman), and the whole of our artillery.

My officers kept on bringing me more and more disastrous news from the Marshal, and I asked General Wolff if he was disposed to support me vigorously with his cavalry. On his replying in the affirmative I ordered the commander of the artillery to follow me with eight twelve-pounders, the two battalions of infantry in their turn to follow and protect the artillery, whilst General Wolff was to cover our movement, and advance as far as the outlying forces of the Prussians. I urged the greatest care in pointing the artillery, and almost before the enemy had noticed our arrival eight or ten of their guns were put hors de combat, whilst their lines were greatly broken. This vigorous and unexpected attack from us only lasted a few moments before Bulow's columns were put to rout, and Marshal Oudinot was rescued, though he had already had many men killed and no fewer than 400 wounded. We spent the day after this disagreeable affair at Hojersverda.

The 12th corps left Hojersverda on May 31st, to continue its march on Velau, and it was a few leagues from that town that I had an opportunity of giving the Marshal the chance of taking a grand revenge for his sufferings outside Hojersverda.

He had halted at the village of Protha, and his three divisions were marching in advance of him. I was going round the outposts of the advanced guard when I discovered that General

Bulow, in his turn, was marching in columns half a league in advance of our divisions, also on the way to Velau, and that his flank was exposed to us in a very unfortunate manner for him.

Our three generals noted this fact at the same moment that I did, and were impatient to profit by it, so I galloped back to ask Marshal Oudinot to give the order for the attack to be made.

The Marshal, always brave enough where he himself was concerned, hesitated now to give the word, and, anxious to be sure things were as we represented them, he climbed into a belfry to see for himself. He soon shouted down to me, 'Yes, you are right; go and order the three divisions to attack!'

I galloped back, but everything had changed in the short interval of my absence. The enemy had got out of the awkward position they were in, our three generals were convinced that the moment had gone by, and that to act now would be as useless as dividing water with a sword.

We therefore continued our march on Velau, where the enemy had taken up their position, and from which we only dislodged them with difficulty. During the struggle the extensive suburb at the base of the hill caught fire, and we fought for a long time in the thickest and blackest smoke I ever saw.

Towards the end of this affair the infantry were obliged to form in squares against constant charges from the Russian cavalry, many of whom were brought down by us, but we lost several guns, and in the end both sides drew back without any very definite result.

On June 9th, General Guilleminot with a French division joined us at Herzberg, bringing us the news of the armistice just concluded.

On the 10th this fine division took up its quarters in the château of Annaburg, which had been converted into a military college.

We made our troops camp, and did all we could to provide them with healthy amusements during the pause in hostilities. We organised sack races and merry-go-rounds beneath a carefully balanced tun full of water, the contents of which would deluge clumsy competitors.

Our cares were not, however, all for the men; we looked after ourselves too, and had many a pleasant water picnic or fishing expedition on the picturesque Elster, in which some of the people of the country, including various charming ladies, took part.

Thus slipped by the 11th, 12th, 13th, 14th, and 15th of June. The Staff were all quartered in the fine manor house of Lubbenau, belonging to the Countess of Schoenberg, who did the honours of her house most gracefully, and we had some delightful open-air fêtes, dancing on lawns or in arbours bright with flowers, with noble and bourgeois dames.

During the spring of 1813 public feeling in Germany was so bitter against the domination of the French, that a secret association was formed, to which nearly all the young fellows in the universities belonged.

The name given to this association by its members was Tugendbund, or the League of Virtue. The handsome young husband of the Countess of Schoenberg who entertained us so kindly was one of the most ardent partisans of the Tugendbund, and whilst we were enjoying the society of his family in his beautiful home of Lubbenau, he was making every preparation to wage war to the knife with us as soon as the armistice ended. Owning a large fortune, he had just levied a regiment of hussars numbering 1,500 men and horses.

To leave no doubt as to the spirit animating his troop, he made his men wear black uniforms, whilst their shakos were surmounted by black plumes and decorated with a badge representing a death's head with its long teeth resting on two crossed bones. Every member of the regiment had to swear never to surrender and to make no prisoners.

We danced on gaily enough, however, at the residence of the Countess whilst the Count, inspired, like all the rest of his countrymen, by the terrible ballad just written by Goethe, the young poet whose verses were then rousing up all the patriotic ardour of the Germans, was preparing a dance of death for us on the resumption of hostilities.

On June 19th we went to visit the battle field of Lukau,

where so much blood had been shed on the 4th, and almost every day we made some excursion up or down the Spree duck shooting, or we went in large parties for long rides, held reviews of our troops, &c.

In the review of June 29th, Pactod's division, in spite of its terrible suffering at Bautzen, figured in brilliant force; the Guilleminot division, still undecimated, presented a most imposing appearance; whilst General Raglovitch's Bavarian division came on to the ground in the very finest condition, evidently well prepared to take the field again.

On August 12th all was ready for the resumption of hostilities, and on the 16th we were all awaiting the reopening of the war.

On August 17th the enemy everywhere anticipated us by attacking our outposts and driving them back.

On the 18th our position was changed by the unexpected arrival of a considerable reinforcement, for the Emperor placed under Marshal Oudinot's orders the Reynier corps, consisting of two French divisions and the King of Saxony's corps, collectively called the 7th corps. To these troops Napoleon also added the 4th corps, commanded by General Bertrand, consisting of two French divisions and the King of Würtemberg's contingent.

To these two corps, the 4th and the 7th, were attached two cavalry corps under the orders of some French generals and the Duke of Padua, the whole, with my corps, the 12th, forming, as stated in a letter from Major-General Prince Berthier, an army of no less than 80,000 men with Marshal Oudinot as commander-in-chief.

After verifying the numbers of the troops as they arrived, however, it was found that there were really not more than 60,000 combatants bearing arms.

The Emperor now ordered Marshal Oudinot to march on Berlin and take possession of it, the same letter mentioning the various dispositions of the movement Napoleon himself would make.

On August 17th, then, the first day of the resumption of hostilities, our army began its march, and we soon came in contact with the Russian corps under Bülow and Tauenzien, who offered a stubborn resistance to our advance, but were driven back on the third day beyond the Spree, across which we at once flung some bridges, so as to pursue them in the direction of Potsdam and Berlin. Our army continued its march ignorant of what was before it, and it was only from the prisoners brought in by our scouts that we learnt that the enemy had taken up a position between Spandau and Berlin, so as to bar our approach to the capital.

The 12th and 7th corps crossed the Spree in the presence of the enemy, who at first defended the passage but feebly. The 12th corps had crossed easily enough about two o'clock in the afternoon, and driven the Prussians defending the heights beyond to a considerable distance from the river; but Marshal Oudinot, before venturing to pursue Bülow, wanted to wait for news of the two corps manoeuvring on his right.

A little before nightfall an officer came from General Reynier, bringing very bad tidings. The General, who had been advancing, as arranged, in the direction of Klistov and Grossbeeren with the Saxons as advanced guard and the French divisions in reserve, had come upon a corps of the enemy. The Saxons had been easily beaten and driven back in disorder upon the reserves, which fortunately had remained unbroken.

This repulse, of course, destroyed the unity of the concerted movement which had been so successfully begun by our left, and an idea occurred to me which I hoped might put things right again all along the line. It was not yet night, and I proposed that the 12th corps should halt and prepare their soup for supper, whilst I should go and ascertain the exact condition of General Reynier's corps. That done, I would at once find General Bertrand and see if his troops were in good heart after their achievements of the day. If they were ready to take the offensive, I would tell him to give there the order to prepare for an attack at daybreak on the front and flanks of the enemy, who would probably be rather off guard after the success of the evening before.

I felt pretty sure that such a surprise would put the enemy to rout, especially as it might catch them asleep, resting on the laurels they had won.

Marshal Oudinot was very unwilling to listen to my advice, and retarded my departure on one pretext or another, so that it was not until quite late that I started, bearing his orders for the attack to the 7th and 4th corps.

I was accompanied only by a very few horsemen, whom I had obtained with difficulty from the Duke of Padua, commanding our cavalry, and for whom he made me wait a very long time. I arrived about midnight at Grossbeeren, near to which General Reynier was hard at work restoring order amongst the Saxons, who had been repulsed that evening. I told him of my scheme for the attack by the three corps, and of the dispositions that the Duke of Reggio (Marshal Oudinot) had instructed me to arrange in concert with him and the General in command of our right, with a view to the making of this attack at daybreak. General Reynier fell in most cordially with the project, hazardous though it doubtless appeared to him when I first broached it. He assured me that his Saxons, though they had been repulsed, had lost very few men, and that they were in good heart now they had recovered breath. He had placed them behind the two French divisions, which were sure to fling themselves upon the enemy with extraordinary vigour. He therefore placed no obstacles in the way of the Marshal's project, and said he felt sure of success if only the 12th and 4th corps on his right and left marched simultaneously and co-operated cordially with him.

Delighted with the good spirits in which I found General Reynier, and with the fresh proofs he gave me of his continued devotion to the cause of the Emperor, I hurried on to Suthen to take the good news to General Bertrand, whose co-operation it was absolutely essential to secure.

As soon as I reached General Bertrand, I told him of the plan of attack for the morning, and also said that the Emperor's dispositions for our march on Berlin were more skilfully combined than any operation he had ever conceived. His orders were that General Gérard from Magdeburg and Marshal Davout from Hamburg were to march with the corps under them upon Berlin, so as to arrive on the west of that city at the same time as the three corps of the Duke of Reggio appeared on the east. The orders, which I had myself written down in cipher, had been received, I knew, for the fact had already been notified to me. The moment of departure was mentioned to each general, with the approximate time required for marching the dozen leagues between us and Berlin, and overcoming the obstacles which were sure to be thrown in our way. Rarely indeed had a great enterprise been more carefully and skilfully organised, and the only things which seemed in the least likely to jeopardise our success were the courage of the enemy and the difficult nature of the ground to be traversed. I felt how great would be the disgrace to our army if a slight check and the loss of a couple of hundred of our allied troops should lead to a retreat all along our line. That this would come about was, however, inevitable if our right wing failed to co-operate with our centre, or our centre with our left, and so on. But nothing I could urge could convince General Bertrand, though I advanced at least a thousand good reasons for his taking the course I wished.

It was with immense regret that I returned to General Reynier to tell him of this refusal. He was so full of fearless devotion to the Emperor's interests that he was terribly disappointed when I said, as I took my leave of him, 'As our right wing will not take part in the suggested attack, I think the risk would be too great with only the 12th and 7th corps; so if you agree with me, I will tell Marshal Oudinot that I think it will be better to abandon the idea of our enterprise.' General Reynier realised sadly enough what a brilliant chance we were losing, but he made no effort to detain me, and let me go back to Marshal Oudinot with the bad news. Whilst waiting for my return, the Duke had been consumed with anxiety for the result of the operation which he supposed would take place. It was late when I got back from my fruitless efforts to arrange for the simultaneous advance of the three corps, for it was a very dark night, and not easy to find the way through the woods.

We passed the rest of the night in a state of painful agitation, and at daybreak the next morning the Marshal realised with infinite regret that there was nothing for it but to order a retreat all along his line. An hour later we sadly re-crossed the Spree, and the enemy lost no time in following us. The fine French army, which ought and so easily might have marched triumphantly into Berlin, was now compelled to retreat without having been beaten on Damm and Wittenberg.

Marshal Oudinot left Suthen on August 24th, and reached Gakow the same day, where he halted for the night. On the 25th, the 12th, 7th, and 4th corps came into line in good order at Riersdorff and Speremberg, though they were pursued and fusilladed all day long by the enemy.

On the 27th, whilst forty leagues behind us Napoleon was winning the great battle of Dresden, our three corps reunited at Riersdorff. Perno and Verben once more assumed the offensive, and marched on Insterburg, a town of considerable size, easily driving out the enemy and taking possession of it.

The 28th was passed near Insterburg in renewing our stock of provisions and trying to find out something about the movements of the enemy. Unfortunately we were quite ignorant of the very navies of the generals opposed to us, of the number of their troops, or the positions they occupied. There is no doubt that the Emperor provided ample means for organising an efficient system of espionage and paying for secret service of various kinds, but the avarice of many of those in command of the French forces led them to appropriate the money to their own use, when they ought to have expended it lavishly in obtaining information about the enemy. We really did not know whether we were about to fight Russians, Prussians, or Austrians. In spite of my patriotism, in spite of my keen sense of what loyalty to the Emperor demanded of me, I found it extremely difficult to secure at any price an intelligent peasant or two to risk venturing into the enemy's lines to collect information for us. We therefore had to manoeuvre altogether in the dark during the following days, though we did manage to gather that a general engagement was approaching, and the Duke of Reggio gave orders for all the non-combatants, carriages, and other impedimenta of our three corps to be withdrawn to Wittenberg, and there shut up out of the way of the fighting.

On the evening of the same day, the 28th, the 4th corps was ordered to march towards the left of the enemy's forces, which at once prepared to attack us.

On the 29th Marshal Oudinot placed his forces as follows: the 12th corps at Eckmandorff, the 4th in the rear of that village, and the 7th with Wittenberg as a support. He had scarcely made these dispositions when he was vigorously attacked. Our three fine cavalry divisions, finding themselves within range of the firing, dashed upon the enemy, driving them back as far as Mazanne, and protecting the reconnaissance. A Polish officer had orders to push from that point to Warbeck, where he found a body of Russian troops encamped.

On August 30th our three corps were reunited at Mazanne, and a very strong force was sent out to reconnoitre the enemy's position. Our troops were surrounded throughout the march by Cossacks, who gradually withdrew before them. They were, however, compelled to return without ascertaining anything, and were hotly pursued by such a strong body of artillery and cavalry that we concluded considerable forces were coming up to attack us. Our artillery was hastily placed in line, and we opened a brisk cannonade, which compelled the enemy to retire.

On the evening of the 30th, the 12th corps slept at Mazanne, the 7th at Feldheim, and the 4th at Tiessintz. September 1st and 2nd were quietly passed by the three corps at Kropstadt in making reconnaissances and preparing for the coming struggle.

On September 3rd our united forces established themselves at Teutchel, near Wittenberg, and whilst the troops were taking up their position the 4th corps was vigorously attacked by the enemy, who were, however, repulsed all along their line.

It was during the manoeuvres of September 3rd that Marshal Ney, whose approach had been notified to us the evening before, arrived with two or three officers. Finding the troops under arms when he came up, Marshal Ney at once rode along the front, took over the command, and ordered the advance to begin.

Ney had received at the same time as Oudinot the plan of campaign the Emperor intended to follow, and the exact part in it his corps was to take. General Jomini, chief of the staff to Ney, and a distinguished writer, not caring for the active share which would fall to him in the bloody struggle about to ensue, sought safety in taking the plan of campaign, which had been placed in his hands as in mine, to the Emperor of Russia. Jomini disappeared suddenly, and the details the traitor supplied to the Russians enabled them to circumvent all the skilful combinations arranged by Napoleon, whose difficulties now became immense, though he was still as undaunted as ever.

But to return to Marshal Ney. In his haste to execute the orders of the Emperor, he ordered the 4th and 7th corps to advance and attack, but did not give the same order to the 12th, which was marching in line with the other two. Marshal Oudinot was left in command of this 12th corps, and I remained with him as chief of his staff. The other two corps came up with the enemy, and a hot struggle at once began. The 12th corps meanwhile, restless and indignant at not having received the same orders as the others, listened attentively to try and find out if the right of the army were engaged. The wind blowing strongly from the west carried away the noise of the cannonade, and we could hear nothing. The appearance of a few Cossacks opposite our front, however, led us to suppose that the army to which they belonged was not far off, and we at once marched in the direction of Dennewitz.

We had scarcely issued from the wood which covered our front, before we found ourselves face to face with the combined Russian, Prussian, and Swedish forces, which were deploying a formidable body of artillery as they advanced upon us. A strong wind blew clouds of blinding dust in our faces, and balls and grapeshot mowed down our ranks, throwing us into such great disorder that it was only with considerable difficulty that we managed to form our infantry divisions into squares so as to retire before the numerous cavalry galloping up to surround us.

Meanwhile General Reynier with the 7th corps had flung himself into the village of Dennewitz, which the enemy was endeavouring to retake. The Guilleminot division performed prodigies of valour, but was unable to hold the village. On the right and at the same level the Würtembergers, commanded by General Bertrand, were fighting on the plain under great disadvantages and losing many men, and Marshal Ney, finding himself in a very critical position with no forces in reserve, was compelled, as we had been, to retire after displaying the most heroic courage.

In our retreat, Marshal Oudinot and his staff had to take refuge in the infantry squares, upon which the enemy was pouring a murderous fire.

Thus hotly pursued, we reached the edge of a vast morass or sheet of water called the Schwartz Elster, of the depth of which we were totally ignorant. A few minutes before, the horse I was riding had received seven balls in the neck and one in the leg, which made him limp. Nevertheless, I did not hesitate to make him go into the black mud of the marsh to test the depth of the water and see if it would be possible for our infantry to ford it and get by a short cut to Torgau, before which they were to take up a position.

On this occasion I had a striking proof of the fact that a man who shows the courage of a hero one day may be a coward ever after. General Fournier-Sarlovèze, commanding one of our divisions of cavalry, was a noted duellist and bully, the terror of all peaceable men, but to-day he was in a state of trembling nervousness, and to the disgust alike of his subordinate officers and of our infantry, who depended on his support, he led the 6,000 cavalry under him so badly that on September 6 they did no good service whatever.

Though pursued by the Russians, the army retired in fairly good order on Damm, Wittenberg, and Torgau.

On September 8th the news of the disaster which had befallen the left wing of his army in Saxony, every position it had held having been lost, reached the Emperor, and he sent for me to give him an account of how it had come about. I left Torgau in haste, and travelled all night through a terrible storm, arriving at Dresden wet through at five o'clock in the morning on

September 9th. Without halting I pushed on thence to Dona, where I was assured I should find the Emperor, and I came up to him just as he was receiving the news of the defeat of Vandamme's corps.

I therefore returned to Damm by way of Meissen, Wurschen, and Eulemburg, arriving at two o'clock in the morning at Mürzen, where I learnt that my corps had been ceaselessly pursued by the enemy during my absence. Every day attacks had been made by the French on the Prussian corps under Bülow and Tauenzin, but without effecting any change in our position.

Several days more were occupied in a continued struggle, many men being lost on both sides without any definite results for either army.

Marshal Ney had meanwhile been recalled by the Emperor, who ordered him to break up the united corps he had recently been commanding, and to resume the direction of the 3rd corps, with which he was to co-operate on the same line as Marshal Oudinot had done.

On the breaking up of the 4th, 7th, and 12th corps, the Duke of Reggio (Marshal Oudinot) was reinstated in the command of the grenadiers of the Imperial Guard, and the 12th corps was incorporated with the 7th and 4th under Generals Reynier and Bertrand.

I now became attached to the 7th corps, and commanded a brigade of 6,000 men belonging to the Guilleminot division. This brigade was made up of five regiments of infantry, namely the 52nd and 64th French, the 111th Piedmontese, the 7th Croatian, and the 3rd Illyrian. Each regiment had a good French Colonel, and the one at the head of the Illyrians was a very witty Breton named De Trommelin, a French émigré, who had formerly been aide-de-camp to Sir William Sidney Smith when that admiral was aiding Sir Ralph Abercrombie in the war with the French in Egypt.

After the breaking up and rearranging of the various corps, we left the banks of the Elbe to march towards Dessau and Leipzig, leaving our baggage at Torgau and Wittenberg. A Piedmontese adjutant of the 111th Regiment came and begged me to let him use my carriage because he was ill, and he promised to look after it and my horses as if they were his own.

I saw no reason not to trust him, and gave my consent. Unfortunately he kept his word much better than I expected. We had scarcely left Torgau and Wittenberg when those towns were blockaded by the enemy. The people in the invested cities soon began to suffer from famine; two of my horses were killed and eaten, whilst my Piedmontese friend sold the rest, hired some post horses and with them made his way in my carriage, and of course at my expense, to Turin, whence he had the impudence to write and tell me that he had had to sell all my belongings so as to be able to live in comfort himself. I answered him in a very polite letter, in which I hid a skilfully laid trap for him.

I told him in this letter that I was the more concerned for the loss of my carriage because I had hidden a sum of 20,000 francs in gold in certain secret recesses of it. As I expected, and heard afterwards, the thief at once had the carriage smashed up, finding nothing, but completing my revenge.

For more than a month after we left the Elbe, the days and often also the nights were passed in marching and countermarching, and in bloody skirmishes with the Prussians and Russians, an account of which would alone make up a deeply interesting volume, but it would weary the reader if I were to attempt to add a description of them to these brief Memoirs. I was no longer an aide-de-camp in a position to judge of the manoeuvres we were going through as a whole, for I saw nothing but what took place close to my own brigade, and all I could do was to make notes day by day on the number of men each day's fighting cost me. All my regiments, though of such mixed nationalities, behaved admirably, and the 4th and 7th corps especially distinguished themselves on October 3rd, when the drove the Russians back in the greatest disorder on the Elbe near Dessau. On that one day alone I lost 360 of my brave fellows.

Well seasoned by all our hard experiences, we came up at last with the rest of the French army, concentrating near Leipzig, on the eve of the awful days of October 18th and 19th, during which raged the terrible battle named after that town. Although on the 18th my regiments were engaged, and I lost many men in the suburbs of Leipzig, I do not feel equal to describing the grand tragedy in which Napoleon's courage and genius were alike displayed in the very highest degree, and in which he put forth all his strength, turning every resource at his command to account.

The battle, which lasted two days, ended between two and three o'clock on October 19th, when quiet was restored upon the blood-stained field. The enemy endeavoured, however, to intercept the troops under Lefebvre-Desnouettes, whom the Emperor had ordered to march on Weimar to cover our retreat, and on Erfurth to get a fresh supply of ammunition, ours being exhausted.

The division to which I belonged was sent to the Saale to prevent the Austrians from taking possession of the Koesen bridge, where they hoped to cut off our retreat on Frankfort and Mainz. The banks of the Saale are very steep, but I managed to place my brigade in ambush behind some inequalities of the ground, and I kept the Austrians at bay opposite the bridge for twenty-four hours. I had such a well-established and protected position on the plateau above the river, that there was no fear of the enemy's balls reaching me, so I was able to give my officers a good meal, of which we all stood sorely in need. The Austrians, massed in great numbers on the opposite bank, did not gain an inch of ground, but fired over our heads from below, the balls only falling amongst us after describing a regular parabola. Our light repast was therefore eaten beneath a hail of steel and lead which did us but little harm, though it worked great havoc amongst our plates and glasses. The ground all about us was riddled with little holes like a stable sieve, but this did not damp our spirits in the least.

Just as it began to get dark, I received orders to march towards Hanau and take up a position between it and the banks of the Saale. I afterwards left this position to cover the pass of Guelhausen and the Hanau woods. One battalion on October 30th I stationed in the village of Saalmünster on fey left, and bivouacked with the rest of my troops on a dry healthy spot a few paces off.

During the night the Austrians crossed the Saale, and at day-break our camp was roused by the approach of their skirmishers.

I must explain here that I had as aide-de-camp a young officer in whom Marshal Oudinot was deeply interested. He had begged me to receive him, and do all I could for him. He came to me absolutely penniless, but with all the pretensions of a scion of a noble family. I welcomed him kindly, filled his purse, bought two good horses for him with saddles, harness, &c., and sent them to him as a gift.

I expected, of course, to get a little active help in return, and to find him zealous in my service. Not a bit of it. I suppose he found his sense of gratitude oppressed him, for he disappeared without taking leave of me. I heard afterwards that he was aide-de-camp to the Duke of Valmy.

There was no officer at hand to fill his place when we were thus surprised by the Austrians, so I went myself to reconnoitre the position the Austrians had just taken up round our bivouac.

Separated from my troops, I galloped about amongst the enemy's skirmishers, and soon saw that I ran great danger of being shot down or taken, so I hastened back to camp to order the brigade to take up arms and join the principal corps of our division.

What was my astonishment when I got to where we had bivouacked to find it wholly deserted, and to be compelled to ride a long way in the track of my own men before I came up with them!

It turned out that whilst I was amongst the skirmishers General Guilleminot had received orders to march towards Hanau, and had sent a message to my brigade instructing it to follow his movement. This order had not reached the battalion I had stationed in Saalmünster, which had for the moment been forgotten, and I had the greatest difficulty in saving it, for the village was already surrounded. I was intensely annoyed at this incident, and bitterly reproached General Guilleminot, who had been a great friend of mine for many years.

On October 31st we reached the Hanau woods, twenty-four hours after the great battle which had taken place there, in which Napoleon defeated the allied Austrians and Russians under Von Wrede, and the brilliant details of which are related by many French historians.

The Bavarian corps had not yet abandoned the hope of cutting off our retreat on Frankfort and Mainz, and Marshal Marmont was left in the Hanau woods to protect us and circumvent the efforts of the enemy. Having heard that a strong force of Bavarians occupied the streets of the suburbs of Frankfort, he flung a number of shells amongst them, setting fire to the houses.

On the same day, October 31st, the Guilleminot division took the place of that under Marshal Marmont, which was ordered to retire on Mainz, whilst my brigade took up its position in the woods on the banks of the Kinzig to defend its passage. I had scarcely reached the river, when a brisk cannonade from the Bavarian camp broke many of the trees above our heads. The branches and pieces of shells rained down upon us, revealing that the enemy was about to make a fresh attempt to cross, and very soon a considerable body of Bavarians on rafts and in small boats came in sight on the little stream.

My troops were well in ambush, and their courage was heightened by their eager desire for vengeance on the treacherous Bohemians, so lately our allies. Two thousand of them managed with infinite difficulty to gain our bank, where the dead silence which reigned evidently intimidated them. All of a sudden, as they hesitated to advance, our regiments flung themselves upon them, overthrew them, and drove them, covered with wounds, back into the river, where they were nearly all drowned, though some few got off on the rafts and in canoes.

I thought the struggle was over, and had a canteen opened, inviting several colonels to come and share its contents with me; but just as we were emptying our first flask a burning shell fell at the feet of Colonel Limousin, of the 52nd Regiment. I called out to him to draw off his grenadiers, for I should have been deeply grieved if one of them had been wounded. All the brave fellows, however, absolutely refused to move out of danger, and though I was some fifty paces away I was struck by a fragment of the shell, which cut through the double felt of my hat like a razor, and tore open my forehead. I fell like an inert mass amongst my comrades, who hastened to help me up. The wound was severe, but with their aid I managed to walk to the ambulance, some hundred paces in the rear, and have it dressed.

As we went along an officer in the French uniform approached me, tore up a white handkerchief he held in his hand, and made a bandage of it for me. Deeply touched at this kind thought, I begged him to tell me his name, and he replied, 'I am Louis of Lichtenstein.'

The doctors made a very deep crucial incision about my wound, an operation in which I lost a great deal of blood, and I was so much weakened that I was unable to return to my post. I therefore sent a message to Colonel Robillard, of the 111th Regiment, asking him to take command of my brigade during my absence. I then went to Mainz, where I arrived the same evening, and remained several days. Colonel Limousin, who had been severely wounded by the same shell as I had been, was presently brought to my lodgings. His injuries were more dangerous than mine, but I am glad to say that I had the pleasure of meeting him several years later in good health, though he limped a little, in his native town of Angoulême, where he was held in high esteem by all his fellow-citizens.

Very soon after the arrival of Colonel Limousin, General Montelégier and several of his brave colonels of cavalry were brought in, so that we soon formed quite a staff of crippled officers.

I had scarcely left for Mainz when our brigade, joined to the Guilleminot division, went to garrison the fort and defend the entrance to the Cassel Bridge at the mouth of the Main opposite Mainz.

Typhoid fever raged severely in the hospitals and the town, making terrible ravages amongst the many sick and wounded brought from Leipzig, Hanau, and Frankfort.

Some of my young servants took the fever, and sometimes I had the grief of seeing them come into my room in their delirium wearing nothing but their night shirts, and looking like mere ghosts of their former selves as they seemed to appeal to me to deliver them from the malady tormenting them.

Such was my condition and such were my surroundings during the closing scenes of the overthrow of the great French Empire, when the power of Napoleon beyond the Rhine was destroyed.

Once more I lost my horses and carriages, and after all my terrible experiences I returned to Paris much poorer than I left it and very weary of war.

It was long since I had got any satisfaction out of the glory of war, or received any reward for my zealous service, or for the many sacrifices I had made in the cause of the Emperor. My chiefs had again and again applied to him for recognition of what I had done, but nothing came of their efforts on my behalf, and I felt the neglect keenly.

But I was still young, my energies were by no means exhausted, and I was glad to have a chance at last of freely indulging my passion for painting everything I admired. Love of nature and of reproducing nature now became a religion with me. I gave myself up entirely to painting as soon as I got back to Paris, and my one ambition was to distinguish myself in that deeply interesting and most fascinating branch of art. Thanks to this occupation, I was happily enjoying the tranquil time which succeeded my adventurous career, when the events of 1814 took us all by surprise in the very heart of France, for Paris itself was besieged. All was changed, and an altogether new state of affairs inaugurated.

LEONAUR

ALSO FROM LEONAUR
AVAILABLE IN SOFTCOVER OR HARDCOVER WITH DUST JACKET

CAPTAIN OF THE 95th (Rifles) *by Jonathan Leach*—An officer of Wellington's Sharpshooters during the Peninsular, South of France and Waterloo Campaigns of the Napoleonic Wars.

THE KHAKEE RESSALAH *by Robert Henry Wallace Dunlop*—Service & adventure with the Meerut volunteer horse during the Indian mutiny 1857-1858

BUGLER AND OFFICER OF THE RIFLES *by William Green & Harry Smith* With the 95th (Rifles) during the Peninsular & Waterloo Campaigns of the Napoleonic Wars

BAYONETS, BUGLES AND BONNETS *by James 'Thomas' Todd*—Experiences of hard soldiering with the 71st Foot - the Highland Light Infantry - through many battles of the Napoleonic wars including the Peninsular & Waterloo Campaigns

A NORFOLK SOLDIER IN THE FIRST SIKH WAR *by J W Baldwin*—Experiences of a private of H.M. 9th Regiment of Foot in the battles for the Punjab, India 1845-46

A CAVALRY OFFICER DURING THE SEPOY REVOLT *by A.R.D. Mackenzie*—Experiences with the 3rd Bengal Light Cavalry, the Guides and Sikh Irregular Cavalry from the outbreak to Delhi and Lucknow

THE ADVENTURES OF A LIGHT DRAGOON *by George Farmer & G.R. Gleig*—A cavalryman during the Peninsular & Waterloo Campaigns, in captivity & at the siege of Bhurtpore, India

THE COMPLEAT RIFLEMAN HARRIS *by Benjamin Harris as told to & transcribed by Captain Henry Curling*—The adventures of a soldier of the 95th (Rifles) during the Peninsular Campaign of the Napoleonic Wars

THE RED DRAGOON *by W.J. Adams*—With the 7th Dragoon Guards in the Cape of Good Hope against the Boers & the Kaffir tribes during the 'war of the axe' 1843-48

THE LIFE OF THE REAL BRIGADIER GERARD - Volume 1 - THE YOUNG HUSSAR 1782 - 1807 *by Jean-Baptiste De Marbot*—A French Cavalryman Of the Napoleonic Wars at Marengo, Austerlitz, Jena, Eylau & Friedland

THE LIFE OF THE REAL BRIGADIER GERARD Volume 2 IMPERIAL AIDE-DE-CAMP 1807 - 1811 *by Jean-Baptiste De Marbot*—A French Cavalryman of the Napoleonic Wars at Saragossa, Landshut, Eckmuhl, Ratisbon, Aspern-Essling, Wagram, Busaco & Torres Vedras

AVAILABLE ONLINE AT
www.leonaur.com
AND OTHER GOOD BOOK STORES

LEONAUR

ALSO FROM LEONAUR

AVAILABLE IN SOFTCOVER OR HARDCOVER WITH DUST JACKET

THE COMPLEAT RIFLEMAN HARRIS *by Benjamin Harris as told to & transcribed by Captain Henry Curling*—The adventures of a soldier of the 95th (Rifles) during the Peninsular Campaign of the Napoleonic Wars

WITH WELLINGTON'S LIGHT CAVALRY *by William Tomkinson*—The Experiences of an officer of the 16th Light Dragoons in the Peninsular and Waterloo campaigns of the Napoleonic Wars.

SERGEANT BOURGOGNE *by Adrien Bourgogne*—With Napoleon's Imperial Guard in the Russian Campaign and on the Retreat from Moscow 1812 - 13.

SWORDS OF HONOUR *by Henry Newbolt & Stanley L. Wood*—The Careers of Six Outstanding Officers from the Napoleonic Wars, the Wars for India and the American Civil War, with dozens of illustrations by Stanley L. Wood.

SURTEES OF THE RIFLES *by William Surtees*—A Soldier of the 95th (Rifles) in the Peninsular campaign of the Napoleonic Wars.

ENSIGN BELL IN THE PENINSULAR WAR *by George Bell*—The Experiences of a young British Soldier of the 34th Regiment 'The Cumberland Gentlemen' in the Napoleonic wars.

HUSSAR IN WINTER *by Alexander Gordon*—A British Cavalry Officer during the retreat to Corunna in the Peninsular campaign of the Napoleonic Wars.

NAPOLEONIC WAR STORIES *by Sir Arthur Quiller-Couch*—Tales of soldiers, spies, battles & sieges from the Peninsular & Waterloo campaingns.

JOURNALS OF ROBERT ROGERS OF THE RANGERS *by Robert Rogers*—The exploits of Rogers & the Rangers in his own words during 1755-1761 in the French & Indian War.

KERSHAW'S BRIGADE VOLUME 1 *by D. Augustus Dickert*—Manassas, Seven Pines, Sharpsburg (Antietam), Fredricksburg, Chancellorsville, Gettysburg, Chickamauga, Chattanooga, Fort Sanders & Bean Station..

KERSHAW'S BRIGADE VOLUME 2 *by D. Augustus Dickert*—At the wilderness, Cold Harbour, Petersburg, The Shenandoah Valley and Cedar Creek.

A TIGER ON HORSEBACK *by L. March Phillips*—The Experiences of a Trooper & Officer of Rimington's Guides - The Tigers - during the Anglo-Boer war 1899 - 1902.

AVAILABLE ONLINE AT
www.leonaur.com
AND OTHER GOOD BOOK STORES

LEONAUR

ALSO FROM LEONAUR

AVAILABLE IN SOFTCOVER OR HARDCOVER WITH DUST JACKET

SEPOYS, SIEGE & STORM *by Charles John Griffiths*—The Experiences of a young officer of H.M.'s 61st Regiment at Ferozepore, Delhi ridge and at the fall of Delhi during the Indian mutiny 1857.

CAMPAIGNING IN ZULULAND *by W. E. Montague*—Experiences on campaign during the Zulu war of 1879 with the 94th Regiment.

THE STORY OF THE GUIDES *by G. J. Younghusband*—The Exploits of the Soldiers of the famous Indian Army Regiment from the northwest frontier 1847 - 1900..

ZULU: 1879 *by D.C.F. Moodie & the Leonaur Editors*—The Anglo-Zulu War of 1879 from contemporary sources: First Hand Accounts, Interviews, Dispatches, Official Documents & Newspaper Reports.

THE RECOLLECTIONS OF SKINNER OF SKINNER'S HORSE *by James Skinner*—James Skinner and his 'Yellow Boys' Irregular cavalry in the wars of India between the British, Mahratta, Rajput, Mogul, Sikh & Pindarree Forces.

TOMMY ATKINS' WAR STORIES 14 FIRST HAND ACCOUNTS—Fourteen first hand accounts from the ranks of the British Army during Queen Victoria's Empire Original & True Battle Stories Recollections of the Indian Mutiny With the 49th in the Crimea With the Guards in Egypt The Charge of the Six Hundred With Wolseley in Ashanti Alma, Inkermann and Magdala With the Gunners at Tel-el-Kebir Russian Guns and Indian Rebels Rough Work in the Crimea In the Maori Rising Facing the Zulus From Sebastopol to Lucknow Sent to Save Gordon On the March to Chitral Tommy by Rudyard Kipling

CHASSEUR OF 1914 *by Marcel Dupont*—Experiences of the twilight of the French Light Cavalry by a young officer during the early battles of the great war in Europe.

TROOP HORSE & TRENCH *by R. A. Lloyd*—The experiences of a British Lifeguardsman of the household cavalry fighting on the western front during the First World War 1914-18.

THE EAST AFRICAN MOUNTED RIFLES *by C. J. Wilson*—Experiences of the campaign in the East African bush during the First World War.

THE FIGHTING CAMELIERS *by Frank Reid*—The exploits of the Imperial Camel Corps in the desert and Palestine campaigns of the First World War.

AVAILABLE ONLINE AT
www.leonaur.com
AND OTHER GOOD BOOK STORES

Printed in the United States
75698LV00002B/154

9 781846 771668